Discovering
Britain & Ireland

Discovering
Britain & Ireland

National Geographic Society

Discovering
Britain & Ireland

Published by
The National Geographic
Society

Gilbert M. Grosvenor
President

Melvin M. Payne
Chairman of the Board

Owen R. Anderson
Executive Vice President

Robert L. Breeden
*Vice President,
Publications and
Educational Media*

Prepared by
National Geographic
Book Service

Charles O. Hyman
Director

Ross S. Bennett
Associate Director

Staff for this book

Jonathan B. Tourtellot
Editor

Mary B. Dickinson
Assistant Editor

David M. Seager
Art Director

Robert W. Madden
Illustrations Editor

Melanie Patt-Corner
Chief Researcher

Lynn R. Addison
Thomas B. Allen
Ross S. Bennett
Edward Lanouette
Elizabeth L. Newhouse
Shirley L. Scott
Editor-Writers

Paulette L. Claus
Mariana Tait Durbin
Lydia Howarth
Mary R. Lamberton
Mary Luders
Maura J. Pollin
Suzanne Kane Poole
L. Leigh Skaggs
Penelope A. Timbers
Anne Elizabeth Withers
Editorial Researchers

Paulette L. Claus
Style

R. Gary Colbert
Illustrations Researcher

Diana E. McFadden
Joris Minne
Illustrations Assistants

Mary R. Lamberton
Map Coordinator

Charlotte Golin
Design Assistant

Karen F. Edwards
Traffic Manager

John F. C. Frith
Production Manager

Richard S. Wain
Assistant Production Manager

Andrea Crosman
Production Assistant

Georgina L. McCormack
Teresita Cóquia Sison
Editorial Assistants

John T. Dunn
Ronald E. Williamson
Engraving and Printing

Maps by
John D. Garst, Jr.
Judith F. Bell
Peter J. Balch
Gary M. Johnson
Patricia K. Cantlay
D. Mark Carlson
Donald L. Carrick
Hildegard B. Groves
James V. Mauck
Robert W. Northrop
Daniel J. Ortiz
Nancy S. Stanford
Kevin Q. Stuebe
Marguerite I. Suarez
Martin S. Walz
Publications Art

Relief maps painted by
Robert Hynes

Jolene M. Blozis
Martha K. Hightower
Indexers

Contributions by
Jennifer G. Ackerman
Patricia Bangs
Caroline Hottenstein
Gwenda L. Hyman
Devon Jacklin-Madden
Kathleen M. Kiely
Linda B. Meyerriecks
Bonnie Piper
Deborah L. Robertson
Lise Swinson Sajewski
Margaret Sedeen
Susan E. Sidman
Andrew J. Swithinbank

United Kingdom Office
Jennifer Moseley
Valerie Mattingly

First edition
455,000 copies

442 photographs, 28 maps

Copyright © 1985
National Geographic Society,
Washington, D. C.

Library of Congress
CIP data page 448

Tudor building at Windsor
Castle, England (right). By
James L. Stanfield, National
Geographic Photographer.
Pages 2-3: Evening mist in an
Irish valley. By Farrell Grehan.

Contents

By Peter Crookston

Introduction

We British are a strange lot; we don't have a noun to describe ourselves in the singular. Someone from the United States can say that he or she is an American, whether from Honolulu or Hackensack. But in these islands no one calls himself a Briton or a Britisher. We say we're English, Scottish, Welsh, or—if from Northern Ireland and "loyalist" (British rather than Irish)—an Ulsterman. The Irish of the independent Republic, who don't care for the British after what Cromwell and the Black and Tans did to them, are of course indubitably Irish.

Newspaper headline writers use the word Briton for brevity, but it's usually about people from Britain in trouble abroad, as in "Spanish Police Arrest Nudist Britons," and the reader knows this can mean anyone whose passport reads "United Kingdom of Great Britain and Northern Ireland." People from our former colonies often call us "Brits," a word many of us don't like. When naming ourselves we are on the whole fiercely proud of the individual countries to which we belong. For example, when the poet Rupert Brooke went off to World War I he wrote:

If I should die, think only this of me:
That there's some corner of a foreign field
That is for ever England.

Not Britain—England. We can reach ludicrous extremes of *local* patriotism. I was once having a pint of ale in a pub in Blackburn, Lancashire, with a local reporter, and I referred to "the people of this area," meaning Lancashire. In

6

A village in Cornwall. By Patrick Ward

an accent as meaty as a Lancashire hot pot he stopped me short and said, "But aa don't coom from this area." He said he was an Accrington man—from all of five miles away.

This sectional chauvinism must have developed from the invasions and migrations that began after the Romans left. The Britain that Rome colonized was made up of Celts (some of whose closest descendants are still alive and well in Wales and Cornwall). Celtic Gaels (hence the Gaelic language) maintained small independent kingdoms in Ireland; the Irish Scotti tribe eventually joined native Picts in the mountainous north of Britain to become the Scots.

From A.D. 43 to 410 central Britain enjoyed a prosperous civilization as a province of Rome. The native British chieftains and their courts, many of whom had not long since been sitting on rush-covered earthen floors in rural wattle huts, now luxuriated on couches above heated mosaic flooring in stone town houses.

But Roman rule ended, and the Middle Ages plunged Britain into centuries of invasion and subjugation. The Venerable Bede, the seventh-century Northumbrian monk who was England's first major historian, maintained that the foundation of the English-speaking people lay in the migration of three hard-fighting pagan tribes from Germania—the Angles, the Saxons, and the Jutes—beginning in the fifth century.

These invaders, known collectively as Anglo-Saxons, colonized most of southern Britain. They interbred with the Romano-Celtic people who had not been slaughtered in the conquests or driven into the moors and mountain fastnesses of Cornwall and Wales. Thus was England born.

Another invasion four centuries later, more bloody and brutal than that of the Anglo-Saxons, gave a further stir to the racial mix: The Vikings sailed in. After an era of vicious raiding, they settled parts of England and Scotland. In Ireland they founded the cities of Dublin and Cork.

The last invasion, 200 years after the Vikings, added the final strain to the English and Irish bloodlines: The French-speaking Normans conquered England in 1066 and held large tracts of eastern and southern Ireland by 1172.

That, briefly, is how we became who we are. But what are we like? I think we're as full of contradictions as the four lands we inhabit. Reserve and the stiff upper lip are characteristics for which the English and Scots are famous. Both may be generally true, perhaps caused by the uncertain climate, which inculcates an inwardness of the spirit, a psychological clenching of the teeth. Yet the Welsh and Irish, beset by the same weather, tend to be more casually sociable and more voluble.

We British seem to be thought of as a gentle, polite nation. Our police rarely carry guns; we do a lot of obedient standing in lines (but as Norman descendants we call them "queues"); we are almost obsessive about holding doors open for each other as we leave the cinema. Yet the worst football hooligans in Europe are rampaging British soccer fans. Two gentle, contemplative hobbies, gardening and fishing, are the most popular. But we have always been a combative bunch or we could never have acquired an empire. So many men volunteered for World War I that the army could not at first supply enough rifles or uniforms. And when the British Navy sank the Argentine cruiser *General Belgrano* during the Falklands war, our biggest selling newspaper, *The Sun*, tastelessly disregarding over 300 Argentinian deaths, yelled GOTCHA! in a banner headline more suitable for a football victory.

So we're hard to pin down. But I believe that this book will lead you to a better understanding of us and of the lands that helped shape us. You'll learn much about how we view ourselves—and each other—as we introduce our homelands to you, for the 12 chapters that follow are written by five Englishmen, one Scot, one Anglo-Scot, two Welshmen, one Irishman and, for transatlantic perspective, two Americans of Irish and English descent. Someday, if you haven't been to Britain or Ireland, I hope you'll follow in their footsteps. You will be made welcome; if there's one thing the English, Welsh, Scots, and Irish enjoy, it is showing off their countries to foreigners, to those people whom Shakespeare—our ultimate chauvinist—described as the inhabitants of "less happier lands."

Two nations fly their flags over these islands: the Republic of Ireland and the United Kingdom of Great Britain and Northern Ireland. The U.K. itself comprises four lands of varying autonomy: England, Wales, Scotland, and Northern Ireland; the Isle of Man and the Channel Islands are self-governing crown dependencies.

In troubled Northern Ireland, which remained with the U.K. after the rest of Ireland won independence, a Protestant majority loyal to Britain vies with a large Catholic minority (which prefers to call the area "the six counties") seeking to join the Irish Republic.

In Britain, county boundaries reflect a reorganization ordered by London in 1974, often over local objection. Counties such as Westmorland, Pembrokeshire, and Argyllshire vanished entirely.

Red borders correspond to the 12 chapters of this book. The map supplement accompanying it offers a traveler's guide and a history chart.

Populations
United Kingdom 55,776,000
England 46,363,000
  London 6,696,000
Scotland 5,131,000
Wales 2,792,000
Northern Ireland 1,491,000

Republic of Ireland 3,443,000
  Dublin 526,000

ORKNEY

10° 8° 6° 4° 2° 0°

58°

WESTERN
ISLES

St. Kilda

Outer Hebrides

HIGHLANDS
AND ISLANDS

HIGHLAND

GRAMPIAN

SCOTLAND

Grampian Mts.

Inner Hebrides

TAYSIDE

56°

SCOTTISH
LOWLANDS

FIFE

CENTRAL

STRATHCLYDE

★ Edinburgh
LOTHIAN
• Glasgow

ATLANTIC
OCEAN

NORTHERN
IRELAND

BORDERS

LONDONDERRY
(DERRY)

DUMFRIES
AND
GALLOWAY

NORTHUMBERLAND

ANTRIM

Newcastle
upon Tyne •
→ TYNE AND WEAR

DONEGAL

UNITED KINGDOM OF GREAT BRITAIN

DURHAM
CLEVELAND

TYRONE

Belfast ★

AND NORTHERN IRELAND

NORTH
COUNTRY

ULSTER

DOWN

CUMBRIA

The Pennines

NORTH
SEA

SLIGO

FERMANAGH

AR-
MAGH

ISLE
OF MAN • Douglas

NORTH YORKSHIRE

54°

MAYO

LEITRIM

MON.

CAVAN

LOUTH

IRISH SEA

LANCASHIRE W. YORKS.

HUMBERSIDE

ROS-
COMMON

LONG.

GR. MANCHESTER

ENGLAND

CONNAUGHT

WESTMEATH

MEATH

MERSEYSIDE

Manchester •

S. YORKS.

GALWAY

OFFALY

DUBLIN
⊕ Dublin

Anglesey

Liverpool •

DERBYSHIRE

LINCOLNSHIRE

*Aran
Islands*

KILDARE

CHESHIRE

NOTTS.

LEINSTER

LAOIS

CLWYD

MIDLANDS

EAST ANGLIA
AND THE FENS

CLARE

WICKLOW

GWYNEDD

STAFFORD-
SHIRE

The Fens

NORFOLK

MUNSTER

TIPPE-
RARY

KIL-
KENNY

CARLOW

THE EAST
OF IRELAND

Cambrian Mts.

LEICESTERSHIRE

LIMERICK

WEXFORD

SHROPSHIRE

W.
MIDS.

NORTHANTS.

CAMBS.

SUFFOLK

REPUBLIC OF IRELAND

52°

KERRY

Shannon

WATERFORD

POWYS

HEREFORD
AND
WORCESTER

WARWICK-
SHIRE

BEDS.

CORK
• Cork

WALES

GLOS.

ENGLISH
HEARTLAND

BUCKS.

HERTS.

ESSEX

THE WEST
OF IRELAND

DYFED

GWENT

OXON.

Thames

GREATER LONDON

W. GLAMORGAN
MID GLAMORGAN
S. GLAMORGAN

Cardiff
★

AVON

BERKS.

⊕ London

SURREY

KENT

WILTSHIRE

SOUTHEAST

SOMERSET

HAMPSHIRE

W. SUSSEX E. SUSSEX

Strait of Dover

WEST COUNTRY

DORSET

ISLE
OF WIGHT

50°

DEVON

CORNWALL

E n g l i s h   C h a n n e l

*Isles of
Scilly*

2°

SHETLAND

*Shetland
Islands*

60°

• *Fair Isle*

*Orkney
Islands*

ORKNEY

SCOTLAND

Same Scale as Main Map

County Abbreviations

England:
Beds. *(Bedfordshire)*
Berks. *(Berkshire)*
Bucks. *(Buckinghamshire)*
Cambs. *(Cambridgeshire)*
Glos. *(Gloucestershire)*
Gr. Manchester *(Greater Manchester)*
Herts. *(Hertfordshire)*
Northants. *(Northamptonshire)*
Notts. *(Nottinghamshire)*
Oxon. *(Oxfordshire)*
S. Yorks. *(South Yorkshire)*
W. Mids. *(West Midlands)*
W. Yorks. *(West Yorkshire)*

Ireland:
Long. *(Longford)*
Mon. *(Monaghan)*

0 ——— KILOMETERS ——— 200
0 ——— STATUTE MILES ——— 100

ENGLAND

ISLE
OF WIGHT

2°

50°

English Channel

Guernsey ⬗ St. Peter Port

CHANNEL
ISLANDS

⬗ St. Helier

Jersey

Same Scale as Main Map

FRANCE

By Norman Shrapnel
Photographs by Jodi Cobb,
National Geographic Photographer

London

We must be free or die, who speak the
 tongue
That Shakespeare spake; the faith and
 morals hold
Which Milton held.

WILLIAM WORDSWORTH, 1802

Veterans assemble in Hyde Park for the Combined Cavalry Old Comrades' Parade.

W hy, Sir, you find no man, at all intellectual, who is willing to leave London. No, Sir, when a man is tired of London, he is tired of life; for there is in London all that life can afford.

SAMUEL JOHNSON, 1777

St. Paul's Cathedral in the City of London

T he Monarchy is our last stronghold
of romantic extravagance.

WILLIAM DAVIS, "The Monarchy Show," 1984

Coldstream Guards of the Royal Household Division march from St. James's Palace.

A dead king stares imperiously down Whitehall, looking more alive than any of the other static figures in which central London abounds, and for that matter, some of the walking ones too. London's best statue commands London's best street.

It is not easy for a London statue to command anything. Admiral Nelson, up on his column in Trafalgar Square, 300 feet away, has had to climb pretty well out of sight to be noticed at all. But King Charles I, astride his mount on a normal pedestal and only a little larger than life, is different. The top of Whitehall, with Trafalgar Square behind it, provides about as dominant a site as could be contrived. Charles has made sure nobody upstages him.

It is a revenge of sorts. The king gazes with forgivable intensity toward what in his day was Whitehall Palace. The only substantial part that survives, ironically, is the Banqueting House built in 1622 by master architect Inigo Jones. Outside of it on a bitter January afternoon in 1649, to a deep groan from the watching crowd, Charles I's head was struck off. His fine statue, horse and all, was itself sentenced to death-by-melting under the Commonwealth of the 1650s, when Britain tried to do without a king. But the statue was hidden, to be triumphantly produced after the monarchy's restoration in 1660. And here it is, outliving them all. Members of the Royal Stuart Society court their own deaths by traffic each year to lay a memorial wreath at the statue's foot.

As for the family living in Buckingham Palace, half a mile away over Charles's right shoulder—naturally he would know nothing of them. Their house wasn't even built in his day.

But why begin this story with kings instead of Cockneys? In their own view at least, it's Cockneys who have always ruled in this town. Yet the two are closer together than you might think. The Cockneys, those down-to-earth East Enders who regard themselves as the only true Londoners, have always assumed a special relationship with royalty,

The Thames was shallower in the 1st century A.D., when the Romans built a town, Londinium, at a ford 40 miles from the river's mouth. London expanded from that base, swallowing up other towns and villages; Greater London today covers 610 square miles. At its heart is the old City of London, a semi-independent square mile with its own Lord Mayor; finance and law now center there. The posh West End, once the City of Westminster, boasts royal palaces and parks, theaters, smart

shops and residential areas. The South Bank mixes theaters and concert halls, office buildings and suburbs. The East End is working-class London, Cockney territory. Most of Greater London's 6,700,000 residents live in its outer boroughs.

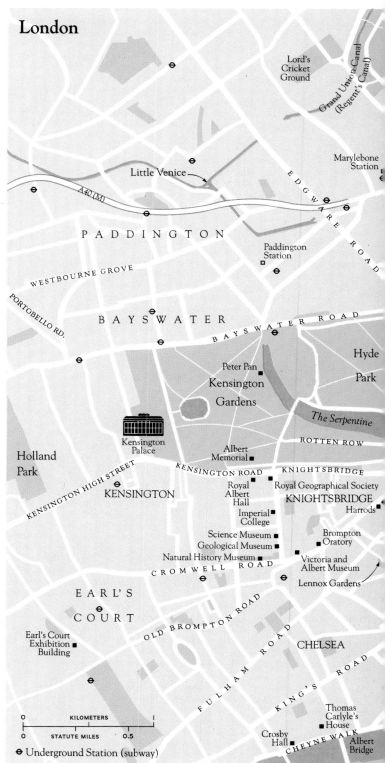

London

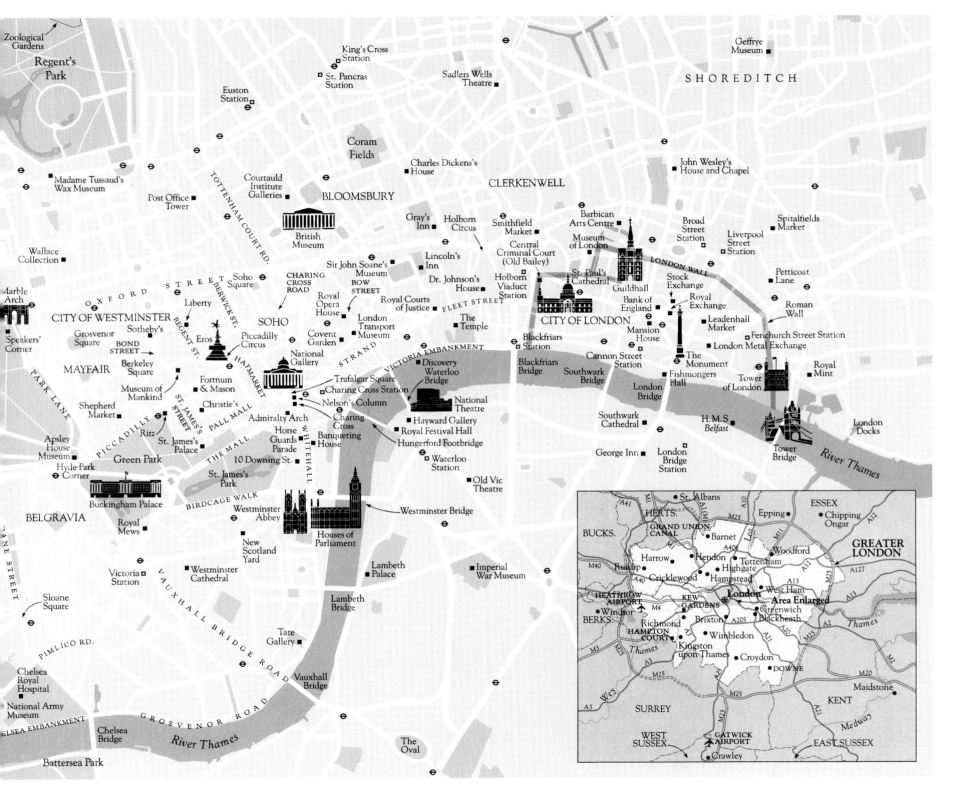

Zoological
Gardens

Regent's
Park

Madame Tussaud's
Wax Museum

Post Office
Tower

Wallace
Collection

Marble
Arch

CITY OF WESTMINSTER

OXFORD   STREET

Grosvenor
Square

Speakers'
Corner

MAYFAIR

PARK LANE

Shepherd
Market

Apsley
House Museum

Hyde Park
Corner

Green Park

BELGRAVIA

Royal
Mews

ANE STREET

Sloane
Square

PIMLICO RD.

Chelsea
Royal
Hospital

National Army
Museum

CHELSEA EMBANKMENT

Chelsea
Bridge

Battersea Park

Sotheby's

BOND
STREET

Berkeley
Square

Museum of
Mankind

Liberty

Eros

Piccadilly
Circus

Fortnum
& Mason

Christie's

Ritz

PICCADILLY

ST. JAMES'S STREET

REGENT ST.

BERWICK ST.

Soho
Square

SOHO

National
Gallery

HAYMARKET

St. James's
Palace

THE MALL

St. James's
Park

BIRDCAGE WALK

Buckingham Palace

Victoria
Station

Westminster
Cathedral

VAUXHALL BRIDGE ROAD

New
Scotland
Yard

Westminster
Abbey

10 Downing St.

Houses of
Parliament

WHITEHALL

Horse
Guards
Parade

Admiralty Arch

Banqueting
House

Charing
Cross

Nelson's Column

Charing Cross Station

Trafalgar Square

Hungerford Footbridge

PALL MALL

TOTTENHAM COURT RD.

Courtauld
Institute
Galleries

BLOOMSBURY

British
Museum

CHARING
CROSS
ROAD

Sir John Soane's
Museum

BOW
STREET

Royal
Opera
House

Covent
Garden

London
Transport
Museum

STRAND

Royal Courts
of Justice

FLEET STREET

King's Cross
Station

St. Pancras
Station

Euston
Station

Coram
Fields

Charles Dickens's
House

Gray's
Inn

Holborn
Circus

Lincoln's
Inn

Dr. Johnson's
House

The
Temple

VICTORIA EMBANKMENT

Discovery

Waterloo
Bridge

Hayward Gallery

Royal Festival Hall

National
Theatre

Waterloo
Station

Old Vic
Theatre

Westminster Bridge

Lambeth
Palace

Imperial
War Museum

Lambeth
Bridge

Tate
Gallery

Vauxhall
Bridge

GROSVENOR ROAD

River Thames

The Oval

Sadlers Wells
Theatre

CLERKENWELL

Smithfield
Market

Central
Criminal Court
(Old Bailey)

Holborn
Viaduct
Station

St. Paul's
Cathedral

Blackfriars
Station

Blackfriars
Bridge

Southwark
Bridge

Cannon Street
Station

London
Bridge

Southwark
Cathedral

George Inn

London
Bridge
Station

Geffrye
Museum

SHOREDITCH

John Wesley's
House and Chapel

Barbican
Arts Centre

Museum
of London

Guildhall

Bank of
England

Mansion
House

Fishmongers
Hall

Broad
Street
Station

Liverpool
Street
Station

Stock
Exchange

Royal
Exchange

LONDON WALL

The
Monument

Leadenhall
Market

Spitalfields
Market

Petticoat
Lane

Roman
Wall

Fenchurch Street Station

London Metal Exchange

Tower
of London

H.M.S
Belfast

Tower
Bridge

Royal
Mint

London
Docks

River Thames

CITY OF LONDON

GREATER
LONDON

St. Albans

HERTS.

BUCKS.

GRAND UNION
CANAL

ESSEX

Epping

Chipping
Ongar

Barnet

Harrow

Hendon

Highgate

Hampstead

Woodford

Tottenham

West Ham

Ruislip

Cricklewood

HEATHROW
AIRPORT

Windsor

KEW
GARDENS

London

Area Enlarged

Greenwich

Blackheath

BERKS.

Richmond

Brixton

HAMPTON
COURT

Kingston
upon Thames

Wimbledon

Croydon

DOWNE

SURREY

Thames

KENT

Maidstone

WEST
SUSSEX

GATWICK
AIRPORT

Crawley

EAST SUSSEX

Medway

17

more intimate than suburbanites could even begin to understand. Not that it was always as cordial as in recent years. No doubt the wartime Blitz, endured by royals and rag merchants on something like equal terms, had a good deal to do with it. Perhaps a shared interest in horses counts too.

Also they appear to enjoy the same sort of joke. Prince Philip came out on American television with the modest and seemingly harmless remark that times were tough and he might have to think about giving up polo. It was irresistible. No sooner did the news reach London than a group of East End dockworkers got together in a pub and floated a fund to buy the prince a polo pony. He had to move fast to divert their charitable urges.

Hard times or no, there has been no sign of the royals becoming an endangered species; but what of the Cockneys? With major areas of their natural habitat, dockland in particular, rapidly going out of business and universal television blunting their accent, they are harder to find nowadays. Not that you can ever mistake a true Cockney when you do meet one. He disobeys most of the English rules. He lacks reticence and deference; he enjoys "taking the mickey" out of someone, exploding pretensions; he is a performer and wastes no time going into his act.

And you can, after all, still meet him in his natural surroundings. The docks may dry up but the street markets sail on, strips and corners of London that have echoed with generations of spieling and dealing in places with famous names—Portobello Road, Berwick Street, Petticoat Lane.

The last time I went to Petticoat Lane I was astonished by its vitality; I had forgotten the urgency of the place, the sheer pressure of this torrent of East End humanity sweeping you along between the banks of stalls. Turn out of the main road at a corner pub called Dirty Dick's and the human flow propels you past surreal rows of whelks, shirts, apples, fur coats, flashy rings, and perkily dressed live monkeys. Here is a market deep in the bloodstream of Cockney London. The barkers sound like men with centuries of practice behind them; theirs is an art form with its own artful rhythms. "I'd *like* to charge you twenty," one of them

David Burnett, Stock Boston

18

Cascading fountains of famed Trafalgar Square frame a memorial to Horatio Nelson, hero of the 1805 Battle of Trafalgar. His statue reaches skyward atop a 167½-foot pedestal and column. The square, a rallying place for pigeons, demonstrators, and footsore visitors of all sorts, links four of London's most important streets: the Strand, Charing Cross Road, Whitehall, and The Mall.

chants; "I *could* charge you twelve; I *will* charge you ten." It's a poem—one that sells. Discreetly clutching my wallet, I enjoyed and admired this turbulent place, firm evidence that the traditional London and Londoners still live.

For me the significance of these markets—as of that royal statue—is that they are anchorages, holding points in the tide of change that has been sweeping over the metropolis. I am always surprised when visitors expect to find the British clinging nostalgically to the past and its trappings. On the contrary, London has long seemed almost profligate in the way it divests itself of its treasures and flings off its architectural clothes without bothering much about what it is likely to get in their place.

Watchdog bodies like the Royal Fine Art Commission were always willing to turn a dutiful ear to complaints and anxieties, but too often the ear turned out to be rather hard of hearing. The aims of the redevelopers were furthered by the fickle eye of the British, with whom building fashions seem to change every few decades. Georgian sobriety gave way to Regency stucco; then Victorian Gothic was all the rage, soon to be spurned in its turn by the simple-life advocates and the functionalists.

Sometimes taste undergoes a two-way switch, and buildings that can survive long enough may come into their own again. The grandiloquent Royal Albert Hall and Albert Memorial, after being music-hall jokes for half a century, are now hero-structures of the Victorian Gothic Revival. And it is amusing, in light of the current reaction against tall buildings in London—where anything over 20 stories is reckoned a "skyscraper"—that a constant Victorian criticism of the National Gallery was that it was too low.

Restless and wasteful though this waywardness can undoubtedly be, it has a good side. It shows vitality, a reluctance to be imprisoned in the past. It has always seemed to me that cities are organic in the sense that they and their inhabitants have a profound effect on each other's growth and development. If Londoners have a collective virtue that stands out, it is a kind of obstinate hopefulness, a willingness to cast their bread upon the water. Their town

Temples of gustatory delight,
the Food Halls at Harrods department store captivate soul,
stomach, and eye amid pillars
of marble and walls of tile.
The clerk at right slices smoked
salmon. Above, shanks and
roasts adorn the tiers of a marble counter. Founded in 1849
as a grocery store, Harrods
today occupies a 4½-acre block
in Knightsbridge. It has been
described as a "cross between
a pre-war ocean liner and an
Oriental bazaar."

both gains and suffers from it. Certainly this cavalier attitude toward its own physical history makes it all the more necessary to preserve what's left of its basic bones, and all the more surprising that there are any left to preserve.

The Romans began that history. There was no London other than a few minor Celtic settlements before they came. The city they developed was, broadly, the "square mile" now known as the City of London, the financial center. But nowadays the Roman profile is low—mostly well below modern ground level. The places where the bones break surface are so few that it is all the more exciting to track them down: a massive slab of Roman wall near the Tower, another in a City churchyard, a section of Roman wharf. Hunting the other fragments is a private-eye job, taking you to places like an underground car park, a post office basement, the Central Criminal Court.

Add to these, in the casual London way, the various finds that have accrued over the years: a bronze emperor's head fished out of the Thames, a Roman barge, a temple, various ornaments and weapons, a leather bikini. And any number of coins, particularly around London Bridge, suggesting either that the Roman British were remarkably careless with their money or, more likely, that they threw coins from the bridge into the river to propitiate the gods.

That first wooden bridge was, literally, the making of London. Nobody knows how long it lasted. The first stone London Bridge, the famous one with shops and houses, was begun in 1176 and lasted six centuries. The second stone bridge emigrated to America after its retirement in 1968, to be reerected at Lake Havasu in Arizona, and was replaced in London by a prestressed concrete structure that looks unlikely to collect either ghosts or votive offerings.

People still hunt for Roman relics buried in the Thames mud, and more will no doubt be found. But already enough has been unearthed for the imagination to work with in reconstructing London's four Roman centuries. Two miles of wall, some twenty feet high and eight feet thick, enclosed the city of Londinium and, for fourteen centuries, that was virtually the entire city.

Sunday morning brings throngs of bargain hunters to the East End's Middlesex Street, dubbed Petticoat Lane by 17th-century Londoners who came here to haggle over second-hand clothing. Today's Cockney pitchmen still set up stalls in their venerable street market, hawking everything from clothes to food to toys. Wall clocks, barometers, and violins vie for attention at another street market, Portobello Road, on the western outskirts of central London.

Hand signals and shouts buy and sell during Open Outcry, the frantic five-minute dealing session held twice daily by the London Metal Exchange. With members from companies in a dozen or more nations, the L.M.E. leads world trade in nonferrous metals like zinc, copper, aluminum, and silver.

Such commodity markets help make the square-mile City of London the world's most powerful financial center. Courts and legal services also concentrate in this area—in a surprisingly sylvan setting. The robed and bewigged barrister at right leaves his Lincoln's Inn chambers for court.

There's still a road called London Wall—a pretty dull one now, though it should make any historically sensitive feet tingle. The signals intensify in Leadenhall Market, a spacious emporium where quails' eggs, oysters, and other necessities of life are available for city aldermen and top directors—not so different, perhaps, from the procurators, governors, and other important people who gathered here in Roman times. For here was the basilica, London's city hall, with the huge forum adjoining.

The City's population then may have been as high as 40,000, much greater than today. Despite the efforts to bring residential life back into the square mile, its human flow consists almost entirely of commuters crowding into the banks and commercial houses in the morning and back to their suburbs in the evening. They are the crowd that flows over London Bridge in T. S. Eliot's *The Waste Land:* "I had not thought death had undone so many."

Most of the Roman population was spared the ordeal of commuter travel; they lived within the walls and, so to speak, over the shop. They seem to have been a fairly sophisticated mix of British and immigrants from various European and North African regions—a multiracial society from the start. Many of them enjoyed central heating and bathing facilities to an extent that the city was not to know again until our own day, if then.

It couldn't last, of course. "Things were never the same, I always say, after the Romans left," a lady once remarked to me at a Guildhall reception.

Evidently she disliked the Normans, as did most of London. Small trace is left of the Dark Ages that preceded the Norman arrival, when Britain was wide open to Vikings, Saxons, and other invaders. But it was a united nation, however precariously united, that William the Conqueror invaded in 1066. And it must have been a prosperous and self-confident London that felt capable—indeed, was capable—of bargaining with the Conqueror. William was prepared to trust the Londoners' undertakings but decided to build the White Tower just in case. This was the first structure of the complex now called the Tower of London.

I must confess to a sense of unreality whenever I look at that old-established horror factory. Can this be the place where half the dire deeds of English history were performed? "Ye towers of Julius, London's lasting shame," wrote the 18th-century poet Thomas Gray (sharing the common delusion of his day that the Tower was a Roman enterprise), "With many a foul and midnight murder fed." There were certainly plenty of those. You'd never think it to look at the place now. It has been to the cleaners; it no longer reeks of blood. It looks more like a child's super-castle. And up there on Tower Hill, where heads used to fall with sickening regularity, they now have a kind of Speakers' Corner for public orators like the more famous one in Hyde Park. Now they talk their heads off instead of having them chopped off, which is an advance of sorts.

What they chop now are buildings. These have been kept fairly well culled by war, fire and other disasters, human avarice, and that inordinate lust for change. Medieval, Tudor, and Jacobean London were virtually destroyed by the Great Fire of 1666; much of what was left fell victim to Georgian and Victorian speculative and industrial builders; Georgian and Victorian London were in turn casualties of Hitler's bombers and 20th-century property developers. But enough survived these successive purges and calamities to provide a mix of all the styles there ever were.

The result is varied and often exciting, but it has a breathless air, a sense of jostling for space. London is no city for vistas; it frankly lacks panoramic views. When you find a rare vantage point like Westminster Bridge, where Wordsworth produced his celebrated sonnet, you see how crowded the townscape has become since his day, how overladen with unashamedly utilitarian blocks and rectangles. Though magically transformed by night into something that even Wordsworth could never have imagined, London by day looks like a warehouse littered with huge boxes. Its mixed-up look, its proclivity to sudden and even convulsive physical change, reflects (if my theory is right) the profound social and psychological changes that have happened to the British within a single lifetime.

A modern-day lamplighter, replacing a bulb, earns a bird's-eye view of the Tower of London (opposite). Its highest turrets are part of London's oldest building, the central White Tower built in the 11th century by William the Conqueror. At various times a fortress, palace, prison, mint, and arsenal, the Tower of London is now a museum—and a stronghold for the Crown Jewels, such as St. Edward's Crown (above), used for coronations. Yeoman Warders who guard the Tower wear Tudor-style uniforms and live in Tudor lodgings within the Tower's moated walls.

In some quarters, like St. James's, these changes manage to disguise themselves with professional skill. This was establishment London, habitat of the higher administrators who ruled areas of the world many times the size of Britain, and the faces you used to see looked well aware of it. With all that parkland, St. James's had the air of a country estate come to town—spacious, serene. It has changed very little—less, certainly, than most other parts of London. And that goes for the faces as well. They have managed to retain their proconsular expressions, but now they wear their assurance like a habit or a mask. They aren't going anywhere any more. They and their scene have switched into reverse. Instead of going out to the Empire, they watch what used to be the Empire coming to them. But it's different now—no duties, no obligations, no strings.

They would, if it were permissible, look lost.

When there is nowhere else to go, you go to your club. Nothing could look more gentlemanly, more unchanging than Pall Mall, the street where most of these establishments are. Not gambling or drinking clubs, though both activities may well occur; just clubs. Above the entrance to the most famous of them, the austere Athenaeum, stands a golden girl, Pallas Athene. A little ungentlemanly to leave her there? If she were invited inside it would have to be to the Ladies' Annex, and her helmet and spear, even in these days, might cause a bit of a stir.

Neighboring clubs are less classically inclined. Bursts of radical thinking are still likely to break out at the Reform Club. The Travellers' Club looks less weatherbeaten now

Saturday sightseers and shoppers jam world-famous Regent Street in Mayfair. London's crowds swell with the arrival of foreign visitors, more than 8 million each year. The city's more colorful residents are themselves tourist attractions. Disaffected—or merely modish—young people in punk attire (right, upper), carefully outrageous and a bit menacing, sometimes charge fees to pose for tourists' cameras. Cheerful pearly kings and queens— Cockneys in button-covered costumes dating from a fad of the 1880s—are star attractions at fetes and parades, helping to raise money for charity.

27

that its members are no longer required to have ventured 500 miles from London as a qualification for joining. At the worldlier end of the street, a plaque on the wall of Number 79 reveals that Nell Gwyn, King Charles II's mistress, once lived in a house on this site, though it is not so insensitive as to add that the king visited her there.

St. James's is predominantly masculine territory. The Belgravia and Mayfair quarters, to its west and north, pay more attention to the memsahibs and their high-spirited daughters—with equally high credit ratings. Here is London's fashionable playground, the hotel and shopping sectors, still physically handsome though transformed within living memory as completely as the Empire itself.

Mayfair as the patrician forefathers knew it really died in the First World War; the lack of servants and the increase in taxes killed the great private houses, dislocating the social life that gathered round them. The era of the big hotels, nightclubs, cabarets, and gambling houses was upon us, and Mayfair never looked back. Gloss succeeded style, though a little of that survived. Recently I found a 30-yard stretch of the old domestic Regency facade in Park Lane—bows, canopies, verandas, and all. It looked like a visitor, some fragile stranger, lost and vulnerable.

Nobody could say that West End shopping lacks scope or imagination, particularly if you have a few thousand to spare for, say, a set of Chinese ceremonial pikes and axes at Harrods. When it comes to tiger skins and javelins you might prefer a shop in New Bond Street that specializes in such items. Some of Bond Street's jewelry is labeled exclusively in Arabic, for oil sheiks.

The best known West End streets—Oxford, Piccadilly, and Regent—provoke yawns in some observers. Oxford Street is in truth rather a bore; I doubt if it has aroused much emotion since the days when it led convicts to the Tyburn gibbet. Now it is an interminable middle-class shop window, lurching down-market into the cheap and raucous. Regent Street has Liberty's, eccentrically mock Tudor on the outside, but offering some of the most elegant merchandise of all the great department stores.

Actors on roller skates await their cue in Starlight Express, an innovative musical show staged at a theater near Buckingham Palace. In a somewhat more traditional performance, Italian tenor Luciano Pavarotti (opposite) sings in Verdi's Aïda at the Royal Opera House in Covent Garden. London's 50 or so theaters, located mostly in the West End, offer a wide variety of entertainment, usually including a Shakespeare play. Work is now under way on the reconstruction of Shakespeare's circular Globe Theatre on the banks of the Thames.

Piccadilly set out in life centuries ago as a country lane, growing up into a highly fashionable thoroughfare and still anxious to keep up with the old times. Where else but in Fortnum and Mason's famous food hall would you find attendants still wearing frock coats?

The handsome St. James's Church, once the most modish church in all London, was not content to expire when the spread of shops and businesses dissolved its rich congregation. It has turned itself into a bustling spiritual and social awareness center and a forum for the arts. Where elegant worshipers once paraded their gowns you may find some equally attractive market stalls, as well as the London Brass Rubbing Centre ("Take Home a Knight from Mediaeval England"). The church has services, too.

But Piccadilly's main significance now seems to be that it leads to Piccadilly Circus, that magnet for all visitors to the capital—undeservedly, many insist. Rude things are constantly said about the Circus, and most of them are true. It lacks spaciousness; it is plagued by murderous traffic and vulgar advertising displays. Yet the magnetism of the Circus holds. The crowds of young people who cluster here are irresistibly drawn to the place, probably without knowing why. (Their whimsical dress would have appealed to Robert Baker, the local tailor who sold frilled collars, called "piccadills," to young dandies centuries ago, supposedly giving the place its name.) Here is the true heart of London. This Circus—which looks more like a square, cramped and rather tawdry, a gathering place where there is scarcely any room to gather—is a kind of symbol of

London's elite inhabitants include so-called Sloane Rangers (left, upper), the near equivalent of American preppies, here gathering at a chic pub near Sloane Square. Many of Belgravia's 19th-century stucco mansions are now divided into luxury flats; former mews (stables) have become expensive living quarters. Tree-lined streets and private parks grace Knightsbridge (opposite). The two town-house crescents of Lennox Gardens front a fenced park equipped with dog loos. Only residents have keys to the park gates.

London's restless vitality, its determination to look haphazard, to break up patterns.

The Circus is where paths cross. Here, cheek by jowl, are the Two Worlds—the London of the rich spenders, the London of the dropouts and derelicts. One offers brilliant entertainment, some of Europe's best food, and a few hotels where you can buy the dearest things in London—quiet and personal attention. In the other world you may find yourself sleeping on benches or even sidewalks.

And now the Third World has come to join them.

London was always cosmopolitan. It has now become so multiracial a society that its older citizens must sometimes wonder whether it is they who have dropped in from another country. A few hundred yards from Piccadilly Circus is a part of Soho where almost every sign is in Chinese—not just restaurants, but banks, beauty salons, cinemas, travel agents—even, strangest of all to the Cockney wanderer abroad in his own country, a Congregational church with the authentic air of an English Sunday morning, except that the church announcements are in Chinese too.

Ethnic restaurants abound. They always did, though they used to be called "foreign," which somehow sounded more appetizing. Now there are far more, and of far greater range. They cater in their own terms, without obvious salesmanship or competitive lures to tourists. I have explored Indian, African, Greek, Japanese, Lebanese, Caribbean, and many other menus, often with pleasure and usually with repletion. Nothing was explained unless I asked. I was left to find my own way, and quite right too. Explorers should not be pampered.

You will hunt hard, and perhaps in vain, for an English restaurant, though I did find an authentic charmer in Covent Garden, full of old oak and old prints and old waiters.

For the rest, you begin to understand why in nearby Park Lane, another area effectively liberated from the British, a high-rise American hotel boasted of having equipped itself with a bar "designed to give the atmosphere of an English pub." Much the same eerie impression of being a tourist at large in his own land might come to a Londoner in so

Sikhs demonstrate outside India House in London, protesting Indian government policies in the Punjab, where Sikhs make up a majority of the population. Sikhs also make up a sizable portion of London's large community of South Asians, West Indians, and Pakistanis. Most live in inner-city areas or in enclaves such as Brixton, with poor housing and rampant unemployment. Government-sponsored mural art (opposite) can sometimes express antigovernment sentiments.

Since the early 1970s a new kind of immigrant has arrived in London—oil-rich Arabs. Their numbers and wealth are evinced by the new mosque built in Regent's Park (right).

contrasting an area as Brixton, where a third of the population is black and the splendid market has a pronounced West Indian stamp. I saw young white stallholders selling yams to black customers; everybody looked warily happy in an area that was shaken by fierce racial riots in 1981.

Many of the Asians and West Indians in London now have proprietary interests. They are second generation Londoners, often with Cockney accents indistinguishable from those of the whites. So the return journey is complete. The Empire has come home. With such economic and ethnic differences, aren't clashes inevitable? Well, they have happened, and no doubt they will happen again. Londoners have always been a turbulent lot, whether they derived from Bow, Brixton, Dublin, or Montego Bay. Medieval battles between rival trade guilds tended to be more violent than any local football derby today; West Ham versus Tottenham can provide nothing to match the turmoil when the goldsmiths met the tailors. And so it went, through the ages of elegance and moral ascendancy. London, even Victorian London, was a dangerous town.

Why, then, the widespread notion that it is more dangerous than it used to be? It depends what is meant by "used to be." There was a period of abnormal social serenity between the World Wars and on into the 1950s. British domestic behavior (on the surface at least) was exemplary, and no comparison, before or after, could stand against it. London acquired a reputation as a place so well conducted and civilized as to put other cities to shame.

But now, they all warn, you must guard your pockets, see to your burglar alarms, think twice before going out at night if you are old and frail, learn karate if you are female, put chains on your doors. The hazards have surely been exaggerated. Londoners can still for the most part number their burglaries, like their marriages, on the fingers of one hand. Violent crime has increased, here as elsewhere. Terrorists have claimed victims in the heart of London. Yet the odds against falling victim to violence are still long. In 1983 London had 149 murders; New York City had 1,622. True, things are not what they were. Graffiti, not all of

it amusing, covers many a wall; slashed seats disfigure the commuter trains; on days of emotional football matches, unpredictable crowds roam the streets. As for demonstrators, these have become such a regular part of the London scene that people scarcely bother to look.

The town is less easygoing, more tense and tetchy than it used to be. A new conformism has reinforced its class consciousness; the amiable bohemianism that used to offset this in central areas like Soho and Bloomsbury is harder to find, particularly with the spread of fashionable wine bars and the steady, relentless gentrification of pubs.

I do miss the tea shops. There used to be one every few hundred yards, or so it seemed. It was one of the few classless areas London permitted. You would drop in to take the weight off your feet, drink your "cuppa" (real tea made from tea leaves), and be called "luv" by a waitress in cap and apron, all for a few pennies. You can still go to the Ritz and enjoy, at a price, the sort of spread that would make a schoolboy's heart sing, but it isn't the same thing.

London is nevertheless full of hidden appeal, round-the-corner surprises. You can get an appetizer by walking behind that vast, low National Gallery and finding streets of little shops. A few yards off the unlovable Oxford Street are narrow, elegant lanes you would need to get lost to find, if you didn't know they were there. Equally hidden, though no farther from respectable Piccadilly, is the less respectable though entirely charming Shepherd Market, a time-trapped morsel of the 18th century that is no market in the usual sense—cafés and shops line its alleys—and certainly has nothing to do with sheep.

The most extraordinary contrast of all is to be found farther east. Ten paces from the Strand and Fleet Street, possibly the noisiest thoroughfare in London, lies the secluded Temple, which might well claim to be the quietest. This is lawyers' territory, and lawyers know how to look after their own. Here is a sizable slab of old London immaculately repaired and preserved: free from traffic, carpeted with collegiate lawns, unbelievably peaceful. So decent of the lawyers, I always think, to let the rest of us in without a

33

fee. I have often played truant here, a refugee from Fleet Street's newspaper treadmill, loitering around the Temple Church of the Crusaders and Middle Temple Hall, or surveying the ancient gardens where, in *Henry VI*, Shakespeare launched the Wars of the Roses.

The place for peace and quiet on a more domestic basis used to be a house in the suburbs, until the motor age ended all that. Nevertheless, London suburbs—or "villages," as they like to call themselves—deserve a place on the asset side of the metropolitan balance sheet. Ask Londoners where they would like to live if they had the choice and a surprising number would not want to change from where they are now—usually in a suburb. This appreciation is quite new; until recently sophisticated Londoners affected to despise the suburbs, and it took foreigners to assess them at their true worth. Now suburbanites are likely to be fiercely appreciative about their home "village."

Certainly I felt like that about Blackheath, where I lived for 20 years. Unfashionable south side of the river it may be, but most of my neighbors and I were convinced that we lived in the most interesting village in London—possessing a stretch of turf unrivaled in historical associations, where armies camped and highwaymen rode, where kings were welcomed or dispatched abroad, where, it is claimed, golf was introduced into England and the first rugby club was formed. . . . This, with or without encouragement, is the way metropolitan villagers tend to go on.

Everyone's personal suburb may be the best, but this doesn't prevent them from having an accepted pecking (or

Brian Seed, Click/Chicago

Four royal parks provide mid-city refuges in London. Boaters and sunseekers in popular Hyde Park (opposite) enjoy the Serpentine, an artificial lake that curves across the spacious grounds. Beyond it tower the high-rise barracks of the Household Cavalry. Weary students (right, lower) rest on the steps of the ornate Albert Memorial, one of many monuments and statues in Hyde Park and in the adjacent Kensington Gardens. Smaller and wilder Green Park (right, upper), once used for aristocratic duels, offers grassy meadows and tree-shaded paths.

35

Crowded with memorials and graves, Poets' Corner in Westminster Abbey honors Britain's literary giants from Geoffrey Chaucer to Dylan Thomas—and some nonliterary and non-British ones, too. The face of German-born composer George Frederick Handel's statue (upper right corner) was modeled from a death mask. Below it is a bas-relief of Swedish singer Jenny Lind.

Built in the 11th century, rebuilt in the 13th, with many additions since, Westminster Abbey has been the coronation site for all but two British monarchs. Pupils of Westminster School, founded by Queen Elizabeth I, gather for morning services in the abbey (opposite).

snubbing) order. Postal codes can be as eloquent as letters after your name; NW3 is likely to carry at least as much social cachet as MBE (member of the Order of the British Empire). Everyone knows that NW3 is Hampstead, but approximations don't count: NW2 is only Cricklewood and that (except to Cricklewoodians) doesn't do at all. Likewise SW3 is Chelsea; SW2 is Brixton.

Contemporary poets and other writers appear to be happy, as happy as their nature allows, in suburbs. Other fauna—foxes, owls, squirrels, even the rare badger—have lately attracted attention by moving into London suburbs from the outer agricultural belt, possibly to benefit from the ecological interest that has swept the urban areas.

Fauna that change habitat could never, one would think, include Trafalgar Square pigeons. Authority looks at them askance: They scare as many kids as they delight, they mess everything up, they humiliate the dignified statues round the square. But they are a part of the London scene, and, like other Londoners, they sometimes behave in an eccentric and mysterious way. I have myself seen a pigeon boarding a train on the underground at Trafalgar Square. Are they abandoning their wings?

Eccentricity is tolerated by Londoners, expected, even. I remember seeing a man leaving home one morning with briefcase and umbrella, dressed like anyone setting out for the office except for one thing—he was on roller skates. Nobody was rude enough to stare. London is full of loners. Some of them tend to talk to themselves or their pets. "Don't get restless now," I heard a woman in a café saying to her old dog, gently and even lovingly, "or I'll shoot you. I will—I'll shoot you dead." The dog obviously didn't believe a word of it.

Even violence is sometimes touched by the bizarre. A Bulgarian exile was murdered with a poisoned pellet shot from an umbrella. In the Victoria Embankment Gardens, vandals or metal-looters demolished a bronze statue, leaving only the feet. It made a curiously malign sight.

In contrast, the statue of Boadicea, Queen of the Celtic Iceni, by Westminster Bridge always seemed to me to look

Tea dancing at the Ritz, a Sunday pastime for romantics, is back in full swing now that the hotel has been restored to its turn-of-the-century splendor. More exotic parties take place at the St. James's Club (right, upper), which caters to show-business and jet-set people, and the occasional python.

The St. James's took its name from a Piccadilly gentlemen's club, now defunct. The profusion of such clubs before World War II made London the club capital of the world. High costs have forced many of these venerable institutions to close, merge, or even admit women.

Other clubs, like the Connoisseur on Kensington High Street (right, lower), exist for a special reason: gambling. Foreigners may join for a fee, but must wait 48 hours to gamble. This rule—to discourage impulsive gambling—and others make British gambling the world's most tightly regulated.

eccentrically serene for a tribal leader driving a chariot, a woman contemporaries described as "huge of frame, terrifying of aspect." She looks more like some president of a women's institute, and you would never suspect her of burning Roman London with such ferocity that the scars are visible to this day.

London's recent artistic achievements have been massive; its culture complex on the South Bank of the Thames is unmatched anywhere in the world in its offering of plays, films, art, and music—now reinforced at the Barbican, the new residential and arts center up in the City. These, together with a prestigious national opera, are costly. The roars of hunger and sometimes anger when the government doles out subsidies suggest the feeding of lions.

Londoners are expansive in their enthusiasms. The Cockneys in the markets, the Irish in the pubs of Camden Town, the West Indians in Brixton and New Cross, the rock and disco scene, the buskers (street entertainers), the student soloists who play violins or guitars in the underground passages—all these are part of London's culture. And so, it seems to me, is the public's support for these private enterprises despite official discouragement. Even Bach is banned in the subways, but the hurrying audiences who drop coins in the instrument cases are clearly of a different mind. They like what they hear, and often it's good. "The best acoustics in London," one soloist observed.

Then there is Covent Garden, more than ever a cultural asset. The old produce market—famed for its baffling mixture of grand opera, cabbage leaves, and Cockney wit—has moved to Battersea, but a whole new complex of shops, retail market stalls, cafés, and assorted entertainments has now cleverly fitted itself round the piazza. It was a bold move, to snatch this rich scrap from the jaws of the property marketeers. The complex caters to a range of tastes and pocketbooks rare indeed in class-stratified London.

London's museums and art collections are so impressive and daunting a part of its culture—and the world's—that they can get little attention here. The British Museum is too vast to be conquered in a visit (Continued on page 43)

Everyone's Home Away from Home, the British Pub

Jodi Cobb, National Geographic Photographer (all)

The pub is an idiosyncratic British institution. It cannot be re-created outside its native lands, because a pub is made by the people who drink there. "The local" is an organic part of the community.

No wonder that the focal point of Britain's longest running TV series, "Coronation Street," is a pub called the Rover's Return. And it's a matter of crucial concern to residents of the street when a new landlord moves in. For if he is uncongenial, the pub will decline.

A real pub has a landlord who cashes the writer's paychecks, a barmaid who takes messages for the artist with no phone, three hardhats in a corner picking the pub's football team, a stockbroker canvassing for a charity bicycle ride, and an old lady with a hat full of cherries who comes in at nine every night to drink a bottle of stout and take another home for her dog. All this because a pub is, truly, its full name: a public house.

A real pub has regulars who "prop up the bar," like these (right) seen through the bottle glass windows of a London pub. That's another idiosyncrasy of the pub—people stand to drink, particularly in the "public" bar. Most pubs have a second bar as well: the "saloon" or "lounge" bar, with slightly higher prices and—for frustrated foreigners and the like—more seats.

And while on the subject of frustrations: Britain's archaic liquor licensing laws—not applicable in major Scottish cities—permit pubs to open only for a few midday hours and then again from 5:30 or 6 until 10:30 or 11 at night. The landlord's traditional proclamation of the inevitable is "Time, gentlemen!" followed by the draping of the bar towel over the pumps.

Undraped, the pumps (left) serve up pints and half-pints. The most popular brew is called bitter—golden, hop-flavored—but you can also try mild ale, barley wine, stout, lager, or cider (see glossary).

Two points of etiquette for

neophytes: People pay for drinks in rounds; if you accept a drink, buy a round in return. And don't tip the landlord (he is, after all, your host).

If you go sampling in London, you'll find pubs patronized by doctors, boxers, printers, lawyers, bookmakers, seamen, journalists, mailmen, to name but a few. The Salisbury, for example (below), is in the heart of theaterland, in St. Martin's Lane, and is full of actors and stage people.

Yet if you, a stranger, happen by, you will not be treated as an alien. A good pub must make everyone welcome. The regulars may form a coterie, but intermingling with it are the irregulars who just drop in for a drink or a plate of bangers (sausages) and mash. The barmaid will still beam you a smile through the press of people at the bar and call out "What'll you drink, ducks?"

That is the magic of a pub, the kind of thing that perhaps moved our greatest regular, Dr. Samuel Johnson, to remark: "There is nothing which has yet been contrived by man, by which so much happiness is produced as by a good tavern or inn."

PETER CROOKSTON

41

or a dozen visits; you could comb it every day for a year and still miss a lot. Here is the world and its treasures—its loot, some say, like the Greeks who would like the Elgin Marbles back. Hardly less immense, the Victoria and Albert Museum is decorative and domestic; you might think it was parading the home life of rich, highly cultivated giants. The new Museum of London brilliantly presents the city's past; sound and light take you back 300 years to experience the Great Fire. Of the great art galleries, the National specializes in classical and the Tate in modern pictures. My own favorites are more modest affairs, more like private houses, which they once were: the 18th-century Wallace Collection and the 19th-century Soane Museum.

But for me, the streets and parks are the best museum. Walking in London is a pleasure. You couldn't do better in the country. In a sense you *are* in the country. Every visitor to London is proudly told that he can walk all the way from Westminster to Bayswater or Kensington without stepping off grass (except for crossing a couple of roads).

I must have told this to a dozen people, one time and another. Now seemed to be the time to try it myself, and I found the boast perfectly true. St. James's Park, Green Park, Hyde Park, Kensington Gardens are like continuous movements in a green symphony. You start in St. James's Park, ideally on a sunny day in May. The blossoms shout, the water birds shine, pelicans bask on their rocky island. The view from the bridge, dominated by the strut and glitter of the Horse Guards Parade grounds, could be the last blast of Edwardian imperialism. No wonder this park is addicted to brass bands.

In Green Park the key is lower, the brass more muted. By the time you reach the wide open spaces of Hyde Park the mood is almost pastoral. Over the Serpentine and into Kensington Gardens you move into genteel Victorian country, where superior nursemaids keep watch over affluent babies. Sometimes you will see protest marchers; always you will see joggers.

Turf is fine, but the streets are best after all. "Get lost"— that is the only advice to offer a stranger footloose in

A powerful backhand helps the young Swedish contender Carina Karlsson reach the quarter-finals at Wimbledon— the All England Club's annual Lawn Tennis Championships. Played in the London suburb of Wimbledon, this prestigious competition was first held in 1877, four years after tennis was introduced in Britain. All courts are busy (opposite) as the fortnight of matches begins. More than 300 players compete; more than 30,000 spectators come daily to watch them—and feast on traditional strawberries and cream.

Beside himself, prominent photographer Patrick Lichfield poses with his double at Madame Tussaud's waxworks. Behind him, the royal family stands in stately tableau. Madame Tussaud's exhibits, a London institution since 1835, include both historical and contemporary people, the famous and the infamous, all modeled and dressed with true-to-life detail. Sculptor Judith Craig (left) used photographs and measurements to create her wax model of Lord Lichfield. American entertainer Liza Minnelli contributed the false eyelashes for her effigy; President Ronald Reagan sent one of his neckties.

At Christie's auction house (opposite), another London institution, solemn dealers pay close attention to a sale of paintings. Christie's (properly Christie, Manson & Woods) and the rival Sotheby's both sell art, antiques, books, and jewelry; both have been in business for over 200 years.

London. Allow it to happen and it will, in this most incoherent, shapeless, and fascinating of capital cities, in no time at all. The dome of St. Paul's will bounce about the sky like a great ball, now over your right shoulder, now your left. Take no notice. A map will solve all.

But the most devoted foot slogger can hardly be expected to tramp the 35 miles that Greater London is now reckoned to span. You must seek public transport. The system is huge, complex, and undervalued. Bear in mind that traveling Londoners observe certain powerful customs. Take conversation. In surface trains and in buses occasional remarks are permitted, usually about the weather or the waywardness of the service. But down in the "tube," travelers never talk to each other; the rule is absolute. Tubes are tediously efficient and, of course, have no weather.

That, in theory. In practice I found myself on an underground journey that soon broke out into the sunshine. The expedition was to Ongar, Essex, in the far northeast, 38 stations away from West Ruislip at the other end of the line and almost, you might think, qualifying you for the Travellers' Club. My tube train was like a worm suddenly endowed with wings, skimming through gardens, woodland, and open fields, past Woodford and bosky Epping (Churchill country), and so to Ongar. Only 20-odd miles from central London, but it might have been 200.

This experience led me to believe what I read about an MP (member of Parliament), Enoch Powell, who actually went fox hunting by underground. It was soon after the war. He found a hunt he could reach by public transport and, according to the writer Andrew Roth, "travelled out to it on the Tube, in full hunting kit. He returned the same way, often muddy and battered from having been thrown."

Indeed, I soon discovered when I worked as a journalist at Westminster that MPs are as prone to bizarre behavior as the rest of their fellow citizens. That, actually, is a considerable understatement. The system they obstinately work under, the jealously maintained parliamentary antics that keep the ancient machine turning, would be regarded as collective insanity in any (Continued on page 53)

Royal London: Ancient Pageantry of a Modern Kingdom

"Elizabeth the Second, by the Grace of God of the United Kingdom of Great Britain and Northern Ireland and of Her other Realms and Territories Queen, Head of the Commonwealth, Defender of the Faith"—traces her ancestry to King Egbert, the first king of a united England, who reigned ten centuries ago.

Only one episode broke the monarchy's continuity during those centuries—the Civil War won in 1649 by Oliver Cromwell, the controversial parliamentary leader who ruled England for nine years under the Commonwealth. But the power of the throne has changed considerably. The absolute monarchy of the 17th century has evolved into the limited constitutional monarchy that governs today.

The Queen, it is often said, "reigns but does not rule." But though Her Majesty's role in government is minor, she plays a major role in boosting the morale and unity of a realm beset with myriad problems. At a time of low public confidence in other British institutions, the monarchy's prestige and popularity remain high. The colorful pageantry of the Trooping the Colour each June and the Queen's glittering procession to open Parliament in autumn have been known to stir even the most cynical hearts.

The Queen's subjects take considerable interest in the public activities—and private lives—of royalty, particularly in the doings of the popular Prince Charles and Princess Diana. (The Queen finally asked the press to allow the beleaguered couple some privacy.) Stories real or fanciful—of royal romances or squabbles or impending abdications—are trumpeted daily

British Grenadiers parade before their Commander in Chief, Queen Elizabeth II (left), honoring her birthday with one of London's most spectacular state events, Trooping the Colour.

in the tabloid newspapers.

Two London papers run more respectable "Court Circular" sections that announce the royal family's official activities—Princess Anne to attend a meeting of the Save the Children Fund (of which she is president); Princess Margaret to appear at the annual party of the Royal Hospital, Chelsea (she is Colonel-in-Chief of the Royal Army Nursing Corps); Prince Philip to lunch with the Royal Marine Officers' Dinner Club (he is Captain General of the Royal Marines).

London's royal rituals center in Westminster, once a royal city in itself. King Edward the Confessor built a palace here in the 11th century, on the site now occupied by the Houses of Parliament (still called the Palace of Westminster). Across the street is Westminster Abbey, where all but two of Britain's monarchs were crowned. About half a mile away is the present royal residence, Buckingham Palace. Built in 1703 as a private home, the mansion was purchased by King George III in 1762. George IV undertook major changes and additions, but died before they were completed. Queen Victoria made it her palace.

Buckingham Palace draws a mob of sightseers on summer mornings, come to see the Changing of the Guard. The crowd waits patiently, jammed against the high iron fence, or perched on the massive Queen Victoria Memorial in front of the gates. At last, from nearby barracks, comes the parade of guardsmen, splendid in red tunics and tall bearskin hats, led by the music of the regimental band. Into the palace forecourt they march and, with complex and precise maneuvers, the new guard replaces the old. The band, meanwhile, entertains with martial music and pops.

Royal guardsmen may look like toy soldiers, but they are real military troops, members of five infantry and two cavalry regiments, serving tours of duty with the Queen's Household Division. The regiments are distinguishable by the colors of their tunics or the

Guards and spectators line The Mall as the Princess of Wales and other royalty return to Buckingham Palace after the Trooping the Colour ceremonies. The West Front of the palace (far right) faces a 39-acre garden where as many as 8,000 guests wander during each of the Queen's three annual garden parties.

spacing of their buttons. They take turns with sentry duty and other assignments.

The Queen herself does not appear at the Changing of the Guard, but you know she is at home if the royal flag is flying over the palace. One part of the palace is open to visitors —the Queen's Gallery, where paintings and furnishings are displayed. The Royal Mews, behind the palace, exhibits the state carriages.

A broad ceremonial avenue, The Mall, extends from Buckingham Palace to Admiralty Arch. This is the route for royal processions. On the right is green St. James's Park, with its duck-filled lake and tourist-filled Cake House. On the left are St. James's Palace, built by Henry VIII and now used for court ceremonies, and Clarence House, home of the Queen Mother.

Royal processions make a right turn into the Horse Guards Parade ground, stop-ping there for Trooping the Colour or continuing on to Whitehall and the Houses of Parliament for opening day.

A more solemn and simple parade takes place on Remembrance Day in November, when the Queen arrives by limousine at Whitehall to lay a wreath at the Cenotaph, a monument honoring the dead of World Wars I and II.

Londoners may also see their Queen at such events as the Chelsea Flower Show and command performances at theaters. Any event attended by royalty is a royal event, and a strict etiquette is observed. No one speaks to the Queen unless spoken to; no one touches her; no one turns their back. However awkwardly, women curtsy and men bow. Whether in full regalia at the opening of Parliament or in quilted coat and head scarf at a horse race, she is the Queen.

SHIRLEY L. SCOTT

Symbol of London, the Clock Tower of the Houses of Parliament sounds the quarter hour with a famous bronze bell—Big Ben. A palace once occupied this site; both legislative houses—the hereditary Lords and the elected Commons— have met here since 1547. The present structure, built after a fire in 1834, includes magnificent rooms for the monarch, who comes here each year to open Parliament. At right, the Queen presides over her assembled Lords (including archbishops and bishops of the Church of England) and Commons.

other calling. It exerts a theatrical mesmerism. The solemnity of the Speaker's procession on its way to the Commons can have strange effects. They still tell of an MP on the fringe of the watching crowd who caught sight of a friend and called "Neil!," whereupon several awed spectators obediently fell to their knees. Do I believe it? Let me say I believe it could happen.

Some aspects of the ritual are less dignified—the all-night wrangles, the rehearsed outbreaks of spontaneous fury, the anxious vigilance of the party whips to ensure that the expected number of members tramp through the "aye" and "no" lobbies when a vote is called. The stage for this curious variety show extends beyond the parliamentary building itself to bars and restaurants, and even some private houses and flats, in the immediate neighborhood. Whenever a vote (known as a "division") is called, warning bells ring, shattering the peace of this enclave in the shadow of the looming Westminster Abbey. Whatever the MPs may be doing, they drop it and go rushing back, to file dutifully through the appropriate voting lobby (joining the wrong queue is considered unforgivably careless). Ambushes have been arranged, the minority party lying low to give the enemy a false sense of security, then descending on the lobbies from their hiding places with, so to speak, cries of triumph and cobwebs in their hair.

The Houses of Parliament were the first high-rise challenge to the twin towers of Westminster Abbey. But the ancient abbey stands grandly aloof from such upstarts. Inside, its atmosphere—compared to the austere St. Paul's, many centuries its junior—is as far from aloof as an atmosphere can get. It throbs with the pressure of humanity, living and dead. Visitors throng the nave and the aisles, crowd the abundant chapels and monuments, and stare at congregations of white marble figures, some of them frozen in quite unnerving postures. No wonder ghosts are on record here: A medieval monk is said to have once talked severely to tourists, of whom he evidently disapproved; but they sensed nothing unusual until he departed by walking through the wall.

Michael St. Maur Sheil

Hampton Court Palace, situated beside the Thames about 12 miles southwest of central London, has been described as "more like unto a paradise than any earthly habitation." Built by Cardinal Wolsey in 1515, the magnificent palace was soon appropriated by Henry VIII. It served as a royal residence for more than two centuries. In 1838 Queen Victoria opened the palace and its gardens to the public. The monarch's apartments in the right-hand wing face the forested Privy Garden and the stately geometry of the Pond Garden (above).

53

Tropical trees and plants fill the lofty Palm House in the Royal Botanic Gardens at Kew. Redwoods and rhododendrons, bamboo and bluebells also thrive in the greenhouses and gardens of this 300-acre preserve, once the grounds of two royal residences. Visitors can stroll from the Lily Pond to ferneries to the 163-foot-high Pagoda flanked by a garden of heath plants. More than a pleasure park, Kew Gardens also serves as a major international center for botanical research, education, and conservation.

I have left to the end what I obstinately regard as London's greatest asset, shared alike by princes, politicians, Cockneys, and suburbanites, and now neglected alike by all but the tourists who chug along on the sightseeing riverboats that alone animate the near-moribund Thames.

Who would think, to see it now, that the river gave London its birth, its shape (such as it has), its wealth, and for centuries its main system of transport? High Street, London, they called it once; now it has been bypassed.

For decades the tidal Thames was grossly overexploited—befouled until it was little better than an open sewer, its breath thickened into fog, its waterway as overcrowded as the land highways are now. Then—suddenly and quite recently—the fogs cleared to reveal a virtually empty river: the great ships gone, the upper docks dead.

The Thames—it is a consolation of sorts—has never been so clean in our time, or our fathers' time. The fish are swimming back, which is fine for the fish. But Londoners don't seem much interested in their river any more.

Those tourists in their riverboats are the wise ones. The best trip in London can't after all be done on foot. It is the water journey from Hampton Court in the west to Greenwich in the east, with a different prospect round every bend: stately parkland, riverside suburbia, the great buildings of central London like Westminster and the Tower, seen at their best from the water; then dead docks, dereliction, the eerie beauty of abandoned wharves. The last bend lifts the heart, with the former Royal Observatory dominating its hill in Greenwich Park and the soaring masts of that fine old tea clipper, the *Cutty Sark.*

No great vistas, did I say? Except one. The Greenwich waterfront, ruled by the Royal Naval College where the palace of the Tudors once stood, provides one of Europe's great views. Even though London tends to shun the grand gesture, here, sounded in a single major chord, are the echoes that have dominated its life—echoes of kings and Cockneys, suburbanites and scientists and sailing men, merchants and dockers, the highly assorted characters who are still proud to call themselves Londoners.

By Geoffrey Moorhouse
Photographs by Dan Dry

The English Heartland

Even when the sun is obscured . . . these walls
are still faintly warm and luminous, as if they
knew the trick of keeping the lost sunlight of
centuries glimmering about them. This lovely
trick is at the very heart of the Cotswold mystery.
It is this, and not the green hills, the noble
woods, the perfect flowering of architecture, that
makes these villages so notable an enchantment.

J. B. PRIESTLEY, 1934

Saintbury, Gloucestershire, a village in the Cotswolds

And strange enchantments from the past,
  And memories of the friends of old,
And strong Tradition binding fast
    The flying terms with bands of gold,—
All these hath Oxford. . . .

ANDREW LANG, 19th century

Oxford students end the annual Eights Week rowing regatta with the traditional burning of a shell.

It was late in March when I set out to rediscover the English heartland, and the ornamental cherry trees were already beginning to blossom around the eastern bottoms of the Chiltern Hills. By the time I had worked my way along the Thames Valley, up through the Cotswolds, and into Shakespeare country, the blossoms everywhere had been joined by a counterpoint of village daffodils. And the big black acres of Bedfordshire, where the last of the Brussels sprouts were being harvested and where plows were readying the ground for fresh crops, had given way to pastures dappled with the year's first appearance of lambs—at least a month earlier, these, than those born in the harder climate of the North.

Although some would dispute the title of this chapter, perhaps out of local patriotism, it is hard to see how any other area can claim to be more the heart of England than the tract that encompasses both the Chilterns and the Cotswolds and stretches from the valley of the Thames to that of Shakespeare's Avon. True, the village of Meriden—traditionally reckoned to be at the geographical dead center of England—had the county of Warwickshire pulled from under its feet and replaced by that of West Midlands when Parliament approved a bureaucratic rearrangement of English county boundaries in 1974. But my heartland occupies the ground between the monstrous urban sprawls of London and Birmingham; it probably contains more significant English history than anywhere outside the capital; above all, its model image of English countryside still dominates the impressions of the visitor, both foreign and homemade.

Its detractors (rude Northerners like myself) often refer to it as "chocolate box England," because the packagers of Christmas confectionery are still apt to use sentimental illustrations from the rural 19th century, British versions of Currier and Ives, with the thatched cottage and hollyhocks up the garden path most prominent among them; and the heartland abounds in such dwellings even now, or

variations on the same theme. It is, blessedly, a largely rural area still, blotched infrequently by industry, badly tainted only along its southeastern edges by the contaminations of the great metropolis.

And all of it in a relatively small space. The area is less than 70 miles from top to bottom, no more than 100 miles from east to west. This is all of a piece with the scale of the landscape itself. By any continental standard, both the Chilterns and the Cotswolds are comically modest ranges of hill country. The Chilterns never go higher than 860 feet above sea level, and the Cotswolds barely manage to top 1,000 feet. Yet in relationship to their surroundings, they can be impressive, offering a steep edge above a ravine, a towering skyline seen from a valley floor. What J. B. Priestley wrote of England as a whole is particularly true about this part of it: "The magic starts in the astonishing difference between the geographical size of England and her *real size*. She is just pretending to be so small."

The heartland's magic consists in the astonishing variety to be found within such geographical smallness. Take, for example, the matter of architecture. In Hertfordshire they built churches for hundreds of years with a rectangular tower topped by a tiny spire, known locally as a "snuffer," a style found nowhere else in Great Britain. A few miles to the west, where the Chilterns have at last got into their stride, the old churches are not only snufferless, but mostly built with walls of flint, because the Chilterns are based on chalk. Chalk provides both flint deposits and soil favored by beech trees—thickly clad hillsides of them—but little in the way of substantial masonry. When Buckinghamshire has been left behind, Oxfordshire and Gloucestershire betray the presence of solid limestone underground, part of a

Three young misses, dressed for a Hertfordshire wedding, exemplify the English heartland's tidy charm. Variety marks this region between the Thames and Avon Valleys. Beechwood cloaks the Chiltern Hills, thatch and timber cottages distinguish Warwickshire, and limestone built the Cotswolds' splendid steeples. This gentle countryside has seen the birth of Shakespeare and much of England's most significant history.

61

belt running diagonally across England through the Cotswolds. It provided the ancient churches and homes with great silvery or honey-colored building blocks. Thatched roofs, which have appeared intermittently thus far, are more heavily spread through Warwickshire. So is the black-and-white half-timbered construction of old cottages and the appearance of mellow brick, which is missing from the Cotswolds. Brick is the great building material of Bedfordshire, because that county is rich in suitable clay.

Navigating through the English heartland therefore is often, visually, like going from one country to the next, instead of merely stepping across county boundaries. But the charms of this countryside are subtle, and you have to keep your eyes open to appreciate them properly. They do not bang you over the head, demanding your attention.

It was a few years since I had roamed round here, and at first I was faintly depressed by what Progress had done. At St. Albans, Hertfordshire, the Roman settlement of Verulamium, with its mosaic floors and half-tumbled walls, remained unchanged, and in the cathedral some careful restoration had uncovered even more of the medieval wall paintings than I recalled. But only a mile or two away, in the small town of Hoddesdon, some authorized vandal had demolished the inn that Izaak Walton frequented when he fished the River Lea before writing *The Compleat Angler*, in order to make room for a supermarket.

The northern edge of the Chilterns revealed further menace. Already the commuter bungalows have crept along the Hughenden Valley as far as Bryants Bottom.

Patrick Rance samples one of the more than 200 cheeses that make his nationally renowned Streatley store a favorite Berkshire tourist stop.

Tourism also brings new life to the Cotswolds. The region began a long decline in the 1830s, when the once prosperous textile industry collapsed

from too many mills and too little power to run them. In the busy town of Winchcombe (left), a painter touches up the clock of St. Peter's, a 15th-century church built with wool money. The tall gables and steep tiled roofs on Chipping Campden's High Street (opposite) typify Cotswold villages.

Who knows how long it will be before they climb the hillside and wriggle into the hollow that at present conceals Great Hampden, with its flinty church standing sentinel over the mortal remains of John Hampden, who challenged King Charles I in 1637. The monarch had devised a new tax to pay for his navy; the Chiltern squire refused to pay it, and the consequent parliamentary uproar eventually turned into a bloody struggle, the English Civil War.

Such dissonances echo from time to time wherever you go across the heartland. There are cruise missiles now in Berkshire, not so very far from where the rudimentary outline of the White Horse was cut, perhaps in the first century B.C., into the grassy slopes of the chalk Downs that rear above Uffington. The Cotswolds are sometimes made hideous with the sound of military jets that have taken off from the airfield at Fairford, whose 15th-century church contains its original stained glass, some of the most magnificent glazing in the whole country. From the battlements of Berkeley Castle, in whose dungeon Edward II was slowly and painfully done to death by his queen and her lover, it is difficult not to get an eyeful of a nuclear power station on the gleaming edge of the River Severn not far away.

Yet even within spitting distance of London, where the heartland has been ravaged most by the march of time, it is surprisingly easy to hide from what jars and imagine that time has stood still. A little to the north of Hoddesdon, nothing much has been disturbed for ages at Ayot St. Lawrence, least of all in the house where George Bernard Shaw once dwelt. There, just inside the front door, is the contraption (a sort of bicycle without wheels) on which the dramatist used to keep fit, and on his desk are still the preprinted postcards he would send to correspondents who were not personal friends. ("Mr. Shaw regrets that he cannot contribute to your charity, as he earns only enough to keep himself in bread and butter," is typical of the putdown that came most naturally to him.) Just outside Chalfont St. Giles is Jordans, the Quaker meetinghouse in whose burial ground William Penn was laid after his return from Philadelphia, and close to it the barn whose timbers, it is said, belonged originally to the *Mayflower*.

I descended those beech-blurred Chiltern slopes and came down to the Thames where the river neatly bisects the towns of Windsor and Eton. For all that the first of these is smothered in tourists for most of the year, it is impossible not to be awed by the sheer bulk of the castle, straggling mightily across 13 acres above the river bank. Fortification may have been Henry II's first objective, but the truth is that here is a very remarkable hybrid: a military headquarters, a royal palace, and a so-called chapel as intricately furnished as any cathedral in the land. It is best appreciated in all its English pomp and circumstance when a Garter investiture is being held in St. George's Chapel, and the Queen leads her knights in gorgeous procession down the walks within the battlemented walls. But Windsor is at all times a powerful reminder that the British have clung rather fiercely to some very old-fashioned manifestations from their past.

So, for that matter, is exclusive Eton College, actually a secondary school. It lies just across a Thames footbridge from the castle and down a street full of shops, so many of them dedicated to the needs of the most privileged adolescents in the land that one shop—Cobb's Eton College Services—thinks it helpful to keep a notice in the window: "This shop is open to the general public." And no wonder, when at least three-quarters of the people hurrying along that street are uniformed in pin-striped trousers, the sort of tailed coat that orchestra conductors wear, and white bow ties or tabs with starched collars. Eton can be a daunting prospect for anyone less exotically dressed.

There are other Etonians, however, apart from these sons of wealth, also obtaining some learning in the town. "The Porny School," says a notice outside one building, bearing all the marks of the less rarified state education system. I was contemplating this (with raised eyebrows, I confess) when I saw inscribed on the brickwork a hundred yards away, an explanation of that suggestive sign. Here, apparently, was built a school "for the instruction of boys and girls of Eton Parish . . . in pursuance of the will of

Spacious lawns invite some after-school football (soccer to Americans) in suburban Welwyn Garden City, Ebenezer Howard's 1920 landmark in town planning. The abundant greenery and open spaces of his "garden cities" inspired the eight new towns built around London since World War II.

Hertfordshire, "the garden of England for delight" according to a 17th-century writer, offers irresistible appeal to a nation of garden lovers like Donald Mayes (above). So many London wage earners settled there between 1900 and 1950 that its population grew four times faster than England's as a whole.

Mark Antony Porny, formerly French master of Eton School: who Died May 2nd 1802." Noblesse Oblige!—as he probably said himself at the time.

The Thames here is a couple of hundred feet wide, bordered by rowing boathouses and pop-pop-popping with the passage of pleasure launches. For some considerable distance upstream nothing of this is changed, as the river winds gently through Berkshire between fields where cattle browse and screens of poplar stand in long rows at the water's edge. This is most distinctly oarsmen's country, and few spring and summer evenings pass without the sight of racing shells skimming along under the thrust of eight bending backs and sweeping blades, most especially at Henley, where a long, straight stretch in the river is the site of international championship races, in a regatta notable as much as anything for the quantities of champagne and strawberries-with-cream that are consumed. But when I passed through, all the excitement was to do with a gray seal that had been seen in the river a few days before—50 miles or more from the sea. It was convincing proof, together with recent sightings of salmon much lower down the river, that the Thames at London has at last been cleansed after generations of pollution.

The river swings through the gap it has made near Goring, between the western end of the Chilterns and the ampler slopes of the Berkshire Downs. I paused there, in the waterside village of Streatley, to victual myself at the counter of a shop that has made the monocled Mr. Patrick Rance the most celebrated cheesemonger in the land. His counters fairly groan under the weight of all his produce, not a packet of which he will sell until the customer has first tasted a sliver, so that he can be sure it is what he wants. Fortified with a mature farmhouse Cheddar, a sheep cheese from Devon, and Dorset Blue Vinney, I pressed on up the Thames until it brought me to poet Matthew Arnold's great fancy, the "dreaming spires" of Oxford.

The truth is that Oxford is not nearly such a pensive place now as it must have been in 1866. Unlike Cambridge, it has made a compromise between scholarship and

The Queen spends many holidays and weekends at Windsor, her Berkshire castle (opposite). From this rear view, the royal family's apartments overlook a private garden and the Thames beyond. William the Conqueror put up a fortress here about 1070. Successive monarchs built and rebuilt until the 1820s, when George IV remodeled the entire castle, giving it a massive Gothic profile. On most days the public can view Windsor's treasures, such as the exquisitely detailed dollhouse built in 1923 for Queen Mary. Tiny leather-bound books, some in the authors' own hand, fill its library shelves (above).

Thatching:
Storybook Roofs that
Last for Decades

Keeping old-time skills alive, thatchers reroof a house at Great Tew in the Cotswolds. One worker pins overlapping bundles of straw to roof laths nailed over tar paper while another shapes the thatch around a window. A helper on the ground (opposite) keeps the roofers supplied with materials.

Usually made of straw or reed, thatched roofs adorn the heartland and other rural districts of Britain and Ireland. They have become more and more prized in recent years, valued for their quaintness, durability, and insulation from cold, heat, and noise. But thatched roofs are expensive. The wide use of chemical fertilizers, which weaken wheat stalks, and mechanical harvesters has sharply curtailed the supply of materials. The roof shown here, made of wheat straw from the Continent, costs about four times as much as a roof of slate or tile. Straw roofs can last up to 20 years, if maintained. Their longevity also depends on the quality of the workmanship and the amount of precipitation they are exposed to (roofs are steeply pitched to shed rainwater quickly).

Far more durable, with a lifespan of up to 80 years, are roofs thatched with Norfolk reed from East Anglia. In spring the marshes are flooded and then drained. The reeds grow through summer, dry out in the fall, and are harvested the following year.

A special tool, called a legget (opposite, upper), is used by reed thatchers to "beat up" the butt ends of the reed bundles so that they taper smoothly from ridge to eave.

Once a common farmyard skill, roof thatching is now a craft practiced by artisans. A cottage in Banbury (opposite, lower) carries the roofer's distinctive dogtooth "signature" along its crown and a pair of straw birds for a real-life bird to roost on. Closely woven wire mesh protects the thatch from wind and discourages nesting birds, rats, and mice.

EDWARD LANOUETTE

Dan Dry (all)

heavy industry, with one of the country's biggest automobile plants on the outskirts. Yet the view from Boar's Hill remains one of the most beguilingly memorable in England, with the pinnacles of Magdalen College most striking among all the other distinctive outlines—Tom Tower at Christ Church, the spire of All Saints in The High, the dome of the Radcliffe Camera, and the rest. That academic core of Oxford is a place to dawdle through on foot, preferably without being knocked down by bicycles. You see them stacked in dozens outside the entrance to every college during the university's three terms, when the narrow streets are thronged with young men and women pedaling frantically from one lecture or tutorial to another, their black gowns billowing behind, their books and files jammed into baskets on the handlebars. If they are conscious of the singular heritage they enjoy, they do not show it in public, being indistinguishable these days, in speech and behavior, from students anywhere else. But theirs is the second oldest university in Europe, junior only to the Sorbonne, a collection of 40 colleges and halls where 12,000 developing minds are primed to carry on the torch of civilization—should they be so lucky.

The collegiate arrangement of the university is something that strangers have difficulty understanding, and not only strangers. The art historian Sir John Summerson observed quite recently that "Oxford bus-conductors still do not know one college from another." And who can blame them, when usually nothing but a simple gateway in a high wall distinguishes one of the ancient establishments from

A gaggle of geese claims the right-of-way in Bloxham in the Cotswolds, where agriculture dates from prehistoric days. In the Middle Ages, sheep farming brought the area wealth. Monasteries, the largest landowners then, grew rich by exporting Cotswolds fleece to the Continent. When the English textile industry developed, wool production soared. In the 16th century Gloucestershire alone had half a million head, prompting one clergyman to admonish: "God gave the earth to men to inhabit and not unto sheep." Today shepherds still drive their flocks to the farmyard for shearing (upper). But better breeding techniques produce fleece (lower) weighing double what it did a century ago.

OVERLEAF: Sixty pounds of fleece weigh down runners at Tetbury's annual woolsack race, the revival of a Gloucestershire practice dating from the 16th-century wool boom.

71

"That sweet city with her dreaming spires," poet Matthew Arnold wrote of Oxford, whose university has molded many of Britain's elite for 800 years. The university comprises 35 independent colleges; founded in different periods, they reveal a history of architecture in their towers and facades.

Close to half of Oxford's graduates come from exclusive "public" schools, of which Eton, founded by Henry VI in 1440, is most famous. Its alumni include 20 prime ministers. Senior Etonians still attend class in mid-19th-century gentleman's morning attire—stiff collars and tailcoats (above).

the neighboring college just down the street? Step inside that gateway, though, and around the invariable grassy quadrangle are grouped the distinctive college buildings, different in style from the neighbor's, because these places were created haphazardly across several hundred years, from the foundation of Merton College in the 13th century to St. Catherine's and others in the 20th.

It is in Oxford that the limestone country of the English heartland first becomes vividly obvious. Many of those college walls came from a quarry near the Cotswold village of Taynton, which has provided building stone for centuries. A few miles to the north of the city, English limestone architecture achieves its magnificent, arrogant apogee in Blenheim Palace. This, Queen Anne's gift to the Duke of Marlborough for his defeat of Louis XIV's army on the banks of the Danube in 1704, was built by Sir John Vanbrugh. It is a construction so immense that he all but exhausted more than 20 quarries in making it, a palace so extravagant that George III later coveted it above all the palaces he himself owned. The Marlboroughs were Churchills, which is how it came about in 1874 that Winston Churchill was born at Blenheim—accidentally, because his mother was merely visiting that branch of the family when she unexpectedly went into labor. It was within sight of Blenheim that they buried Winston Churchill 91 years later, in the very ordinary churchyard at Bladon, in a coffin made from English oak, setting him down between the graves of his cousin Ivor Spencer Churchill and a Mr. Montague Beechey, with his parents at his feet. Westminster Abbey, where most of the British national heroes are deposited, has rarely been snubbed so grandly.

I abandoned the Thames at Oxford, preferring to potter into the Cotswolds along the valley of the lesser Windrush, so that I could enjoy Swinbrook and Burford. Swinbrook is nothing more than a handful of cottages and a church, but this contains the most enchanting funeral monuments I know: to the Fettiplace family, six of whom, clad in armor and reclining sideways on an elbow apiece, lie one on top of the other, in two groups *(Continued on page 82)*

Spectacles of Sport:
The Upper Crust
at Play

"The object is to eat and drink. . . . We might even do some rowing!" declares a 30-year veteran of the July regatta at Henley-on-Thames.

Known as Henley Royal, the regatta is one of several spring and summer sporting events, most of them held in the heartland, that are as notable for the beautiful people who attend as for the events themselves. The Grand National steeplechase and the Badminton Horse Trials begin the social season in March and April. With May comes the Royal Windsor Horse Show. The Derby, Royal Ascot, Henley, and the Wimbledon tennis matches crowd the June calendar and get July off to a rousing start.

Some of these events have been going on for decades. Henley Royal was started in 1839 "to amuse and gratify the neighborhood and the public in general." Today Henley is one of the world's most famous regattas—and certainly its smartest. Over a four-day period, club rowers, school-

boys, university students, and top oarsmen from around the world compete along a narrow stretch of the upper Thames. But it is the entertainment along the lush Berkshire banks that brings out so many of the upper crust.

In blazers and beribboned boaters, pretty frocks and parasols, they come to see and be seen, and the best place for that is the Stewards' Enclosure opposite the course's end, where admittance is limited to members and their guests. Here champagne is served, and Pimm's punch, a concoction of gin and lemonade with floating fruit; a band of Grenadier Guardsmen plays; and the atmosphere is unmistakably Edwardian.

At lunchtime, thousands of people pour out into the car

Pimm's and champagne, parasols and club blazers (left), and a floating seat on the Thames itself add to the festive mood at the Henley Royal Regatta.

parks to enjoy elaborate picnics, many served on tables laden with linen, silver, and crystal from the trunks of Rolls-Royces.

But the Greatest Show on the Thames is not reserved exclusively for the privileged. Other people come to ogle the swells and perhaps even watch a race from the public stands or the river's edge.

The Henley Regatta earned the title "Royal" after Prince Albert, the Prince Consort, attended it in 1851, but rowing is not Queen Elizabeth's sport. Her favorite is horse racing. She usually attends the Grand National, Royal Ascot, and the Derby.

The Derby has been held at Epsom Downs in Surrey since 1780 and creates probably the largest annual traffic jam in southern England. More than any other top sporting event, the Derby brings together the highborn and the lowborn. Over a century ago *The Illustrated London News* thought it "the most astonishing . . . and most glorious spectacle that ever was. . . . For once people speak to other people and positively hob nob with those palpably inferior to them."

The Royal Windsor Horse Show, held in the Queen's own backyard, attracts top international names in every equestrian event, as well as show business personalities, socialites, and of course, the royal family. Prince Philip often competes, along with Princess Anne and her husband, Capt. Mark Phillips.

But the highlight of the season is Royal Ascot, a four-day racing meet in mid-June for which many royals, aristocrats, gentry, and plain old rich folk turn out in formal dress. It has been called "a garden party with horses."

In 1711 Queen Anne reportedly attended a sports day near Windsor and said, "This is the place to stretch a horse. Let there be a race meeting here." Most years since there has been one. Queen Victoria was not amused that her son, the future King Edward VII, attended so often. In a letter to his mother, he wrote: "It is an opportunity for the Royal

High and low spirits etch vivid portraits at the Henley Royal Regatta (left). Prince Charles (right) helps his team vie for the Royal Windsor Polo Cup. At the Royal Windsor Horse Show (opposite, top and bottom) the Queen holds her gold-plated camera ready. Prince Philip (in sunglasses) makes a splash as he competes in the International Driving Grand Prix.

Dan Dry (all)

Family to show themselves in public—which I am sure you desire—and after all, Racing . . . still remains, I may say, a National Institution. . . ."

Queen Elizabeth, herself a racehorse owner, apparently subscribes to Edward's view; she does not miss a day. Every afternoon before the first race, riders in top hats and scarlet coats lead a procession of five open landaus, each drawn by four horses, down the course to the Royal Enclosure. There the Queen and the Master of the Horse alight from the first carriage, followed by members of the royal family and their guests. The Queen's party retreats into the glassed-in royal box, while around it in the Royal Enclosure sit or mill several thousand souls who had applied for this privilege months ahead of time.

The Royal Enclosure is *the* place to be at Ascot for those who care about being seen. (Heaven forbid that one should end up in the public

Ascot's "Hat Lady," Gertrude Shilling, shows off one of her famous creations. An Ascot racer submits to the crowd's scrutiny (right), while spectators in the Royal Enclosure (opposite) await the Queen.

stands; they are for the parvenus, the middle class, and the hard-core gamblers.) People who gain admittance to the Royal Enclosure must look the part: dresses and hats for the women; morning suits and top hats for the men. Recently the Queen's trustee of the Ascot Society complained that some women's shoulders were too bare and their hats too small to cover the crowns of their heads, as the dress code requires.

One woman who cannot be accused of wearing too modest a hat is Mrs. Gertrude Shilling. Ever since 1961, when she saw the broad-brimmed extravaganzas in the Ascot scene in the film *My Fair Lady*, Mrs. Shilling has come to the Royal Enclosure in a new and increasingly bizarre creation dreamed up by her milliner son. In honor of the 1984 Olympic Games she wore five enormous velvet rings balanced around a red plastic flame. The Ascot song in *My Fair Lady* exaggerates only slightly:

Every duke and earl and peer
* is here;*
Everyone who should be here
* is here;*
What a smashing, positively
* dashing*
Spectacle—the Ascot opening
* day.*
  Elizabeth L. Newhouse

81

of three, their marble faces oblivious to the excruciating discomfort they have endured for the past 300 years.

Burford is chocolate box England exemplified, though its roofs come in solid limestone slabs, not thatch. It cascades prettily down a hill to the Windrush and the church where Anthony Sedley, a soldier imprisoned for four nights on Oliver Cromwell's orders, scratched his name and the date 1649 on the lead lining of the font. In the steeple are other, less desperate inscriptions cast into the metal of the nine church bells. "Sancta Maria," says the great tenor, which weighs nearly a ton. "Come away make no delay. A. R. 1720," says the little sanctus bell, which is small enough to be nursed in the lap. Here, as in churches throughout the land, the ancient art of campanology—change-ringing with bellrope and wheel, something that only the British have ever really taken to—is occasionally still practiced. On those Sundays Burford echoes to short touches of "Plain Bob Minor" or "Grandsire Triples," or some other permutation of the bells, in the half hour or so before matins begins. This is one of the everlasting, haunting sounds of rural England.

The Cotswolds invite pottering, and church-bagging too. Every small valley in these modest hills (and there are dozens of them, at least) discloses some ravishing new harmony. Everything seems organically one. The villages, built entirely from the stone that nature provided, look as if they have grown from the ground they stand in, like the copses of trees which surround them, glowing gently to soothe the eye against the green of watermeadow or sloping pasture. The 20th century might never have come to places like Duntisbourne Abbots or Temple Guiting or the two Slaughters (Upper and Lower) or Slad, of which the poet Laurie Lee has remembered that, within his lifetime, "Quiet incest flourished where the roads were bad."

But the 20th century did arrive and left its mark on innermost places in these wolds. In the tiny Saxon church of Coln Rogers there is a plaque to the twenty-five men and one woman who went to the First World War from that village—"All of whom by God's Great Mercy returned safely." The list includes two Harrises, two Hiscocks, two Pawlings, three Portlocks, and two Stevenses. The parish probably amounted to no more than a hundred souls at the time; it may not be even that many now.

The churches of the Cotswolds tell much of the local history. In the larger villages and the small market towns, they often seem surprisingly big for the communities they dominate. These are the famous wool churches of Gloucestershire, known as such because they were built on the immense wealth that came locally between the 12th and 18th centuries from the sheep's fleece, on which England's prosperity then was mostly based. At Northleach many monumental brasses in the nave and elsewhere celebrate and sanctify this humblest of quadrupeds. At Chipping Campden, just down the exquisite main street from the parish church, there is Woolstaplers Hall, which was built in the 14th century for one of the most important wool merchants in the district, who doubtless contributed a little of his profit to the building of the elaborate church.

Prosperity still clings to some of Gloucestershire's major towns: to Cirencester, Tewkesbury, and Tetbury, which are busy with farmers from the outlying villages on market days; to Cheltenham, elegantly Georgian still, as it began to be in 1788, when its reputation was established as a spa whose peculiar spring water was beneficial to disordered bowels. The prosperity is less obvious in Gloucester itself, a workaday and unexpectedly humdrum place, redeemed by one of England's most glorious cathedrals, whose great east wall consists of little but medieval stained glass. And there, set amidst the tombs of princes and bishops, not far from the effigy of poor Edward II, is a small monument to a local lad who made good, John Stafford Smith, son of the cathedral organist. A popular drinking song he composed made its way to the fairly new United States, where his tune was adopted for "The Star-Spangled Banner."

The classic case of local lad made good is, of course, to be found in Warwickshire. I made for Stratford-upon-Avon along the Fosse Way, the old Roman road that runs straight up the spine of the Cotswolds until, after Moreton-

A wold, or upland, rises behind the Windrush Valley church at Naunton, Gloucestershire. The timelessness of such heartland scenes belies the changes in village life since World War II. Machines have displaced half the farming work force, and old rural trades have vanished, forcing many residents to leave for factory towns. Other villagers stayed and adapted; the smithy of tiny Stagsden (above) now fixes farm machinery. An influx of outsiders has transformed old communities but ensured village survival. A butcher (left) takes time out for a chat in Winchcombe; such market towns usually fared better than agricultural villages.

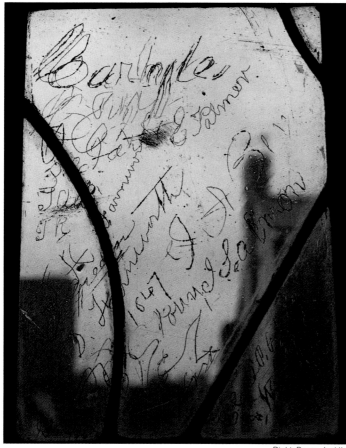

A shop window (right), "as 'twere the mirror up to nature," reflects Shakespeare's much-visited birthplace against a display of modern Stratford-upon-Avon souvenirs. Everything from plates to pillboxes bears the image of the poet. As a young man, Shakespeare left Stratford to seek his fortune but returned in 1610 and died there six years later. On a window in Shakespeare's birth room (above), famous visitors later scratched their names, among them Sir Walter Scott and Thomas Carlyle. When the Birthplace Trust acquired the property in 1847, it put a stop to the graffiti.

in-Marsh, the last slope has been downed and the much gentler undulations of the Shakespeare country lie ahead. Here are "Piping Pebworth, dancing Marston, haunted Hillborough, and hungry Grafton, with dodging Exhall, papist Wixford, beggarly Broom, and drunken Bidford," villages that the playwright is said to have immortalized in this fashion after a drinking bout with some cronies one night in the Falcon Inn at Bidford. He never stuck a label on his hometown, though there has been no shortage of them since, usually composed by those who have found Stratford's total surrender to Shakespeare, its industry in profiting from a historical coincidence, just a little too much to bear. The Stratford Theatre's appearance from the outside has been variously described as a "jam factory" and a "barracks-cum-roadhouse." Of the town as a whole, dainty old Henry James once remarked that "my enthusiasm hung fire in the most humiliating manner."

Yet the world is enthralled by this dapper little place and what it contains. In 1983 more than half a million people trooped through the birthplace in Henley Street. So many were there the day I dropped in that it was difficult to study the contents without being nudged on before I had finished: the copy of Shakespeare's will, beginning "In the name of God Amen . . ."; the translation of *Julius Caesar* into Swahili, made by Julius Nyerere, President of Tanzania; the 18th- and 19th-century graffiti scratched on some of the windows, themselves an object of curiosity now.

On the outskirts of Stratford, at Shottery, a long queue of people waited their turn to stroll through Anne Hathaway's Cottage, the lucky ones managing to shelter from a shower beneath jutting eaves of thick thatch. As at Shakespeare's birthplace, what these people were waiting for was not, I think, so much a chance to enjoy the furnishing and other contents for their own sake. It was so that they could go home and say that they had seen with their own eyes the very bench—high-backed, narrow, and reeking of wax polish now—on which young Will is thought to have sat and courted the older Anne in the inglenook.

So illustrious is Stratford that its county town tends to

The quality of mercy is not strained,
It droppeth as the gentle rain from heaven,
begins Portia in a Royal Shakespeare Theatre production of The Merchant of Venice. *The company performs in Stratford ten months a year for international audiences.*

lie in its shadow, disregarded. Yet Warwick is handsome in a way that Stratford has never managed to be, the second squatting complacently by the Avon, the first standing proudly on a cliff above the river. Proudest of all is Warwick Castle, which William the Conqueror started a couple of years after his victory at Hastings, and which other builders extended in the centuries after him. Some would put it second only to Windsor in the pantheon of British military buildings but, in spite of its appalling dungeons and instruments of medieval torture, it is an engaging place rather than an intimidating one. This is partly because of the peacocks that strut about the park beneath the battlements. But it is more because Warwick Castle over the centuries evolved into a large manor house that just happens to be surrounded by fortified walls.

If you enter that house, you can see exactly what life was like for the English upper classes at the turn of this century. It has retained its period furniture, decorations, and ornaments, and, with the assistance of Madame Tussaud's, its multitude of rooms are populated with wax figures from the not-too-distant past. Here is a servant pouring drinks for a house party given by the Earl and Countess of Warwick in 1898. Other servants pour water into baths for the guests. In the music room, the Duchess of Devonshire and other guests listen to a recital given by Dame Clara Butt. It is bewitching stuff, but it makes the contemporary visitor feel uncomfortably like a voyeur. I had already surprised the waxen Duchess of Marlborough in her dressing gown. I moved quickly to another room, and there caught Lord Roberts intently tying his tie in front of a wardrobe mirror. I turned to one of the attendants the castle now employs to assist visitors and keep an eye on potential souvenir hunters and the like.

"The trouble is," I said, "that I feel I ought to keep apologizing to these people for butting in on them like this."

"That's how you should feel," she replied crisply. "That's absolutely the right attitude."

Now there, I thought, *there* spoke the English heartland—straight from its fairly well-bred heart.

"It was probably much happier to live in a small house, and have Warwick Castle to be astonished at, than to live in Warwick Castle and have nothing to be astonished at," wrote John Ruskin in the 1880s. The mansion's walls and turrets were the best that 14th-century military architects could build. From gaps in the parapet of Caesar's Tower, reflected in the River Avon, the castle's defenders could shower stones, quicklime, and boiling pitch on attackers.

The first fort here was probably Anglo-Saxon. William the Conqueror built another and conferred it, with the title Earl of Warwick, on a loyal follower. The Earls of Warwick kept their fortified mansion for some 900 years, until they could no longer afford to run it. In 1978 Madame Tussaud's of London bought the castle as a tourist attraction.

By Shirley L. Scott
Photographs by Patrick Ward

The West Country

T his Cornwall is very primeval: great, black,
jutting cliffs and rocks . . . and a pale sea
breaking in. . . . It is like the beginning of the
world, wonderful: and so free and strong.

D. H. LAWRENCE, 1916

Land's End, Cornwall

T*ime slowly accumulates in Dorset: the present settles gently into the past without disturbing it.*

ANN JELLICOE, in *Village England*, 1980

The cobbled street of Gold Hill, in the ancient market town of Shaftesbury, Dorset

"Morecaravans, more chalets, every year. . . ." So wrote novelist Daphne du Maurier about her beloved Cornwall in 1980. It was not the cry of an impractical sentimentalist. Du Maurier recognized that change was inevitable. The West Country had been discovered.

In Clovelly, a tiny village on Devon's north coast, I sat on a bench and watched the coach parties arrive. Even on this chilly Monday in May, cheerful crowds edged their way down the steep cobbled street, delighting in the scene: charming little cottages built one above the next, each with a perfect little flower garden. People peered into windows, snapped photos of the patient residents, jammed the little shops. A crowd blocked the street's narrow turning to watch gulls take scraps from the hand of a villager.

Not many years ago, Clovelly was a quiet fishing village. But fishing isn't what it was and, as du Maurier said, "Men must live." Clovelly lives mostly on tourism.

Until recent decades, much of the West Country was isolated by terrain and distance, veiled in misty legends of smugglers and shipwrecks and King Arthur. Railroads and highways began reaching into the area in the mid-19th century. And just in time. Mining and fishing, two mainstays of West Country economy, were beginning to collapse. Today dairy and livestock farming thrive, along with the china clay industry and some shipping, shipbuilding, and quarrying. But since the schools of pilchards unaccountably moved out to sea, fishing has largely been taken over by deep-sea trawlers, many of them from other nations of the European Economic Community—the Common Market. Tin mining fell victim to world competition.

Tourism isn't an easy way to make a living, I mused as I continued down Clovelly's crowded street. The annual summer invasion disrupts life even as it fills empty purses. "I can remember Polperro," wrote poet Sir John Betjeman in 1964, "when it smelt of fresh fish instead of fried. . . ."

The West Country is a popular destination for foreign visitors—Americans like me, for instance—as well as for

the British. Villages like Clovelly are a major attraction; so are the resort towns and sandy beaches, wild sea cliffs and rolling hills and moors, cathedral towns and port cities. And, to a large extent, the fresh, clean air and a dearth of development. Try as it might, the region hasn't been able to attract much industry, which accounts in part for both the fresh air and a relatively sparse population.

The West Country is also rich in prehistoric remains. The builders here had plenty of stone to use, and the region's remoteness helped to preserve their efforts. My first West Country excursion was with a coach tour from London to Stonehenge, one of the most famous tourist attractions in all of Britain, and deservedly so.

Stonehenge stands alone in the middle of the empty Salisbury Plain, a broken circle of mammoth stones, ruins of a mysterious temple begun about 4,000 years ago. A fence has been built around it to protect the monument from the constant crowds, an improvement on the Victorian practice of bringing hammers to chip off souvenirs. We stood in hushed awe, staring at those megaliths. How was it built? The largest stones, some weighing 50 tons, were somehow brought here from 20 miles away, somehow raised, somehow capped with more megaliths.

And why was it built? Most likely Stonehenge was a center for religious rites, and its orientation to sun and seasons indicates a religion closely allied to an agrarian way of life. But archaeologists can only speculate. The mysteries of Stonehenge are part of its enduring appeal.

Two major cities tack the West Country onto the rest of England: the seaside resort of Bournemouth at the southeastern corner; the port of Bristol at the northern. I chose Bristol as a base for further excursions—and discovered a fascinating city. Built where the River Avon nears its end at Bristol Channel, Bristol has been a major port since the tenth century. The shipping now takes place downriver at Avonmouth, where

England's West Country meets the sea in a long peninsula battered by the Atlantic but warmed by the Gulf Stream. It is a land of rugged moors and coastal cliffs, gently rolling pasturelands and picturesque fishing villages. Centuries of isolation helped preserve pre-historic sites and, especially in Cornwall, the independent spirit of a Celtic people never absorbed by invaders. The area has become one of Britain's favorite holiday lands. Summer visitors fill beach resorts like Newquay (opposite) and feast on such regional specialties as cider, clotted cream, and Cornish pasties.

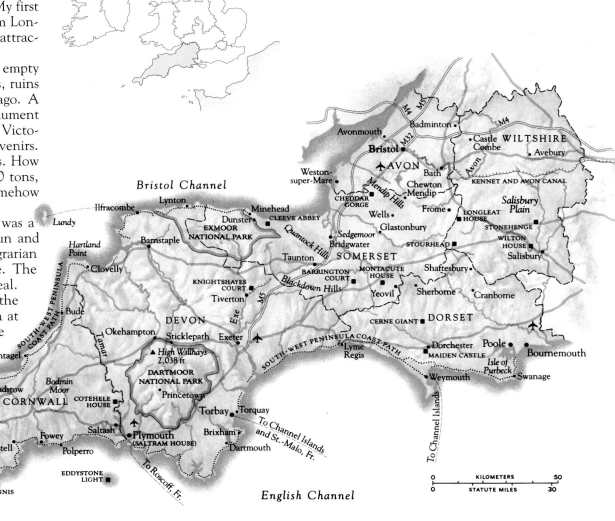

93

Equestrian events lure April visitors to the West Country. The prestigious three-day Badminton Horse Trials (above) bring crowds to the Duke of Beaufort's 52,000-acre Avon estate to watch cross-country contests, dressage, and show jumping. The dapper official at left graces the South Devon Hunt's annual point-to-point races near Brixham.

In another sort of contest, Castle Combe (opposite) in Wiltshire won a poll that chose England's prettiest village.

cranes load containerized goods onto ships too large to navigate the river. Bristol's waterways no longer teem with the "ships of all sizes and rigs and nations" that Robert Louis Stevenson described in *Treasure Island*. Instead, tour boats and pleasure craft fill the channels called the Floating Harbour. Art centers and craft shops line the waterside. Much of central Bristol was demolished in the Blitz, but treasures survived, including the 14th-century Church of St. Mary Redcliffe; the Theatre Royal, one of England's oldest; and the Llandoger Trow, a half-timbered 17th-century pub that may have been Stevenson's model for *Treasure Island*'s Spy Glass Inn.

My stay in Bristol coincided with that of another American, evangelist Billy Graham, who was conducting a series

of open-air revival meetings. Bristol has a long history of outdoor preaching. Denied the use of Anglican pulpits, early Methodist leaders like John Wesley held their meetings outdoors. In 1739 Wesley and his followers built here the first Methodist chapel, a simple stone church that stands today as an island of serenity in the middle of Bristol's largest, busiest shopping mall.

A few miles from Bristol lies the town of Bath, a popular spa since the time of the Romans. Mineral springs, the warmest in Britain, were the original attraction. The Romans built a town here, with extensive baths and a temple. The Saxons built on top of the silted-over Roman ruins. Norman structures swallowed up the Saxon.

When Queen Anne visited Bath early in the 18th century, the town again became an elegant, fashionable resort. It is still popular, crowded in every season. And still elegant, a town which, one modern English writer claims, "likes to think of itself as above the common herd."

I visited the restored 18th-century Assembly Rooms, where Charles Dickens's Mr. Pickwick was bewildered by "the hum of many voices, and the sound of many feet," where "dresses rustled, feathers waved, lights shone, and jewels sparkled." I stopped at the Pump Room, where high society once sipped the mineral waters. Below ground level, in the excavated Roman baths, I dipped a hand into the water to test its temperature. But I was not tempted to taste it. "They found an amoeba in it," the ticket seller told me sadly. New wells have now reached unpolluted springs, and someday soon, visitors may once again sip—and even bathe in—Bath's mineral waters.

The best way to explore the English countryside is by car, ideally with a driver for whom left-side driving and one-lane roads are a way of life rather than a constant challenge. I enlisted my young English friend Andrew Swithinbank to drive for me (and, I confess, to serve as interpreter when I forgot that in England a cookie is called a biscuit, the second floor is the first, and it's the Americans who have the strange accent). After Andrew had politely reminded me that British law requires the use of seat belts,

we headed southward to the Mendip Hills, a high limestone ridge riddled with caves and cut with gorges. Cheddar Gorge is the deepest, about 450 feet. Its gray walls seemed a lot higher than that as we drove slowly down the narrow road to the bottom of the ravine. ("Cyclists are advised to walk," says the road sign.) The caves at the base of the gorge once sheltered Stone Age people. Now they are overwhelmed with tea shops and gift shops—and tourists.

But there were no other visitors at nearby Ebbor Gorge, a 142-acre reserve of wild woodland and rocky slopes, birdsong and breeze. Ebbor Gorge is owned by the National Trust, a private organization that preserves places of natural beauty and historic significance in England, Wales, and Northern Ireland. (Scotland has a separate trust.)

Built by first-century Romans as a swimming pool and social center, the Great Bath acquired its statues and columns from Victorian restorers. The five-foot-deep pool still has its original lead floor and limestone paving. Bath's mineral springs pour forth at a steady temperature of 116°F, a warm retreat for Romans stationed in chilly Britain.

Bath ranks as Britain's most important Roman site. But much is now buried beneath the modern city. A mosaic floor discovered in a pub cellar was excavated, photographed, and then covered up again, to protect the pub's foundation.

Treasures of a later age include the 18th-century Royal Crescent (above), a curving terrace of 30 homes built of the region's honey-colored limestone. This much-copied design by John Wood the Younger was a hallmark in Georgian architecture. One of the Crescent's houses has been restored to its 18th-century appearance; two others are used as a hotel.

97

From the rim of Ebbor Gorge you can see another National Trust property six miles away—Glastonbury Tor, an isolated hill, 520 feet high, topped with the ruins of a medieval church tower—and surrounded by legends. It was used at least as early as the fifth century for religious ceremonies and burials, either pagan or Christian. And we know that a Christian church existed at the base of the tor prior to the seventh century when a monastery was established there. But did Jesus' disciple Joseph of Arimathea visit here? Was King Arthur buried here? Archaeologists continue to doubt, debate, and excavate.

Beginning in the 12th century, an enormous new abbey was built at the base of the tor. Only remnants still stand— a few walls and corners, a chapel, the kitchen building. The magnificent church was abandoned and gradually torn down to build houses after King Henry VIII's edict of 1539 dissolving all the monasteries. Viewing ruin after ruin, visitors soon have that date firmly fixed in their minds.

Somerset rewarded our leisurely ramble: Priory Farm at Chewton Mendip, where we saw Cheddar cheese being made—and sampled it; the little city of Wells with its medieval cathedral; the low-lying Sedgemoor plain, reedy refuge for ninth-century King Alfred between battles with the invading Danes. But the world goes on. In Taunton, an enthusiastic band of marchers protested the stationing of American cruise missiles in England.

At Lynton, on the coast, we encountered the South-West Peninsula Coast Path, Britain's longest footpath. It begins in nearby Minehead and ends 515 miles later at

Conservators at Wells Cathedral tackle seven centuries of weather, air pollution, and vandalism. Only 286 statues survive in the West Front's 461 niches (section shown at far left); many lack a hand, a foot, or facial features. Restoration policy limits the work to cleaning and repairs; missing parts are rarely replaced. The royal statue at left fell from its niche in 1840; the iron dowels used to mend it have caused further damage. Sculptor Derek Carr's replica will serve as a model for restoring the fragile original or, if necessary, take its place.

99

Fireworks swirl as the town of Bridgwater in Somerset celebrates Guy Fawkes' Day, a holiday commemorating the failure of the Gunpowder Plot. In 1605 Guy Fawkes and other rebels tried to blow up the Houses of Parliament on opening day, November 5, when King James I would be there. All over Britain, bonfires, effigies, and fireworks celebrate the rebels' downfall. Children carry a Fawkes effigy from house to house, begging "a penny for the guy" to buy fireworks. Bridgwater's festival, one of the largest, includes a mammoth parade, entertainments, and specially designed fireworks.

Poole in Dorset. In between, the path closely follows the rugged coastline, climbing cliffs and crossing rocky headlands. It is not for the fainthearted or the short-winded. Even Andrew, who has hiked much of this path, admits that some stretches are a bit difficult. But since it frequently intersects harbor towns, even timid walkers can attempt bits of the path without committing themselves to more.

On a sunny afternoon, Andrew and I walked the half-mile from Lynton to the Valley of Rocks. The path here is broad and level, cut deeply into the side of a cliff. Below us, the waves crashed against the rocks. High above, feral goats peered out from the crags. A stiff breeze blew in from the sea. The world seemed new and fresh and glorious. "Makes me proud to be an Englishman," said Andrew.

Inspired by this satisfying sample, we decided to explore the whole coast.

"You won't like Ilfracombe," a Lynton resident warned. "It's a tacky place. Of course," he added, "I take my own family there two or three times a year."

Ilfracombe turned out to be no tackier than large resort towns anywhere in the world. It was comfortably filled, mostly with retired folks (OAPs, the British call them: Old Age Pensioners; the term intends, and apparently gives, no offense). May is much too early for swimming in England, Andrew informed me. In August, Ilfracombe and every other beach would be packed with families on holiday. In the meantime, visitors breathe deeply of the sea air and play bingo and minigolf. From Ilfracombe's harbor, a steamer makes excursions to Lundy, a sparsely populated, rocky little island 23 miles away.

Ilfracombe has been a popular seaside resort since Victorian times. Other towns began more recently to make the change from harbor village to resort. They range from the carefully controlled elegance of St. Ives to the casual seediness of Perranporth to the unstudied charm of little Mousehole (pronounced Mowz'l). Some have broad stretches of sand, others only pebble beaches, some no beach at all. You could spend years visiting these varied places and never weary of it.

Between the towns are areas where few visitors come, where wave and wind batter the crumbling cliffs into a wild and dangerous beauty. Ridges of broken black shale line the coves. Jagged rock piles rise from the sea, wreathed in the spray of breaking waves. It is a savage scene, awesome and wonderful. Rachel Carson, in *The Edge of the Sea*, explained that Britain's exposed coasts receive "some of the most violent surf in the world, created by winds that sweep across the whole expanse of ocean. It sometimes strikes with a force of two tons to the square foot." From the lighthouse on Hartland Point, we watched the sea raging around the promontory—and remembered the lifeboat and crew that waits in nearby Bideford Bay. Every harbor along this rugged coast has collection boxes for the lifeboat fund. I vowed to make a contribution.

About 35 miles of Somerset and North Devon shoreline form the northern border of Exmoor, an area of rocky coastal headlands and hills laced with lush river valleys. Most of this land is protected as Exmoor National Park.

In Britain, national parkland remains for the most part privately owned. Exmoor's 170,000 acres are largely farmland, dotted with villages. Visitors must obey the Country Code: Stay on public footpaths, leave livestock alone, close gates. Park rangers walk a tightrope, balancing the rights of visitors against those of the farmers and weighing both against the preservation of scenery and wildlife.

On our way to visit Andrew's friends the Scotts at their farm in Luxborough, we drove cautiously along the narrow roads, easing past sheep that had perversely broken through the thick hedges to browse along the roadside.

"Well, that's sheep, isn't it," said Malcolm Scott, with a grin, when I mentioned the strays. "Never satisfied. Wherever you put them, they want to be somewhere else."

Malcolm and his father and brother raise sheep and cattle on their 230-acre farm. National park status usually makes little difference to many Exmoor farmers, Malcolm told me as we strolled around the tidy farmyard. But bitter controversies can flare when farmers seek permission to raise a building or clear a new field.

South of Exmoor lies the larger and wilder Dartmoor National Park, its 234,000 acres mostly granite highlands. We drove mile after mile across bleak, rocky moors, past hills topped with weird formations of weathered granite, past treacherous bogs glistening in the waning light. Wild ponies, cattle, and black-faced sheep grazed on the sparse grasses. We stopped to stare at Her Majesty's grim gray prison in Princetown. A mist rose, making the moors seem even lonelier, and a little sinister. This was the setting for Arthur Conan Doyle's *Hound of the Baskervilles:* "Over the wide expanse there was no sound and no movement. . . ."

At Hound Tor the next day there was plenty of sound and movement. Forty-four pupils of nearby Christow Primary School were on a field trip. The children, ranging in age from almost-five to just-turned-nine, had already hiked a mile that morning, teacher Gwen Matthews told me. They had gone to see the flanged granite rails built in the 19th century for the horse-drawn wagons of Haytor Quarry. Now the children swarmed up Hound Tor, accompanied by a dozen teachers and parents, park rangers Mike Barber and Tom Pridmore, and me. From the top, we spotted a circle of small boulders on the other side—the remains of a Bronze Age burial chamber. "Was a king buried there?" asked one child. "Not a king," Tom answered, "but probably an important person, a chief."

Over a rise lay low rock walls, remnants of a dozen medieval longhouses. Tom explained that families lived in the upper part of the sloped houses and kept their livestock in the lower part, which had a drainage channel in the center. "Phew," said the children. They scampered in and out, examining each house, not even noticing the chilly breeze that reddened their noses and kept us grown-ups huddled against the granite outcroppings.

We trooped back to Hound Tor, where Andrew had joined a group from the Dartmoor Outdoor Pursuits Centre. These teenagers had come from London for an adventurous week of hiking, climbing, and kayaking. Now, as a finale, they were traversing two pinnacles with rope and sling. Watched by (Continued on page 111)

Donkeys carry luggage for hotel guests in Clovelly, where the street is too precipitous for automobiles. At Cadgwith (opposite) low tide reveals the harbor's steep slope. The West Country's coastal cliffs compelled fishing villages to grow vertically, not horizontally. Clustered houses and narrow, twisting streets add to the charm of these popular "park-at-the-top" villages. Throughout the West Country—and most of Britain—tourists can enjoy low-cost lodging in private homes.

From Mist and Stone, Remnants of the Old Religion

Puzzles from a misty past crop up throughout Britain and Ireland: giant stone circles, hillforts, and barrows (earthen burial mounds)—vivid reminders of an ancient people and their gods.

Who built Stonehenge and Avebury? How were they used? Is Silbury Hill a tomb?

Writing was virtually unknown in Britain until the Romans arrived. What passed before then lies buried in folklore and oral tradition, embellished by the imaginations of the Victorians. Now, archaeologists are trying to piece together the past.

Neolithic farmers first built chamber tombs around 3500 B.C. (a thousand years before the Egyptians built the pyramids). These elaborate tombs, made of huge stones—megaliths—held as many as 50 dead.

The early Britons also built circular banked ditches, or henges. Bronze Age people began to embellish these henges around 2000 B.C. by arranging enormous mega-liths in circles within them. At Stonehenge, they topped these slabs with lintel stones, raised perhaps by a system of levers, timbers, and ropes.

In the 18th and 19th centuries, heightened interest in these ruins led to many speculations. One man announced that Stonehenge and Avebury were built by the Druids as colleges of philosophy, theology, and sciences—taught

"Observatory, altar, temple, tomb, erected none knows when by none knows whom, to serve strange gods or watch familiar stars. . . ," wrote the poet Sir John Squire about Stonehenge. On the longest day of the year, modern Druids (right) gather here to celebrate the summer solstice and watch the sun rise over the heel stone, perpetuating a discredited theory that Druids built Stonehenge. The original Druids arrived long after Stonehenge was built and worshiped in oak groves, not in stone circles.

Patrick Ward

Patrick Ward (all)

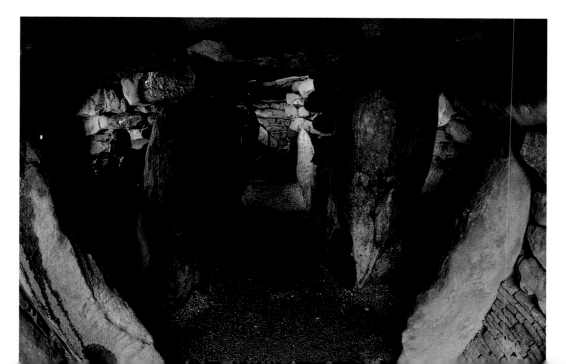

by tutors from Greece. England's first Oxford! Experts now suggest that these henges served as religious temples and as a way of tracking the sun, moon, and seasons.

Silbury Hill, the largest artificial hill in Europe, was built in Wiltshire around the same time as Avebury, but its purpose is still unknown.

The Celtic people of Iron Age Britain (about 700 B.C.) grew rapidly in numbers and began to compete for land. They built many hillforts, which have survived in greatest numbers in the west and south. Huge fortifications like Maiden Castle in Dorset, with multiple rings of defense—ditches, ramparts, and wooden palisades—sheltered inhabitants from intertribal warfare. More remote villages, like Chysauster, were unenclosed and undefended.

With the Roman invasion, pagan Britain was introduced to gods and goddesses with

A modern village lies partly within the Neolithic circle of Avebury (right) in Wiltshire, where stones of 40 to 60 tons dwarf visitors (left, upper).

A modern skylight illuminates the five inner chambers of nearby West Kennet Long Barrow (left, lower).

106

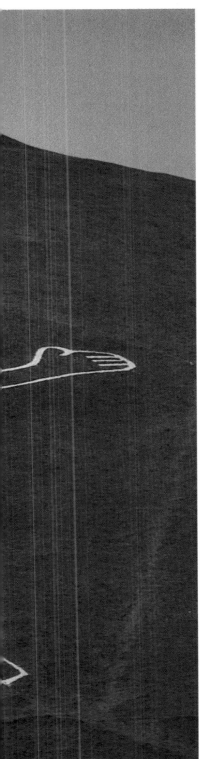

new names and, with the coming of Christianity, to the concept of one god alone (attended by many saints and angels). Missionaries erected churches on pagan holy sites in an effort to exorcise the old gods and wean people from the old religions. Thus you can find the remains of a church tower on top of Glastonbury Tor, the ruins of an abbey at the foot of the Cerne Giant, and an old church within a Dorset henge.

In a way, the old religion lives on, its gods diminished and thinly disguised as fairies, saints, and witches. And every so often the shadows of the old gods show through the mist: Even today, when Gaelic-speaking Scots go to church, they say they are "going to the stones."

MELANIE PATT-CORNER

Affectionately called "our giant" by local villagers, the 180-foot-long Cerne Giant has stood watch on his hill for 2,000 years. This Celtic god of fertility and the hunt was cut from turf to expose the chalk below and kept in trim for centuries by Cerne Abbas villagers, who scoured him every seven years. Even today a visit to the giant is said to bring fertility to childless couples.

Prehistoric Monuments of Britain and Ireland

- Stone circles, henges, standing stones
- Tombs
- Hills
- Forts, hillforts
- Dwellings, villages
- Chalk figures

Prehistoric sites pepper Britain and Ireland, from the Iron Age village of Chysauster near Land's End to Bronze Age Jarlshof in the Shetlands to the Neolithic Legananny Dolmen (above) in County Down, Ireland. Erosion has altered this earthen burial mound, baring its inner stones.

a wide-eyed audience of younger children, they made the perilous crossing with aplomb.

In the northern part of Dartmoor, on the highest, bleakest part of the plateau, the Ministry of Defense has a training camp and firing range. (Royal Marines landing on the Falklands in 1982 were cheered to see that those islands looked just like their familiar Dartmoor.) On a day when the red warning flags were not flying, Andrew and I drove along an empty road not shown on the tourist-brochure map. A military helicopter passed overhead, drowning out the song of a skylark. Two nights before, a platoon of trainees got lost on these desolate moors; search parties found them the next morning. We had been amused by the news reports but now, seeing this landscape, we understood.

Dartmoor is not, of course, all bleak and rugged moorland. Tucked around those empty hillsides are wooded river valleys and dells like Becky Falls and delightful little villages like Sticklepath and Widecombe in the Moor.

West of Dartmoor flows the River Tamar, the border between Devon and Cornwall. Or between England and Cornwall, in the view held by some Cornish people. The Cornish are an independent lot. Their peninsula was one of the last Celtic refuges from the invading Saxons. As late as the 18th century the Cornish people still spoke their own Celtic language, alive today in family names and place-names—Penzance, Pendeen, Pendennis (*pen* here means "headland"). Cornish scholars and nationalists try to revive the language, with some success.

Most visitors in Cornwall go to Land's End, the westernmost point of mainland England. And most get there by car or coach and a short walk through a neat compound of shops and exhibit halls. Andrew and I decided to earn our view. We parked a mile away, at Sennen Cove, and hiked the coast path to the rugged cliffs where England ends. Once there, however, I did what most American visitors do—had myself photographed beside the sign that points to America, 4,000 miles away.

Tintagel vies with Land's End in popularity, not only because of the cove's spectacular beauty but also because

High hedges shelter a field of daffodils on St. Mary's (opposite), largest of the windswept Isles of Scilly. Market flowers are a prime industry on these islands, where a mild, sunny climate enables growers to plant bulbs for winter blooming. The first narcissus buds appear as early as November. Islanders Jonathan and Andrew May (above) gather the last spring daffodils, a sweet-smelling variety called "Cheerfulness," for shipment to mainland markets. Early potatoes provide Scillonians with another profitable crop. But high winds, drought, or low market prices can leave many islanders with only one other source of income: the tourist. Regular visitors to St. Mary's include former prime minister Harold Wilson, who owns a house here, and members of the royal family and its staff; the Prince of Wales, who is also the Duke of Cornwall, owns most of Scilly.

OVERLEAF: Friday-evening gig races off St. Mary's Island recall the days when Scillonian pilots competed to reach incoming vessels. The first gig to arrive got the job of guiding the ship through outlying rocks. Lightweight and swift, gigs were used when the regular pilot cutters were busy elsewhere. Gig crews also rescued shipwreck victims and salvaged cargo.

legend says King Arthur lived here. The sea has cut deeply into the slate cliffs, isolating the castle site. We climbed the harrowing hundred steps to the cliffside ruins and gazed down at the hungry sea. The castle was built by a 12th century Earl of Cornwall. King Arthur lived in the 6th century. But no matter; his spirit is surely here, whether or not he himself was.

Ruins of more recent vintage dot the Cornish landscape: the abandoned engine-houses and stacks of the tin-mining industry that flourished here in the mid-19th century. Only three mines now operate in Cornwall, where once there were two thousand.

Geology has provided another resource—large deposits of high-quality kaolin, china clay, used in making paper, ceramics, and paint. Kaolin is found in the granite base of Cornwall and parts of Dartmoor. Since the deposits are funnel-shaped, narrow end deepest, the huge mining pits cannot be backfilled as they are dug. Instead, until recent years, the waste material was piled into immense white pyramids, the "Cornish Alps." Regulations now require that the waste heaps be lower and flatter and the land reclaimed. But old pyramids remain, a startling sight.

Twenty-eight miles off Cornwall are the Isles of Scilly, accessible from Penzance by steamship (two and a half hours) or helicopter (20 minutes). On my first visit, several years ago, I went by steamship, unaware that it is known locally as the "Stomach Pump." Two and a half hours became an eternity. This time I chose the helicopter for the crossing—more expensive but vastly more comfortable.

Either way, Scilly is worth the journey, fully equal to a jaded urbanite's daydream of a faraway island retreat. Mapmakers count more than a hundred islands before they begin to ponder the distinction between an island and a rock. Only five are inhabited. Most of the 1,500 or so residents live on St. Mary's, the largest island at 1,554 acres.

It is to St. Mary's that steamship and helicopter bring visitors. Many of them, even those who arrived by steamship, head straight for the noticeboards on the quay to sign up for a boat trip. Old folks and young, babies and dogs all

Ancient customs of uncertain origin endure in West Country festivals. Padstow celebrates the traditional first day of summer with a fearsome Hobby Horse (opposite) prancing through the streets, led by a "teaser" and followed by crowds of residents and visitors. In Helston (above), an awed child encounters another May festival, the Furry Dance, when young and old dance in long lines around the decorated town, stopping to sing an ancient May song. The name "Furry" may derive from a Cornish word for a fair.

Heather, gorse, and sparse grasses sustain hardy Dartmoor ponies. Herds roam free until autumn, when owners round them up, brand the foals, and sell some of the ponies at fairs. Cattle and sheep also graze these granite hillsides. Wind, rain, and frost erode the summits, strewing boulders and grinding rock into soil. Harder granite is left behind in high outcrops called tors. Haytor (opposite) displays the vertical joints that formed when the molten rock welled up and cooled.

pile merrily into launches to explore the outer islands and their windswept heaths, rugged rocks, and clean empty beaches. Some boats visit the keeper at Bishop Rock Lighthouse or cruise among outcroppings inhabited only by seals, seabirds, and rabbits. The islands are actually the tops of drowned hills, part of the mainland before the sea rose—which accounts for the rabbits.

Scilly is one of England's prime bird-watching spots, with an impressive 130 species regularly seen there—puffins and shearwaters, hawks and ducks, warblers and sandpipers. About 200 more species have appeared during spring and fall migrations, including an occasional North American bird blown far off course and arriving on Scilly by accident (and, one assumes, with gratitude).

This particular North American found it hard to leave Scilly. Back on the mainland, Andrew and I made our way slowly up the coast and crossed the Tamar into Devon at Plymouth, the port from which the *Mayflower* sailed in 1620. Finally sailed. The Pilgrims had set forth from Southampton, stopped at Dartmouth for repairs and then at Plymouth for more repairs. A memorial stone marks the place on a Sutton Harbour pier whence they departed. Sutton Harbour launched many another famous voyager, including Sir Francis Drake and Capt. James Cook.

In modern times, Plymouth's docks drew the attention of German bombers in World War II. After the fall of northern France, the Germans virtually destroyed Plymouth in a series of 59 air raids. It is a marvel that the Sutton Harbour area, the oldest part of the city, survived.

Exeter also suffered major war damage. Its 14th-century cathedral, itself bombed and painstakingly repaired, dominates a city largely rebuilt after 1945. But evidence remains of a more successful invasion: bits of the wall built by the Romans around the city they established here.

As Andrew and I explored the coast of South Devon and Dorset, the staging area for much of the Normandy invasion force, Britain was commemorating the anniversary of D-day. One woman, who had been a small child then, recalled seeing the English Channel "black with boats."

Turning inland, we rode through the chalk downs—undulating green pasturelands broken by hedges and groves, thatched farmhouses, quiet little villages: Thomas Hardy country, looking much as it did when Hardy began writing his novels in the 1860s. But perhaps Hardy himself would be a little dazed by the madding crowd and rush-hour traffic of Dorchester, the town he used as the setting for *The Mayor of Casterbridge* and other novels.

The south coast rises in high cliffs of red sandstone, gray limestone, and white chalk. Especially around the peninsula called the Isle of Purbeck, the sea has sculpted the soft chalk into pillars and arches, scalloped coves, and wavewashed caves. Long stretches of this coastline are still wonderfully wild and empty.

It always rains on the spring bank holiday weekend. At Swanage on the Isle of Purbeck, holidaymakers strolled from shop to shop and wandered along the beach, ignoring the downpour. Windsurfers in black wetsuits waded into the choppy water. Children dug happily in the sodden sand and begged their parents for ice cream. The rain fell steadily. In a tent beside the beach, the Dorset Blind Society was holding a "sale of work" (handcrafts) and hoping that the weather would drive customers in rather than keep them away. Andrew the Intrepid set off for a hike on the coast path. I set off for a restaurant for tea. It always rains on the spring bank holiday weekend.

We drove to Salisbury, where I would spend my last few days in England. Salisbury's cathedral area is always peaceful, even when the town is crowded and busy. In the soft light of early morning, I strolled in a riverside garden lush with forget-me-nots and buttercups, fragrant with lilies of the valley and lobelias. A mallard floated past, six ducklings in a row behind her. Swallows skimmed the water. Lambs gamboled, just as lambs should, in the meadow beyond. Two swans waddled awkwardly through the grass, to settle gracefully on the water. Above it all rose the glorious spire of Salisbury Cathedral. Idyllic. Impossibly idyllic. Is this the real England? I wondered.

It began to rain again.

Gateway to a changing future, the Royal Albert Bridge brought the railroad across the swift River Tamar from Plymouth to Saltash, ending Cornwall's isolation. Isambard Kingdom Brunel's innovative design used arches made of elliptical hollow tubes to counteract the inward pull of the suspension chains. The 100-foot clearance enabled tall-masted ships to pass below. With the construction of this bridge, the railway linked Penzance to all of England. A century later, a highway bridge joined Brunel's masterpiece.

Michael St. Maur Sheil

Channel Islands: Where Britain Blends with France

My fourth cabdriver in a row spelled out his French surname in an unmistakably English accent—underlining the dual nature of these British islands grouped within 30 miles of France.

Part of the Duchy of Normandy when Duke William conquered England in 1066, the Channel Islands remained loyal to England when France overran Normandy in 1204. Now they are self-governing crown dependencies, divided into the Bailiwicks of Jersey and Guernsey—the latter including Alderney, Sark, Herm, and Jethou.

Prepared to air my French, I was disappointed to find that I would need it only for reading place-names or for attending a session of The States—parliaments—of Jersey or Guernsey, where formal remarks and votes are made in French. But older islanders do still speak varying patois on Jersey, Guernsey, and Sark.

The Channel Islands nurture their continental image to encourage tourism. Most visitors come from Britain, to enjoy the mild climate, splendid beaches, fine scenery, and tax-free shopping and accommodations; duty rates are low and there is no VAT—value-added tax.

Since Jersey and Guernsey have an income tax of 20 percent, with no property taxes or death duties, they also attract bankers and millionaires seeking a tax haven. Tourism, finance, and farming are the chief island livelihoods.

In St. Helier, Jersey's busy capital, banks jostle jewelry shops and luxury hotels. At the harbor mouth rises Elizabeth Castle, now a museum, named by Jersey Governor Sir Walter Raleigh for his queen. Another castle, Mont Orgueil (Mount Pride), looms over the quaint harbor of Gorey.

Pedigree Guernsey cows file across a meadow on 500-acre Herm. A fishing boat (left) threads the rocks off Port du Moulin on Sark, 3 miles east.

The whole Jersey coast is indented with beaches. Inland, soft-eyed Jersey cows graze in green pastures. Pink granite walls line the roads, and the older houses and churches are built of this rosy stone, a Jersey trademark.

Two popular attractions are a 33-foot prehistoric tomb called La Hougue Bie, built of huge cut stones, and Gerald Durrell's zoo for endangered species, set in a lovely park.

On another plane is the large underground hospital built by the Germans, using imported slave labor, during World War II. Britain thought the Channel Islands indefensible and demilitarized them, evacuating many citizens. The Germans moved in and built fortifications.

Alderney, nearest to France, was almost totally evacuated and has a large share of German installations; some have been made into shops, cafes, or beach homes.

Philip Perrée of Little Sark wears his beret with a Gallic flair. He cleared a virtual wilderness to create farmland and his hotel, La Sablonnerie.

The Sark fire engine makes a run (left). Sark bans all motor vehicles except tractors—even the doctor uses a bicycle.

Michael St. Maur Sheil

The Channel Islands shelter in a crook of the French coastline 100 miles south of England, but to islanders "the mainland" means Britain. Regular air service links Jersey, Guernsey, and Alderney with England and France. Car ferry routes shown here may vary seasonally. No cars are allowed on Sark or Herm; you can reach them by passenger ferry from St. Peter Port. Other island-hopping expeditions are readily available in the season by boat, hydrofoil, and small planes.

Visitors at left stroll from Little Sark to Great Sark across La Coupée, a knife-blade of land rising 260 feet above La Grande Grève bathing beach.

Alderney is also ringed by Victorian forts, built during the period when Britain sought to make it the "Gibraltar of the Channel." Remote and quiet, with a single town, Alderney prides itself—justifiably—on its good pubs.

Slightly smaller, Sark requires that visitors walk, bicycle, or travel by horse carriage around its 3 by 1½ miles. Spectacular granite cliffs drop from a high central tableland to jewel-like beaches. Headlands and fields are thick with wildflowers in spring. The 17th-century mansion of Sark's feudal Seigneur faces a walled garden where time stands still amid the heady scent of roses. "You never hurry on Sark," I was told.

Sark has quite a few hotels; pretty Herm has only one. Both islands are popular day excursions from Guernsey.

Natives of Guernsey share

Guernsey's capital, St. Peter Port, climbs steeply behind a harbor marina. Narrow cobbled streets with French as well as English names, white buildings with gay awnings, and open-air markets give the town its continental flavor. Tides as high as 40 feet sometimes threaten waterfront shops, which keep sandbags at the ready.

a joking rivalry with Jersey. "Why is a Guernsey man happy when he sees a red sky at night?" demanded silversmith Bruce Russell. "Because he thinks Jersey's on fire!"

Serious rivals in the business of making a living, both islands woo financiers and tourists, grow vegetables and flowers, raise their respectively named pedigree cattle, and knit their respective sweaters.

For my money, Guernsey, smaller and quieter, has more appeal, despite its many greenhouses and dense housing, its blue-gray rather than pink granite, its lesser number of gorgeous beaches.

What, after all, could be more intriguing than the tiny chapel that a monk built and decorated, inside and out, with shells and bits of broken china? Or more entertaining than the ornate house in St. Peter Port where exiled French novelist Victor Hugo lived for about 16 years and shocked the neighbors by taking a shower on the roof? Or more gratifying than the opportunity, finally, to use my French? I joined a French tour. Hugo was right, I thought happily, when he said that the Channel Islands were little bits of France that had fallen into the sea and been picked up by England.

MARY B. DICKINSON

Michael St. Maur Sheil

125

By Leslie Thomas
Photographs by Michael St. Maur Sheil

The Southeast

Mariner, mariner, furl your sails,
For here are the blissful downs and dales,
And merrily, merrily carol the gales,
And the spangle dances in bight and bay,
And the rainbow forms and flies on the land
Over the islands free;
And the rainbow lives in the curve of the sand;
Hither, come hither and see;
And the rainbow hangs on the poising wave,
And sweet is the color of cove and cave,
And sweet shall your welcome be.

ALFRED, LORD TENNYSON, on the Isle of Wight

Yachts race around The Needles, west of the Isle of Wight.

God gives all men all earth to love,
But, since man's heart is small,
Ordains for each one spot shall prove
Beloved over all.
Each to his choice, and I rejoice
The lot has fallen to me
In a fair ground—in a fair ground—
Yea, Sussex by the sea!

RUDYARD KIPLING, 1902

Bandstand draws a crowd on the Grand Parade at Eastbourne, East Sussex.

Dover is the very cornerstone of Britain. From the ramparts of its Norman castle atop the famous white cliffs, you can see to France across the 20 miles of Channel that separate our kingdom from the rest of the world.

For over 2,000 years this corner of England has been the gateway for traders, troops, and tourists. Today the differing shapes and wakes of ships voyaging between Dover and the European Continent crease the summer sea. To the east the extravagantly funneled ferries tie up. To the west rise the stabilizer fins and huge propellers of their rivals, the big Hovercraft. Between the two landings is the harbor, built to cosset a World War I Grand Fleet, now a haven for fishermen and windsurfers, its shingle beach free from breakers even in the storms of winter.

For such a busy and spectacular place Dover is becomingly modest. It has something to commend it as a resort but knows that most of its visitors are merely going somewhere else. The approach from the sea—the first view for the Romans and many who followed them—unfolds in a splendid panorama. The shoulders of chalk cliffs lift themselves little by little from the sea as the ship nears.

The antique foreshore displays Regency and Edwardian houses, most of them small hotels with cellars dug deep into the backdrop of cliffs, sanctuaries from shelling from Occupied France during World War II. High above them, in the shadow of the massive castle, stands a tower that must be the tallest Roman relic left in Britain—the country's oldest lighthouse. The lower half still stands, a wonderful construction of stone and Roman brick 40 feet high, now a convenient dove-and-pigeon cote. Listen within its hollow trunk and you can hear them cooing.

Most of the earliest arrivals came to Dover uninvited. Julius Caesar and his legions were repulsed here and landed farther along the coast at Deal in 55 B.C.—first of three dates any English schoolchild can recite. Saxons (invited originally as mercenaries), Vikings, and Normans followed, but there the invasions ceased. Neither Napoleon nor Hitler ever attempted to cross that narrow but perilous Channel. Just west of Dover you can see the aborted beginning of a tunnel that for years has been discussed, a link between England and France. Construction may start again one day, but underlying the many arguments for abandoning the idea is the unspoken certainty: Once such a tunnel is completed, this island will be an island no more.

Men and women have sailed, swum, ballooned, and flown to Dover. Peering out from the breezy promenade, looking suitably aerial with helmet and faraway gaze, is a statue of Britain's Charles Stewart Rolls, the first airman to fly the Channel nonstop both ways, in June 1910. Louis Blériot, the Frenchman who made the first one-way solo flight, is commemorated in a curious, even grudging, manner. If you plunge into the woods at the back of Dover Castle, you will come upon a clearing and the stone outline of a full-size airplane, propeller and all—the place where Blériot's flimsy aircraft came to rest on a July day in 1909.

That was before my time, but I was present on the historic morning 50 years later when an inventor named Christopher Cockerell brought ashore an amazing and unwieldy contraption: a Hovercraft, a wingless fuselage

that rides on a cushion of air just above the surface of land or water. He told me that when it was being test-driven down the sand flats at Calais, on the distant side of the Channel, a Frenchman digging for bait refused to move and the huge machine had to be coaxed *around* him. "As we went by," related the inventor, "he did not even look up. He just reached out and drew his bucket a little closer."

The road-building Romans made a highway (now the A2) from Dover to London and beyond. It passed through Canterbury, whose cathedral is the cradle of Christendom in England. The majestic pile stands not far from a church already in use when Augustine, the first archbishop of Canterbury, baptized Ethelbert, King of Kent, in 597. Here it was in 1170 that Archbishop Thomas Becket was murdered at Vespers after King Henry II mused aloud in the presence of four knights, "Who will free me from this turbulent priest?" Canterbury thereafter became a famous pilgrims' destination. Their route across the breastbone of southern England is now part of a long-distance footpath, the North Downs Way. Many made the journey in the same boisterous spirit, we can suppose, as those pilgrims

Target of continental armies from Caesar to Hitler, the Southeast offers tourist legions scenic coasts, peaceful gardens, and hop farms. A vine stringer in Kent works from stilts; the 20-foot vines will bear the hops used to flavor beer.

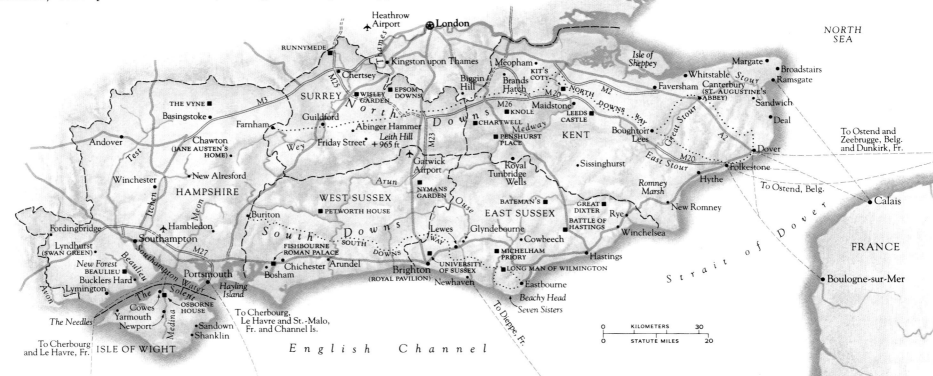

from London Chaucer portrayed in his *Canterbury Tales*.

West of Canterbury you pass near Leeds Castle, which many believe to be the most beautiful in a land of castles (see page 158). It was once a favorite place of Henry VIII, who went there when pain gripped his leg. They say the local doctor worked wonders for him.

There is an American association here, for Leeds Castle was in the 1740s the home of Lord Fairfax, who later moved to Belvoir on the Potomac, one of the few English peers to emigrate to the New World. His family married into that of George Washington. Today an 18th-century sundial on the grounds traces the five-hour time difference between the Fairfax homes in England and in America.

Few castle compounds can match the stunning setting of the place, its crenelated walls set in a mirroring lake graced by black and white swans. Douglas Pack, who has worked the grounds for 25 years, gave me a lift to the distant gate. "Look at it," he said glancing back. "Never will you see anything better." He grinned as if embarrassed by his pride. "Nice little golf course we've got here too," he added. "In the winter you can hit the ball to the second hole, right across the lake—by bouncing it on the ice."

The county of Kent was thick with summer as I traveled its narrow lanes. It is called the Garden of England and with good reason: orchards, farms, and hopyards clothe every hill and falling valley. To the north the River Thames cuts a broad channel. To the east is the old oyster town of Whitstable, and homey Broadstairs (where Dickens lived and wrote), and the sandy (Continued on page 143)

Veiled in mist, the Seven Sisters (opposite) guard the Channel coast near Beachy Head. In the 1800s, smugglers hid among these chalk bluffs, which dwarf Dover's more famous cliffs.

In the 20th century, technology triumphs at Dover Hoverport; from there Hovercraft (above, right) skim across the strait in 35 minutes, riding on a cushion of compressed air at speeds up to 75 mph and shaving an hour off the ferry crossing time to France.

Inside a Coastguard Operations Centre a radar-scanning observer tracks Channel traffic at Dover, one of the busiest passenger ports in Europe.

133

Symphonies in Stone Exalt God in an Age of Faith

Michael St. Maur Sheil (both)

Medieval miracles of art and architecture, Gothic cathedrals like those at Canterbury and Winchester (following pages) focused everyday life for the faithful during the Middle Ages. Carvings of plants and animals, saints and sinners, kings and cobblers; windows glowing with scenes from the Bible: these served the illiterate as lessons in science and history, as sermons in glass as well as stone.

The cathedral was also a source of charity, solace, and sanctuary in a rude and brutal society. It promised hope for the hereafter, and the faithful flocked in from the countryside. With sweat, blood, and fearful devotion they wrestled tons of rock great distances to raise ever larger churches and save their souls. Stone was imported from Caen in France to build Canterbury.

The Gothic cathedral grew out of the earlier English Romanesque, or Norman, style known for its barrel-vaulted roofs supported by squat, massive piers or by walls some-times eight to ten feet thick. Windows, necessarily small and recessed in the stone, let in little light.

In the 12th century, master masons, forerunners of architects, began to adapt a form already old in the Middle East when introduced to Western Europe during the Crusades: the pointed arch. Its natural opposition of forces—like two curved pillars leaning against each other at the top—made it stronger than the round arch. When combined with a light-weight ribbed-vault roof, pointed arches directed pressure downward onto

Canterbury Cathedral, cradle of English Christianity, glows in the setting sun. Henry VIII dissolved the monastic order that served the cathedral, but he founded the King's School, whose students still attend cathedral services. The school's 700 or so scholars can buy their supplies at this sagging shop, built around 1607.

134

slender columns. Narrow buttresses on the outside reinforced the walls, allowing them to be hung as thin curtains of stone that could lend space to stained-glass windows. The artistry of the glazier and the stone mason—and the guilds that preserved their skills from generation to generation—grew apace.

Centuries later, Renaissance critics would contemptuously call this architectural style Gothic, or barbaric—though historian Will Durant in *The Age of Faith* thought the Gothic cathedral the "supreme achievement and expression of the soul of man."

Most cathedrals, as well as other churches, took the form of the Latin cross, its head pointed toward the east. Worshipers entered the long nave and its side aisles from the west portal. In the aisles the arcade enabled the clergy to ambulate undisturbed in meditation. Above rose the clerestory, its colorful windows bathing the nave in light during the day.

The congregation stood in the nave (there were no seats). They faced the crossing which linked north and south transepts under a central tower. A screen separated the people's part of the church from the choir, the domain of the monks or can-

ons. At the far end rose the high altar and, behind it, the *cathedra*, or chair, of the bishop, the seat that transformed the church into a cathedral. Beyond came the apse, the projecting east end of the cathedral, which was semicircular or square in shape.

Every cathedral treasured its sacred relic—the fingerbone or garment or tool of some saint—goal of pilgrims far and wide seeking miraculous cures. None was more venerated than the remains of Saint Thomas Becket enshrined at Canterbury's Cathedral Church of Christ. Canterbury, whose archbishop is the Primate of All England, has been the spiritual home of English Christianity since 597. In that year Augustine, a Benedictine mission-

Tourists close in on Dr. Robert Runcie, Archbishop of Canterbury, at an ordination service. The prelate wears mitre and vestments similar to those that adorned Thomas Becket— portrayed here in stained glass —on December 29, 1170, when ruthless knights killed him in the northwest transept. Brass letters mark the spot in Trinity Chapel where the saint's shrine stood from 1220 to 1538.

ary from Rome, converted Ethelbert, King of Kent, and established a monastery and cathedral at this old Celtic, now Jutish, settlement.

Challenged by York Minster (whose bishop was mentioned in records as early as 314), its primacy was sealed in 1072 by a council of bishops and approved by William the Conqueror. A century later, during a struggle for authority with the crown, Archbishop Becket, "the holy blessed martyr" of Chaucer's *Canterbury Tales*, was cut down by Henry II's knights. Enshrined behind the high altar in a tomb "all over bedecked with a vast number of jewels of an immense price," Saint Thomas rested in peace until the 16th century, when Henry VIII challenged the authority of the Pope, dissolved the monasteries, and ordered the desecration of Thomas's tomb.

Worshipers fill the nave of Canterbury Cathedral as choir and clergy escort the Archbishop to the nave altar. A pointed arch, the structure that enabled Gothic walls to soar, frames the service. Elaborate fan vaulting of the tower ceiling (opposite) distinguishes the Late Gothic, or Perpendicular, period.

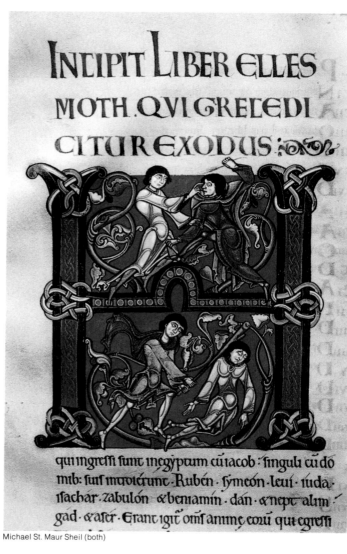

INCIPIT LIBER ELLES
MOTH. QVI GRECEDI
CITUR EXODUS ·

qui ingreſſi ſunt inegyptum cū iacob ſinguli cū do
mib: ſuiſ introierunt · Ruben · ſymeon · leui · iuda
iſachar · zabulon · & beniamin · dan · & nept alim
gad · & aſer · Erant igit oīſ anime eoū qui egreſſi

Michael St. Maur Sheil (both)

140

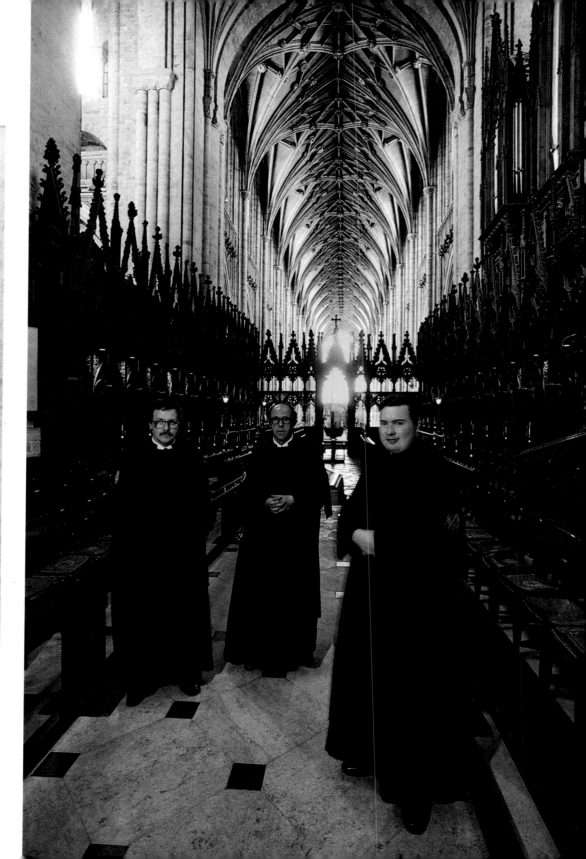

But pilgrims still come; the city welcomes nearly two million tourists a year.

Revered almost as much as Becket was Saint Swithun at Winchester, ancient capital of the West Saxons. Bishop Swithun sought to imitate the humility of Christ. Before he died in 862, he supposedly asked to be buried outside the old Saxon cathedral so his parishioners could walk over him. When, on July 15, 971, his grave was opened to place his relics in a shrine within the cathedral, "the heavens wept . . . copiously." Thus the rhyme: "Saint Swithun's Day, if thou dost rain,/For forty days it will remain." A later shrine met the same fate as Becket's: Henry's commissioners despoiled it.

Compelling for most visitors to Winchester is the nave of the longest medieval cathedral in Britain—556 feet. Its soaring arches draw the eye and heart heavenward, just as they did 500 years ago.

ROSS S. BENNETT

Winchester Cathedral's nave arches beyond vergers standing in the choir. The letter H, painted by 12th-century monks, introduces the Book of Exodus in the Winchester Bible, the church's most valued treasure.

Patrick Ward

Selected Cathedral Towns of Britain and Ireland
Variety of form and function marks the cathedrals of these isles, from Dublin's St. Patrick's, largest Gothic church in Ireland, to the roofless ruin of St. Andrews, once the greatest cathedral in Scotland, and St. Paul's in London, England's only domed Anglican cathedral. Through the ages cathedrals served not only for worship but also as social centers for fairs and festivals. One custom lives on at Salisbury Cathedral: Each May costumed dancers celebrate the ancient right to gather dead wood for fuel "by hooke or crooke."

Kirkwall

Fortrose · Elgin

Aberdeen

Dunkeld

St. Andrews

Dunblane
Glasgow · Edinburgh

Londonderry (Derry)

Carlisle · Durham

Belfast

Armagh

Ripon · York

Tuam
Clonmacnoise · St. Asaph · Liverpool · Lincoln
Clonfert · Kildare · Bangor · Chester · Southwell
Lichfield
Kilkenny
Limerick · Peterborough · Ely · Norwich
Cashel · Worcester · Coventry
Killarney · Waterford · Hereford
Cork · Ardmore · St. David's · Gloucester · St. Albans
London
Llandaff · Bristol
Wells · Winchester · Canterbury
Salisbury · Chichester
Exeter

141

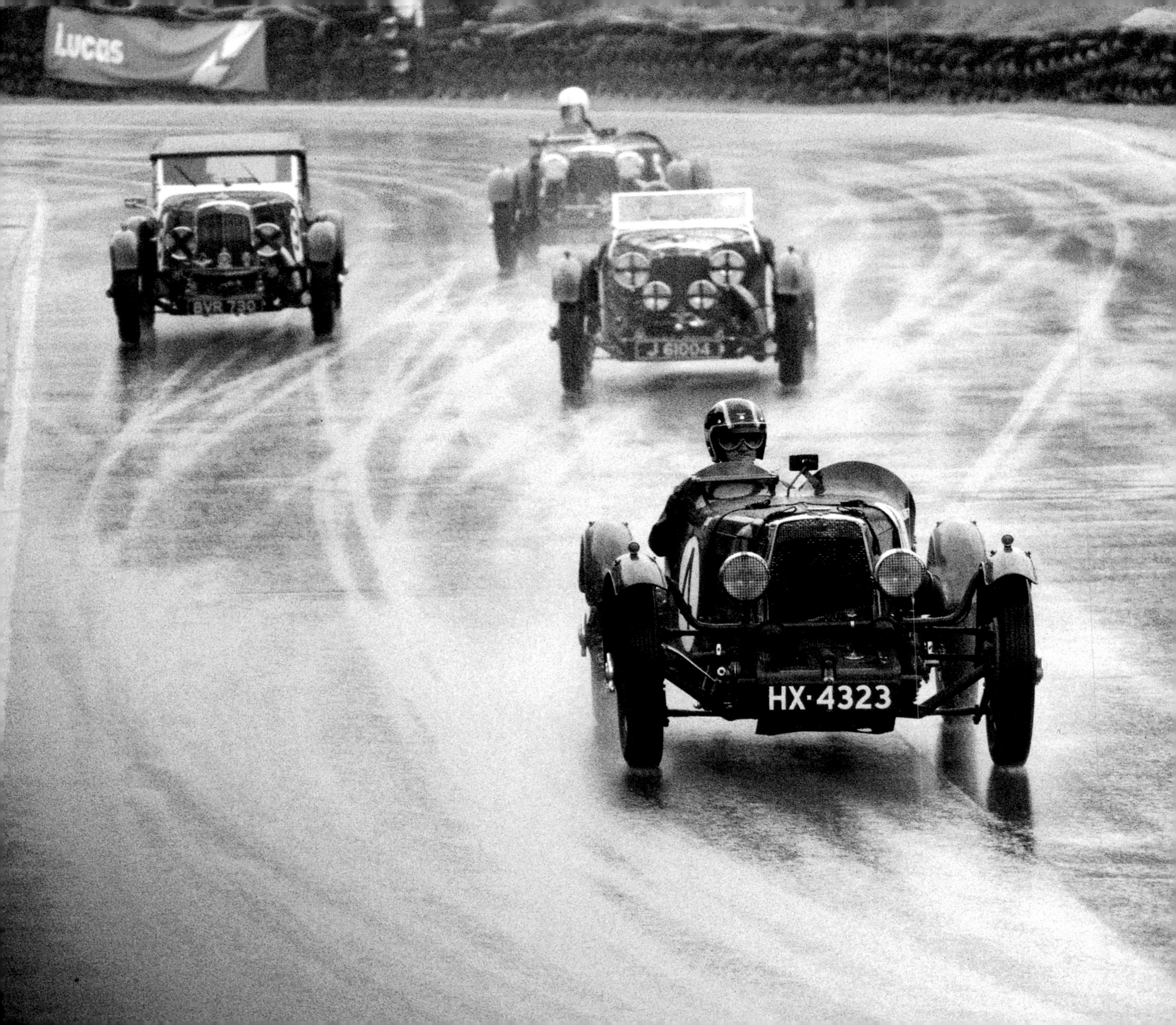
Lucas
HX·4323

shores of Margate and Ramsgate, once the landing places for marauding Danes, but now in summer the goal of armies of sunbathers.

There had been two weeks of fine skies for motoring through the North Downs. To see a sign saying "Biggin Hill" is, to anyone British, an immediate reminder of the battles fought in those skies more than four decades ago. This was one of the most famous of all the RAF (Royal Air Force) fighter stations, whose pilots, scattered up and down the country, inspired Prime Minister Winston Churchill to declare in 1940: "Never in the field of human conflict was so much owed by so many to so few."

Recently I discovered a book, *Country Notes in Wartime*, a collection of articles on gardening lore written in those alarming days by the gifted author Victoria (better known as Vita) Sackville-West. Despite the peril of the times, she tried to keep to her horticulture: "My only excuse can be that the determination to preserve such beauty as remains to us is also a form of courage."

She need not have apologized. The exquisite garden she and her husband, Sir Harold Nicolson, created from a virtual wilderness at Sissinghurst Castle, a former mansion partially restored southeast of Biggin Hill, is there to be seen and enjoyed today, years after their deaths.

The country westward curved and swerved, a green and golden switchback of full fields and ripening orchards. Hopvines on their strings covered the slopes. In prewar days poor East End Londoners spent holidays picking these Kentish hops, which earn British beer the name "bitter."

Classic cars compete on a rain-streaked course at Brands Hatch in Kent during the historic-car racing season in the Southeast. The spring meet organized by the Aston Martin Owners' Club features a 20-lap round of the FIA European historical car championship.

At Epsom Downs, Surrey, *cutups don bobby helmets on Derby Day. Namesake of the 12th Earl of Derby, the world-renowned horse race is held the first Wednesday in June.*

For those who prefer nostalgic train rides, the 1945-vintage Bodmin billows steam near New Alresford, ready for a run in the Hampshire countryside.

143

A string of quiet villages brought me to Royal Tunbridge Wells, where Beau Nash, the dandy of the 18th century, held court to the rich and famous of London who had come to ease their aches and pains at the iron-laced Chalybeate medicinal spring. The bathhouse still stands today at the end of a tree-lined and colonnaded walk paved with square clay tiles from which the area takes its name, The Pantiles. The ghosts of yesteryear rustle below the branches. Edmund Kean, the great 19th-century actor, performed at the theater on the lower walk. The county boundary once ran right through the middle of that house; the stage was in Kent, the audience in Sussex.

The second date every English schoolchild remembers is 1066. In that year William the Conqueror made the last successful invasion of Britain. He came ashore near what is now the resort of Hastings and advanced a few miles inland to confront the Anglo-Saxon defenders under Harold of Wessex. Both armies numbered 8,000 to 9,000 men, but William had a military edge—mounted knights and many bowmen. According to tradition, Harold died with an arrow in his eye, but the Bayeux Tapestry, a 231-foot-long Norman embroidery that chronicles the years leading up to the historic battle, shows Harold cut down by a sword as the Normans rout the Anglo-Saxons.

The site of the victory that changed the face and history of England is today called Battle, and it stirs the imagination. Standing on the ridge where Harold positioned his shieldwall of warriors and looking over the sweeping valley, you can almost hear the clash of metal and the cries of

Minarets and domes bedeck Brighton's Royal Pavilion, a "palace" near the sea. "The dome of St. Paul's must have come to Brighton and pupped," observed a 19th-century wag after seeing the odd summer lodgings of George, Prince of Wales, later King George IV. Arriving in 1783, the resort's famed seasonal resident transformed a timber-framed farmhouse into an Indian mogul's palace.

Simpler sights prevail along the coast at Eastbourne. Here the window of a shelter frames a couple gazing from the resort's thousand-foot-long pier at the waders and sunbathers below.

men. William swore that, if victorious, he would build a monastery here and he kept his promise. Its remains can be seen within the walls of Battle Abbey, now a girls' school.

East of Battle is Rye, one of the most delectable small towns in England. Novelist Henry James once lived here, at Lamb House. It can be visited, but his garden writing room was demolished by a German bomb. Rye suffered the final indignity for any harbor—it silted up and the sea went away. The town now stands on an island surrounded by three rivers and the pale green ocean of a great marsh, a smugglers' landscape occupied by sheep. Rye is a place of cobbles and sly streets, old inns and surprises. Some of the chimneys are wonderfully twisted and many walls bulge like fat men. Its church claims one of the oldest clocks in England still using its original works. When I was there, I also found a town crier named Gus Gale, an old friend.

Gus (an abbreviation of his navy name—Gusty Gale) and I used to be neighbors in distant Hertfordshire. He was a college lecturer then. Imagine my astonishment when I saw him in Rye dressed in a three-cornered hat, an ornate coat, and knee breeches, shouting, "Oyez! Oyez! Oyez!" the traditional town crier's call.

"I saw the job of town sergeant advertised and, since I was tired of college life and lectures, I applied and I got it," he explained. "It's fascinating. I look after the town hall and the mayor, I take visitors around, and I dress up and shout on special occasions."

This exposed corner of the Southeast, always eyed by invaders and raiders, was successfully defended in medieval times by the fleets of seven towns, the five original Cinque (pronounced sink) Ports—Sandwich, Dover, Hythe, New Romney, and Hastings, and the Ancient Towns of Winchelsea and Rye. Their tubby, single-masted ships, depicted on their town seals, took pride in their work, England's wooden walls of defense before there was a national navy.

The coastline hereabouts is also studded with Martello towers, the squat drums built in anticipation of Napoleon's invasion. The ingenious gun emplacements were armed again during the threatening days of 1940. Now they have

Lively opera fills the 830-seat theater at Glyndebourne as performers rehearse The Marriage of Figaro. *A repertory standard for 50 years, Mozart's Figaro opened the Glyndebourne Festival Opera's 1984 season—its golden anniversary. From late May to August, the world-famous festival draws wealthy patrons to this private 16th-century baronial estate in the East Sussex countryside. During the long intermission opera lovers may dine on the lawn, with grazing sheep for quiet company.*

been converted to varied uses—water towers, restaurants, shops, unique round homes.

Chalk cliffs run like bulwarks along most of the Sussex coast. At Beachy Head, from a height of 534 feet, you can view a lighthouse—from the top. Westward, past the array of white headlands called the Seven Sisters, the cliffs dwindle, smoothing to the shingle strand of Brighton.

This lively and unusual town has long been a favorite seaside retreat for Londoners. It was known as Brighthelmstone, a simple fishing village, until the 18th century, when a fashion for sea bathing stamped its future. It was always a brash place, some said brassy. It was called "Doctor Brighton" for the stimulating effect it had on Regency society and the grand people of the London Court who strolled along its promenades. Then, into the 20th century, it became a wider and wilder playground. There were youth gangs and other nefarious folk. Nevertheless, Londoners continued to travel down to paddle their feet in the sea and to eat fish-and-chips in the salt air.

Now it has changed again. The metamorphosis surprised me. It looks brighter and more wholesome than it did 20 years ago. The fish-and-chips and day-trippers are still there, but the long beach was thronged with young and vibrant people, many of them foreign students. The French, Germans, Dutch, and Scandinavians are attending language schools, a thriving industry in these south coast resorts, and the Americans are from the University of Sussex. It was the Fourth of July and the party at the Pink Coconut was lively and late. We could have been in Boston.

British visitors have changed also. Sitting on the terrace of the old Grand Hotel, I watched successive buses bring West Indian families to a gospel meeting at the expansive conference center. They are third- and fourth-generation immigrants, still with the colorful clothes and handsome laughter of the Caribbean but now speaking with the vowels of Bristol, Birmingham, and Cockney London. (Alas, visitors of a grimmer sort were to call at the Grand a few months later: the Irish Republican Army, planting their bomb for Prime Minister Thatcher and her cabinet.)

Among the parks and away from the sea, stands Brighton's most famous building, the Royal Pavilion. There is nothing in Britain to match it. Its domes and minarets and cupolas belong somewhere east of Samarkand. Within, it has huge and gilded rooms full of treasures, ornate and oriental. There is the fabulous banqueting room, with a table set with priceless silver, and hanging from the ceiling a giant palm tree out of which hisses a dragon—originally the outlet for the gaslight!

This extravaganza was fashioned from a farmhouse by George, Prince of Wales, at the turn of the 18th century. He became Prince Regent and eventually King George IV, and had a passion for a Mrs. Fitzherbert and a generally raffish image. With his startling pavilion, his friends, and his zest for living, he put Brighton firmly on the map. Although changed, the town is just as fascinating today. Its elegant crescents and tight lanes, bright with the windows of antique shops, fit rather surprisingly into the large and the modern. It has a vast yacht marina, and, like twin guardians of the resort's past, two great piers extending far into the English Channel. On the Palace Pier, I once went to visit the gypsy fortune-teller and found her with a fishing line dangling through a hole in the floor of her booth. Attached was a little bell that rang when a fish took the bait, although I wondered why someone with extrasensory perception should have needed that.

Brighton is backed by the South Downs, uplands green and smooth, where sheep have grazed for 5,000 years and windmills stand like men with (Continued on page 154)

Fishermen at Hythe (opposite) help keep Southeast resorts supplied with seafood—from snails and cod to "dabs," a flatfish on sale at Ye Olde Fish Shop in Folkestone (above, left). At English's Oyster Bar, a 150-year-old restaurant in Brighton, the chef offers an elegant platter of locally trapped lobster.

148

Michael St. Maur Sheil (both)

A Rose
Is a Rose
Is a National Hobby

A garden is "the purest of human pleasures," wrote English philosopher Sir Francis Bacon in 1625. Many Britishers today would agree. By one estimate, 80 percent of British households and 70 percent of Irish have some sort of garden (compared with 51 percent in the United States), ranging from the determined window boxes of city dwellers to the spectacular terraces of Powis Castle in Wales.

In his book *The British*, Sir Anthony Glyn claims that "the sight of an elderly and aristocratic Britishwoman, in her raincoat and rubber boots . . . weeding the border in the pouring rain is one that should be seen by all those who wish to understand the British character."

Notebooks in hand, more than 200,000 people attend the prestigious Chelsea Flower Show held in London each May. About a million people listen to "Gardeners' Question Time" every Sunday on BBC radio. "The more hours a man spends in the garden," says Sir Anthony, "the more worthy he and his friends feel themselves to be."

Climate encourages this horticultural enthusiasm. Summers are seldom really hot (80°F is a rare heat wave) and winters are usually mild. Rainfall is generous but gentle. There is, of course, less sunshine than most gardeners would like. But palm trees thrive on the southwest coast.

One of the finest results of this zeal is what author Vita Sackville-West called "probably the prettiest form of gardening ever achieved in this country"—the cottage garden: Roses at the doorway, hollyhocks along the walls, and a dense but orderly profusion of flowers, especially in the "herbaceous border"

Britain blooms with gardens like the Hodgsons' charming border (left) and the seven-acre estate, Great Dixter, of gardening authority Christopher Lloyd (right), both in East Sussex.

along the pathway. These delightful gardens make a showplace of every village.

But the formal gardens of stately homes are the biggest attraction, and not only for foreign tourists. Visiting these gardens has been called Britain's national summer sport.

The Romans probably introduced formal gardens to Britain (and, according to one historian, invented the British country gentleman). At Fishbourne in West Sussex, archaeologists have reconstructed the garden of a Roman palace, with its symmetrical clipped hedges, rosebeds, and a seaside terrace.

No evidence suggests that the British created such gardens after the Romans left. Only in monasteries, apparently, were a few flowers grown for their own sake. But the Roman influence reached Britain again. In Tudor times, royalty and noblemen began adding formal gardens to their palaces and castles, inspired by Italian gardens.

Sissinghurst Castle's garden was "crying out for rescue" when Sir Harold Nicolson and his wife, author Vita Sackville-West, purchased the derelict fortress in 1930 and planted its now-famous walled design.

Most Renaissance gardens were rigidly formal and artificial, cluttered with fountains and statues and arbors, topiary and mazes. (Britain's largest maze, with more than one and a half miles of paths, was created at Longleat House in Wiltshire only a few years ago.) Still popular in the 18th century, such stylized gardens even appeared, on a smaller scale, in the North American colonies. The Governor's Palace in Williamsburg, Virginia, for instance, boasts a maze patterned after the one at Hampton Court Palace.

But formality and artifice began to give way to a more natural beauty. One of the geniuses of this "landscape movement" was Capability Brown, so nicknamed because of his oft-repeated assurance to clients that their gardens "had great capability for improvement." In the late 1800s, Brown transformed many formal gardens into open lawns enhanced only by lakes, trees, and a bridge or two. One of his most impressive lakes survives at Blenheim Palace (see page 222).

Large or small, the gardens of Britain and Ireland today combine a variety of styles and reveal a skill and devotion unmatched in any other land.

MARY R. LAMBERTON

Inverewe
Pitmedden
Edzell
Castle
Drummond
Castle • Branklyn
Crarae • Falkland Palace
Woodland EDINBURGH • Tyninghame

Castle
Kennedy
Mount • Threave
Stewart
Castlewellan • Rowallane Levens Studley Royal
Hall Country Park
• Harlow Car

• DUBLIN Bodnant Tatton Park
Powerscourt • Dargle Glen Arley Haddon Hall
Abbey Leix Hall
House Mount • Gwyllt Blickling Hall
Usher Powis Burford
Castle House
Packwood House
Anne's Grove • Kiftsgate Court Hidcote Manor
• Derreen Blenheim Palace • Kew Gardens
St. Fagans of the Rose
Castle Cliveden • LONDON
Montacute House Wisley • Hampton Court
Knightshayes Stourhead Sissinghurst
Court Nymans Great
Barrington Court Cranborne Fishbourne Dixter
Manor Roman
Palace
Glendurgan

Selected Gardens of Britain and Ireland

From charming cottage gardens to the elaborate parks of stately homes, more than 3,000 gardens are open to the public. Visitors stroll to the dramatic grotto at Stourhead, admire the arrangement of red, white, and blue flowers in Mount Stewart's Jubilee Glade, and wonder at Tyninghame's tulips, descendants of bulbs imported by the Romans. The Royal Botanic Gardens at Kew vie for popularity with the formal gardens of Hampton Court Palace, where a maze (left) has bewildered visitors for more than three centuries.

their hands raised. At Arundel the turrets of the castle and the pointed church look over billowing trees, a sweet village, a curling river, and the prettiest cricket ground in England. Arundel Castle is the seat of the Duke of Norfolk, Earl Marshal of England, even though Norfolk lies five counties to the northeast.

I drove down honeysuckle lanes to Bosham, whose church is depicted on the Bayeux Tapestry (which hangs in France but may have been embroidered by English hands from Canterbury). It shows Harold of England, in 1064, embarking on a diplomatic mission to Normandy. Bosham is today a salty village with a cozy hotel, sitting on the edge of a wide and reedy harbor, a haven for winter water birds and those who like to watch them.

Westward, Sussex gives way to the fields and watery meadows of Hampshire, a county of slender rivers. Its two great ports of Portsmouth and Southampton, one naval, one mercantile, lie almost berth by berth, their harbors protected by the rising haunch of the Isle of Wight. Looking out to that large island, misty in the sun, I thought once again how it is a place apart, served only by ferries dependent on good weather. Queen Victoria spent her holidays there and died on the island at Osborne House near Cowes, where each year Cowes Week decorates the sea with grand yachts. In a shed near the house you can see the wheelbarrows and garden tools of the royal children of more than a century ago, each touchingly marked with the small owner's initials.

There are sandy seaside towns on the isle, and Sandown and Shanklin are among the sunniest resorts in Britain. Off the western coast majestic rocks, The Needles, show off their lighthouse best at sunset. There are also quiet harbors and hamlets. At one of these, Yarmouth, I once tied a dinghy to the stone harbor wall, forgetting about the deep fall of the local tides. When I returned the sea had ebbed, leaving the boat hanging by its bow.

An air of mystery pervades the Isle of Wight, a remnant perhaps of smuggling days, when it was busy with the "trade." Its aloneness persists. Brian Freemantle, a writer

Boaters pause on still waters near Romney Marsh, a secluded lowland along the Kentish coast. Romans, Saxons, and Normans all dwelt in these marshy meadowlands reclaimed from the sea with walls and dikes. In Hampshire, a trout fisherman challenges the River Test. Anglers pay property owners dearly to cast dry flies on the world-renowned Test and nearby Itchen to lure the wily brown trout. At Michelham Priory in East Sussex, an archer sights an arrow with puckered precision.

Michael St. Maur Sheil, Susan Griggs Agency

Stately summer sport, cricket dances on village greens throughout the Southeast. At Swan Green, near Lyndhurst in Hampshire, players move through a complex ritual: A batsman (above) defends his wicket—three upright sticks— from a bowler's hurled ball; if it knocks down the wicket, he is out. Cricketers have played Britain's national game in Hampshire for centuries, quenching their thirst at pubs like the Bat and Ball, an old inn at Hambledon. Suburban sprawl enfolds Meopham Green, Kent (opposite), an 18th-century cricket field where local teams play league matches.

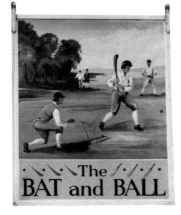

The BAT and BALL

from an old Hampshire family, knows the island well. "When the last ferry goes on a winter's evening," he said, "the island withdraws into itself. The inhabitants regard mainlanders as foreigners. They call them 'Overners.'"

Southampton is a rebuilt city, ravaged by fierce German bombing during World War II. (Residents used to trek each night into the neighboring New Forest and watch from there as fires sprouted over their homes.) It still has ribbons of medieval city wall, however, and I walked below it to view again the modest memorial reminding the world that the Pilgrim Fathers first set sail from here on their journey to the New World. Much more dramatic and colorful departures from Southampton preceded the Pilgrims —Richard the Lion-Hearted on the Third Crusade and Henry V for victory at Agincourt.

Portsmouth's pride is H.M.S. *Victory*, Lord Nelson's flagship in 1805 at the Battle of Trafalgar, where the British fleet defeated the combined fleets of the French and the Spanish. The victory cost Nelson his life at the hands of a French sharpshooter. There was no mistaking the pride of Robbie Hall, a naval airman (he normally serves on aircraft carriers) who took me around the veteran vessel. Craftsmen were caulking the deckboards, using the skills and implements of the early 19th century. Robbie took me below deck to the midshipman's berth where Nelson died (his body was brought home in a barrel of brandy). He spoke of the *Victory*'s superior firepower as if she were one of the cruisers of today's navy, lying beside us in the great anchorage. I sat at Nelson's table and I touched his coffin-shaped hanging cot. "Sometimes on night watch duty this seems a very ghostly place," Robbie admitted. "I've seen that cot swinging for no reason at all."

Guns point through the ports, and cannonballs are piled beside them. "Two girls stole a couple of cannonballs," my guide grinned. "Carried them off in plastic shopping bags, but the cannonballs fell through the bottom." He sniffed. "The girls were French, of course."

Alongside H.M.S. *Victory* is a building containing *Mary Rose*, Henry VIII's sunken flagship recently recovered from

The Solent. After centuries of submersion, the hull is not as spectacular as *Victory,* and the sailors of the latter ship refer to it as "H.M.S. *Driftwood.*"

Many of Nelson's ships, although not *Victory,* were built at Bucklers Hard on the Beaulieu River (pronounced Bewley), south of Southampton. The village is preserved by the Montagu family, who have lived at Beaulieu for almost 450 years. "They built the street so wide," explains the present Lord Montagu, "so that sawn timber from the huge oak trees felled in the New Forest could be piled up for seasoning and later used in shipbuilding."

William the Conqueror designated the New Forest as his exclusive hunting ground in the 11th century. At 145 square miles, it is for southern England a vast area of wild country. There are wild ponies, deer, cattle, pigs, and donkeys, all protected in the forest under ancient laws, and there is a Court of Verderers (magistrates) to see that the laws are observed. I once lived in a Queen Anne house at the edge of the forest, near Fordingbridge. There was an idyllic stream running through the garden on its way to the River Avon. It contained a pike that used to snap at the legs of my dogs. We had a splendid walled garden and an old gardener who told me, "If you want a garden like this, you have to start two hundred years ago."

Northeast of the New Forest is Winchester, the capital of Wessex in Anglo-Saxon days. The massive statue of King Alfred, sword aloft, towers somewhat threateningly over shoppers in its main street. Today the dove gray city's focal point is the square-towered cathedral, with its flying buttresses, its magnificent west window, and the stony poetry of its lofty roof. Among all the kings, queens, and clerics whose tombs are on view, stands a little statue dedicated to a deep-sea diver. Beneath it I read the words: "William Walker the diver who saved this cathedral with his two hands, 1906-1912"—years spent in the water and mud below the walls shoring up sinking foundations built hundreds of years ago over a bed of peat.

The novelist Jane Austen is buried in the cathedral. She spent her last months in the city, but her best remembered

Hot-air balloonists rally at Leeds Castle near Maidstone during the Radio Kent Balloon Race in June 1984. Built on two islands at the site of a Saxon fort, Edward I's stronghold remains one of Britain's finest castles. A 13th-century barbican (gate tower) from his era still stands. The monarch gave Leeds successively to each of his two wives, beginning a tradition. At least eight medieval queens lived here. Tourists now roam the restored castle and grounds, bequeathed to the Leeds Castle Foundation in 1974. The organization sponsors open-air concerts, fireworks displays, and six-course Kentish dinners. In the castle's unusual museum visitors can see a collection of dog collars, one made entirely of silver. Occasionally the castle closes down to host state conferences.

Once owned by Henry VIII, Leeds Castle was named after Led, a royal minister who built the original fort in 857 and protected it by means of a drawbridge over the lake.

house is in the Hampshire village of Chawton. It has the feel of a real home (far more, for example, than Dickens's birthplace in Portsmouth). The door she allowed to creak—so that she could hide her manuscript if anyone approached—still creaks.

Surrey lies northeast, toward London. To many, it means rows of well-scrubbed commuter houses with parks and ordered trees, suburban railway stations, gardens and golf clubs, but it is still fine riding and racing country. On Epsom Downs, Britain's greatest flat race, the Derby, is run every June. It began in 1780. This is a day out for all classes—the upper set in their gray top hats, the ordinary Londoners picnicking and watching the races from the upper decks of open-topped buses, the gypsy fairground families who meet here for the annual tribal gathering. The Queen herself does not miss Derby Day if she can help it.

In former days many iron forges occupied wooded parts of this region. At the hamlet of Friday Street there is a hammer pond, its water once used to power the hammers of the forge. And at nearby Abinger Hammer a mechanical smith on the village clock strikes the bell to ring the hour.

The church of St. Peter's at Chertsey has a curfew bell, inspiration for the American poet Rose Hartwick Thorpe's "Curfew Must Not Ring Tonight." Blanche Heriot, a local girl, clung to the clapper, legend says, so that her lover, due to be executed at curfew, would be saved.

It is at the extreme edge of Surrey, however, that two moments of history, separated by an ocean and many years, are marked. At Runnymede bad King John was forced in 1215 (the *third* date any English schoolchild can recite) to seal the Magna Carta, upon which the basic freedoms of this country are established. Overlooking the Thames, a cupola commemorates the event. Two hundred yards away, on a hillside, rests another freedom memorial, this one to John F. Kennedy—a simple white slab recording that he died at the hand of an assassin. It is shaded by English trees in a rough-cut English meadow, but the land around it belongs now to the United States, one acre ceded by Britain. A piece of America beside the English Thames.

By Edward Storey
Photographs by Michael S. Yamashita

East Anglia & the Fens

I associate "my careless boyhood" with all that lies on the banks of the Stour; those scenes made me a painter, and I am grateful; that is, I had often thought of pictures of them before I ever touched a pencil. . . .

JOHN CONSTABLE, 1821

Willy Lott's Cottage, on the River Stour in Flatford, Suffolk, appears in several Constable paintings.

saw Naples, I smelt Naples,
and I survive to love Southwold.

COL. B. GRANVILLE BAKER, 1931

Clifftop town of Southwold, Suffolk, overlooks a North Sea beach.

They have a beauty of their own, these great fens, even now, when they are dyked and drained, tilled and fenced—a beauty as of the sea, of boundless expanse and freedom.

CHARLES KINGSLEY, 1866

Reclaimed fenland in Lincolnshire meets the sky along a line of trees planted as a windbreak.

There is no obvious starting place from which to explore the ancient kingdom of East Anglia. Each county has its own characteristics, independence, and history. As one of the first regions of Anglo-Saxon settlement, this area of England has strong claims to being the birthplace of the country we now know. Once the home of the East Angles, the region was eventually divided into smaller kingdoms for the North Folk (Norfolk) and the South Folk (Suffolk), which together form East Anglia proper; the East Saxons (Essex); and the Middle Angles, which became Cambridgeshire and the Fens. North of these counties is Lincolnshire, equally steeped in history. Romans, Saxons, Vikings, and Normans have all contributed to the evolution of today's East Anglians.

I began my journey in Essex, at Maldon, a town popular with yachtsmen and shoppers. An epic struggle between the Saxon Earl of Brihtnoth and the Danes took place here in A.D. 991. *The Battle of Maldon,* one of the oldest poems in the English language, commemorates it: "There gainst the fierce ones/Ready was standing/Brihtnoth with his warriors." Essex's contribution to the nation's history did not seem to impress a veteran of the First World War whom I met on the quay at Maldon one Sunday morning.

"Are you an Essex man?" I asked.

"What, me?" he replied, insulted. "Not likely, mate. I'm *English.* Born in London. Where else?"

We English may be parochial even in the capital, but finding a Londoner in Essex is no surprise; the county is often called London's country playground. Here, within an hour of the city, lies the rural England of green country lanes, attractive villages, and 16th-century houses.

Much of the Essex coastline is broken by muddy estuaries, of interest mainly to bird-watchers. Better to explore Colchester, the oldest recorded town in England. Despite its hideous attempts at modernization, Colchester still has visible reminders of its days as Camulodunum, a stronghold of the Roman occupation. There are mosaics, ruins of

city walls and of two temples, a museum full of relics, and a Norman church constructed in part from Roman bricks. The Colchester oyster, famous as a local delicacy since Roman times, is still served at the annual Oyster Feast with traditional pomp and civic ceremony.

Still better is to lose yourself in rural Essex, away from such busy centers, and find delightful villages like Dedham, lively but not yet vulgarized by its popularity. It has a splendid, well-endowed church, good pubs, and a thriving Arts and Crafts Centre where bargains *can* be found.

My wife, Angela, and I stayed for a few days at a quiet and gracious little hotel in nearby Ardleigh, from which we explored the less well-known corners of Essex. The Essex landscape is not spectacular, but nearer to the Stour Valley it takes on a gentle beauty that is typically English. The undulating fields, a mixture of arable and grazing land, are well farmed. There are hedges and trees, and the lanes in spring are embroidered with primroses, cowslips, and bluebells. Little wonder that the landscape artist John Constable (1776-1837) found this part of England, shared between Essex and Suffolk, such a source of inspiration.

There are picturesque villages to enjoy, filled with pastel color-washed or half-timbered houses—Little Baddow, Tolleshunt D'Arcy, Great Bardfield, Felsted, Finchingfield. You will also see houses decorated with an East Anglian architectural specialty, the elaborate relief plasterwork called pargeting. Another local craft, the corn dolly, dates from Neolithic times. Corn dollies are small puppets or horseshoes or cornucopias woven out of straw to preserve the "spirit of the corn" and ensure a good crop next year. Most gift shops carry them.

To pass from Essex into Suffolk is to step into a Constable painting. The scenes he made famous now attract thousands of visitors, who come to see the source of "The Hay Wain," "Flatford Mill," or "Willy Lott's Cottage."

Today Suffolk is as much associated with composer Benjamin Britten, co-founder with Sir Peter Pears of the Aldeburgh Festival. Walk through the reedbeds at Snape, look back at the Maltings concert hall, and you are in touch

Low-lying East Anglia, its watery Fens now largely diked and drained, includes some of England's richest farmland (and jolliest scarecrows), as well as sandy beaches, tranquil villages, and fine cathedrals—the scenes of Britain's early history.

East Anglia abounds in Tudor half-timbered buildings, like those in Lavenham, Suffolk (opposite, upper right), so picturesque that the village has been used as a film set. "Half-timbered" describes a frame built of logs split in half. Spaces between the timbers were filled chiefly with mixtures of mud or clay. As time and weather warped the wood and crumbled the clay, owners remedied the ensuing draftiness by plastering the house. Ivy Tricker's 400-year-old house in Kersey (right) was plastered and then painted pink, a favorite house color in Suffolk since medieval times.

Pargeting, the modeling of ornate designs in the plaster, became popular in Suffolk in the 16th century. The 15th-century Ancient House (far left) in Clare gained its lavish pargeting in the 17th century.

Only one kind of stone was readily available in East Anglia—hard, irregular flint. Builders made flint walls by embedding the stones in mortar and adding rows of brick for strength (opposite, lower right).

with nature and genius at the same time: on the one hand the wide cloud-patterned sky reflected in water over which curlews call, and on the other hand the building, beached like a stranded ark on the edge of the estuary, where some of the greatest musicians in the world have performed.

For music of another sort, go farther up the coast, to the crumbling cliffs at Dunwich, where the encroaching sea has buried the medieval town beneath the waves. Legend says you can hear the town bells tolling beneath the waves on stormy nights (a preliminary visit to one of the local pubs might help!).

Suffolk is slowly losing not only its coast but also much of its pastureland. I asked Michael Stagg, warden for the Suffolk Heritage Coast, about it. Mike is a poet of con-

servation; he deplores the practice of burning stubble after the harvest—"the funeral pyres of the barley fields"—and rhapsodizes about his favorite river, the Alde, "the plaintive river, the voice of Suffolk." But of pastureland he said, "It's frightening how the land is changing. In ten years the character of the county has been transformed." Large areas of heathland have disappeared, mostly under the plow.

Suffolk does have some of the most beautiful villages in East Anglia. Framlingham is a special favorite of mine. I once saw the old year out in the shadow of the town's great castle and heard the peal of nearby New Year's church bells echoing from the castle walls. It seemed as if the castle had its own ghostly bells, as if knights, lords, and ladies still

169

celebrated their own phantom New Year's Eve in the ruined banquet hall.

There are days in East Anglia when you can step back a hundred years or more into an England where time has a different measure. They say people live longer in northern Norfolk than anywhere else in Britain. If there are more centenarians in this county than in any other, I can understand why. It is peaceful, unhurried, and healing.

Norfolk people love to boast of their deep family roots. In a small fishing village I heard the story of the old locals arguing in their pub one day as to how long their families had lived in the area. When one claimed that his folk had been there for 400 years, the squire's wife (who had stopped in for her daily gin and tonic) pointed out that her family had been there longer than any. "You see," she explained, "we have deeds and documents on our estate which prove that my ancestors came over in 1066 with William the Conqueror." At which an old fisherman looked up and said, "Ah, my lady, I know that's right cus my old dad was there and helped to pull the boats in!"

Most of my childhood holidays were spent "at the seaside" in Norfolk, and I am always happy to return. Even the white summer clouds appear to be on holiday as they bask in the sky. Fat and harmless, they remind me of kind, overweight aunts unashamed to expose their generous flesh on the carefree beach. Summer sunlight brightens flint seaside cottages with gardens of hollyhocks and roses. Sailing boats and creeks smelling of samphire (a salt-marsh plant that can be cooked, a bit like spinach), friendly pubs and friendly people—what more could you ask for?

Inland, Norfolk offers the lively city of Norwich, complete with cathedral and churches, a castle-museum, theaters, television studios, and a traditional marketplace, shaded by colorfully striped awnings.

Away from the bustle of modern commerce is an area unique in Britain—the Broads. This complex, 200-mile network of inland waterways links 30 lakes, carved out by centuries of turf cutting during the Middle Ages, when peat was used to fuel fires here. The advent of coal put an

Straight and narrow New Bedford River (left), created by the 17th-century Dutch engineer Cornelius Vermuyden, collects overflow from the Great Ouse. Hundreds of such drainage projects have transformed the soggy Fens into rich farmland.

Racing yachts and cabin cruisers now crowd the Broads, a region of shallow lakes. As hordes of holidaymakers invade this watery world, motorboat wakes erode the shorelines and severe pollution endangers such wetland birds as the grey heron.

171

end to the digging, seawater filled the excavations, and now the Broads are popular with thousands of holidaymakers who, like Kenneth Grahame's Water Rat, enjoy "messing about in boats."

As always in Norfolk, history is just over your shoulder. You can walk along the Roman Peddars Way, or visit the remains of a Saxon cathedral at North Elmham, or explore 18th-century Holkham Hall. The Norfolk home that attracts most attention is Sandringham House, which the royal family owns and uses as a retreat. In late spring the woodland roads there are regal with the purple, red, and pink blossoms of rhododendrons and azaleas.

Not far from Sandringham is King's Lynn, a seaport with a lingering air of old sailing ships and salty sea captains. King's Lynn found prosperity in the 13th century, during the surge in the wool trade between England and the Continent. Today the town is a thriving modern port like Felixstowe and Harwich, linking Britain with the rest of the Common Market. Gantry cranes clang, sea gulls call, and foreign accents echo round the quayside walls.

When King John granted the town its charter in 1204, King's Lynn was almost on the shores of that huge apron of shallow water called the Wash, which then encroached much farther inland than it does today. Here, in October of 1216, as he campaigned against the rebellious barons, John lost most of his treasure when the incoming tide overwhelmed his baggage train as it crossed the Norfolk tidal flats. John himself reached the safety of Lincolnshire, only to die there a few days later, of dysentery.

Most counties in East Anglia have a single distinctive character, but Lincolnshire has two completely different faces—the Lowlands, wide open and flat, and the Wolds, undulating and secretive.

The Lowlands spread around the Wash from Norfolk into Lincolnshire. Some of this rich agricultural area, known for its potatoes and flower bulbs, is called Marshland because its terrain is reclaimed from the sea. It is a beguiling, solitary landscape. In springtime the air smells salty; in summer it is warm and languid, and heat haze

East Anglians, once described as a "wild, amphibious race," meet the North Sea's challenge —and harvest its bounty. At Cromer in Norfolk, a tractor hauls in boats bringing the day's catch of famed Cromer crabs. At Aldeburgh in Suffolk, Vic Smith, a fisherman for most of his 80 years, watches patiently for incoming boats, waiting to switch on the winch engine that will pull them to shore. Both of these ancient towns lost their original harbors to erosion and siltation. Offshore sandbanks and rough seas imperil fishermen, but the sandy beaches lure tourists. Cromer's pier holds both the lifeboat house and a pavilion theater.

PAGES 174-175: *Beach huts at Felixstowe, Suffolk, await the onslaught of summer visitors.*

172

shimmers over dry grass. Autumn brings a dreamy remoteness, and winter turns the place uncompromisingly Siberian, with freezing fogs and icy winds from the northeast.

Although seawalls around the Wash are still being extended to reclaim even more of the salt marshes, the area produces an uneasy feeling, as if it belongs to neither the land nor the sea. Scientists and farmers are working to make this virgin soil as fertile as that reclaimed earlier. But for now, the bleakness humbles and awes. At times North Sea storms temporarily retake these fields. In mankind's conflict with the elements, this is the front line.

But when spared such disaster, the springtime fields of lowland Lincolnshire can take on all the colors of the rainbow as daffodils and tulips burst into bloom. These millions of tulips are cultivated primarily for bulbs; the unwanted flowers are cut to decorate floats in the Spalding Flower Parade, held every May. The festival attracts thousands of visitors to the town, creating for a day the atmosphere of a continental fiesta.

Rising from the fields farther north is a landmark no one can miss: the imposingly elegant tower of St. Botolph's Church, soaring nearly 300 feet above the banks of the River Witham in the town of Boston. Nearby is the 15th-century Guildhall where, the sign on the wall says, "William Bradford, William Brewster and others afterwards known as the Pilgrim Fathers were imprisoned on the 23rd September 1607 after attempting to escape to religious freedom" in the New World. They had made their way successfully to Boston, but the captain of the Dutch ship they boarded there turned them in. Only after several months of captivity in Boston and years of exile in the Netherlands did they manage to join the other Pilgrims who were ready to sail from Southampton on the *Mayflower* in 1620. Because of Boston's American associations, the Stars and Stripes often flies side by side here with the Union Jack.

Beyond Boston you soon begin to discover the other face of Lincolnshire—the Wolds, gentle green hills whose fields are used mainly for grazing sheep and cattle. The

Louth sheep market is a good indication of their popularity in the county. On market days the cacophony of auctioneers, buyers, sellers, and bleating sheep gives the town a taste of medieval England. My wife and I spent a few days exploring the Wolds and were completely enchanted by them. From our hotel in Scamblesby it was easy to walk along the Viking Way, an ancient track that meanders where the invading Danes passed in the ninth century, over farmland and along a stretch of the River Bain.

The city of Lincoln is more up-to-date, but I prefer its older streets, where history is imprinted like a watermark on every cornerstone. To get the full flavor of Lincoln you must struggle up a cobbled street aptly named Steep Hill, to Castle Hill. As you pause to catch your breath, reflect upon the legends associated with the House of Aaron the Jew, a 12th-century moneylender who was said to have become the richest man in England. Or rest a while in the Usher Gallery and view the collection of paintings by Peter de Wint (1784-1849). Another room holds an assortment of hats, cloaks, pipes, and pens of Victorian poet laureate Alfred, Lord Tennyson, born at nearby Somersby in 1809. Or you might prefer to get your second wind at the Wig & Mitre, a licensed (they serve alcohol) eating house with a Dickensian atmosphere, complete with cobwebs.

In addition to the castle ruins and cathedral, Lincoln offers antique shops, bookshops, and, for anyone interested in rare Scotch malt whiskies, the Whisky Shop, which has one of the finest collections in the country.

Heading back south from the Wolds, you can pause near

Lincoln Cathedral (left), one of England's earliest, towers over the town from the hilltop site it shares with a Norman castle. Begun in 1072, the cathedral was largely rebuilt after disastrous fires and an earthquake in the 12th century. Multiturreted Ely Cathedral (opposite), begun in 1083, dominates the flat *Cambridgeshire landscape from its low hill, an island until the Fens were drained. Its unique octagonal central tower, a marvel of medieval engineering, was constructed in the 14th century after the original square Norman tower collapsed.*

Stamford to see Burghley House, the extravagant example of Elizabethan architecture that was the seat of Elizabeth I's Lord High Treasurer William Cecil, Lord Burghley. It is said that the arrogant Nazi marshal Hermann Göring selected Burghley House as the English home that he would occupy once the Germans had won the war. If so, he must have ordered the *Luftwaffe* not to bomb it.

From Stamford we turned east into the Fens. Centuries ago these expanses were a tangle of swamps, but the great drainage operations of the 1600s changed them forever, into a flat, open land renowned for spacious skies.

I was born on the edge of the Fens, in the market town of Whittlesey, and there learned to love the region's qualities of space and light. As a child I could not believe that the earth was round. Each morning I saw the sun rise low in the east and make its slow journey across a continent of sky to set in the west. My world was as flat as a pool table.

Although I have lived with this landscape for more than 50 years, I only recently discovered the advantages of exploring the countryside by boat. My wife and I hired a diesel cabin cruiser named *Tranquil Waters III*, a name we considered a suitably good omen. We began our voyage at Earith on a Saturday afternoon in April, a cool, gray day with a strong northeasterly wind blowing. My mind went back to the day when the young Dutch engineer, Sir Cornelius Vermuyden, stood here in 1630 and contemplated the great task before him—the drainage of the Fens.

The *Oxford English Dictionary* defines a fen as "low land covered wholly or partially with shallow water. . . ." The

Auctioneer and drover sort sheep into batches for sale at the Louth Cattle Market. An average of 500 sheep and 400 cattle are sold here each week at the Friday market that continues a tradition begun in 1802. Its location, where the rolling Lincolnshire Wolds meet the flat coastal marsh, makes Louth the region's major center for livestock trading. It is also one of England's prettiest and best preserved Georgian market towns. The poet Alfred Tennyson and explorers John Smith and John Franklin all went to school here as children.

fens Vermuyden faced had formed after the Ice Age, when melting glaciers exposed a basin where the ground had subsided under the weight of the ice. Rivers flowing from the uplands accumulated here, creating huge shallow, stagnant lakes. Daniel Defoe called the Fens "the sink of no less than thirteen counties."

Vermuyden's great vision and skill made draining this sink possible. He straightened out the winding course of the River Great Ouse and cut new channels to enable all the surplus water to reach the river outlet on the Wash. Windmill-powered scoop wheels would later lift water from below sea level over the silt banks so it could reach the sea. At one time there were a thousand windmills along the riverbanks and dikes.

It was no easy task to dig new waterways across miles of wild bog—made no easier by local opposition. Fen people pride themselves on their independence. They were the last to surrender to the Normans in the 11th century, and boast that they never really gave in to the Romans. They are tough and stubborn, products of years of conflict with nature and invaders. The Fenmen of the 17th century were quite content with the living they made from fishing, wildfowling, and reed cutting. They were so violently opposed to Vermuyden's plans that they not only refused to work for him, they also sabotaged the work once it began. In the end, Vermuyden had to rely for labor on 1,500 Scottish and Dutch prisoners of war.

Nevertheless, during a period of 22 years, hundreds of ditches and new channels were cut. Nearly 400,000 acres were reclaimed in the 17th century alone. Villages and towns expanded, and families moved in from other regions to find work. The Fen Country had a new beginning.

The term "fens" is a misnomer today. They are drained, and their soil is the most fertile in England. Unlike Marshland silt, initially brackish from lying beneath the sea, Fen soil is peat-based—rich and black. I have seen farmers from other countries shake their heads in envy as they looked over these prolific fields.

We steered *Tranquil Waters III* along Old West River to

Rivaling Holland, the fertile Lincolnshire lowlands blossom with millions of tulips. Workers at left gather flowers for markets as distant as North America. Flowers also adorn spectacular floats for the town of Spalding's annual Flower Parade (right). But most of the 10,000 or so acres devoted to this industry grow tulips, daffodils, lilies, and other plants for their bulbs, not their blooms.

join, three hours later, with the Great Ouse. It was so cold and still we could have been gliding on ice. We moored for the night in a sheltered elbow of the river, then set out early the next morning for the Isle of Ely, a low hill that was once a true island but now rises from a sea of farm fields. The city of Ely grew up around the abbey founded in A.D. 673 by Saint Etheldreda, and its cathedral has inspired visitors ever since the 12th century.

Ely has dominated the region's history. Against the backdrop of Ely, characters who have changed our way of life played out their roles: Danish King Canute, who was so impressed by the Ely monks' chanting that he instructed all the monasteries to improve their musical worship; Hereward the Wake, scourge of the Norman invaders when they attempted to conquer the Fens; and Oliver Cromwell, 17th-century villain of the Civil War, whose troops beheaded all the statues and holy figures in the cathedral's beautiful Lady Chapel.

We returned to our boat and drifted downstream to the River Lark, a placid waterway that penetrates deep into the Fens. You do not actually see much of the landscape from the river. High flood banks hide the view. Only when we stopped to climb to the top of the bank could we tell what the world looked like on the other side. The view then is breathtaking: hundreds of acres of rich, soot black soil patchworked with early crops, glowing in the afternoon sun. Such scenes stayed in our minds even after the water gently rocked us to sleep.

The following day we made our way upstream on the Great Ouse to join the treelined River Cam, which took us to the city of Cambridge. The university's origins lie in the 13th century, and some of its colleges are more than 500 years old. Scattered throughout the Cambridge region are reminders of more recent history: The now disused airfields from which Allied bombers flew raids into enemy-occupied territory during World War II. Where the old runways still remain, a sad ghostliness pervades the air. On cold, foggy mornings you can almost see the gray shadows of the planes departing. *(Continued on page 189)*

Cambridge:
Britain's Ancient Colleges
on the Cam

Michael S. Yamashita (both)

There is something especially beautiful about Cambridge. The energy of youth, the elegance of civilization, and the confidence of erudition seem to echo in its courtyards, glow from its spires, and whisper through the trees beside the River Cam. Everyone who was ever a college student recognizes this Cambridge of the mind. Only a few are lucky enough to be educated there.

Approximately 8,000 students apply for admission to the University of Cambridge each year. If they receive high grades on advanced-level secondary-school examinations, they may apply to one of the university's 24 undergraduate colleges. They can improve their chances for admission by taking the Cambridge Colleges Entrance Examination, which identifies the very best among the best. The exam is optional, but encouraged. In the end, only about 3,000 are admitted.

Students are also interviewed by the colleges of their choice. Applicants choose a college, where they will live and study, for any number of reasons—academic, social, or political. Once accepted, the student remains forever loyal. "To the initiated," said one Cambridge-educated American, "it is my college that I mention first; to the stranger, if asked, I announce myself as a Cambridge man."

Undergraduates attend university-sponsored lectures as they please, but do much of

The experienced make punting past the Backs on the River Cam look easy. Balanced on squared-off sterns, they propel their crafts with long wood poles. For the novice, however, an afternoon of punting may involve a dunking—when the pole sticks in the mud and vaults the navigator into the river.

Henry VI founded King's College in 1441; in the 1800s his statue was placed in the courtyard, and the gatehouse, with its cupola and pinnacles, was constructed.

their work within the college, supervised by tutors. In most subjects they write weekly essays, meeting individually with tutors for discussion.

Tradition permeates Cambridge life; some customs are centuries old. At Magdalene (pronounced MAUD-lin) College, students must wear gowns at chapel and in one dining hall where dinner is still served by candlelight.

Such formalities may create an impression of inflexibility. After all, English literature was not accorded equal status with Greek and Latin in the university's curriculum until 300 years after Shakespeare lived. It took until 1969 for a social science department to be established, and until 1972 for any of the all-male colleges to admit women.

But what might appear to be an unwillingness to move forward really is not. Cambridge scientists were the first to split the atom, and have won numerous Nobel prizes for science.

Nor is the system at Cambridge as conservative as it might at first seem. There has always been room for nonconformists. When William Wordsworth came up to St. John's College in 1787 (traditionally, students don't arrive at Cambridge, they come up), he refused to take certain

examinations or show proper respect for his tutors. His unseemly behavior was overlooked, and in 1791 he took his B.A.

The rules at Cambridge, then, are meant to be broken sometimes—and often have been, in a most high-spirited manner. Midnight curfews were once rigidly enforced; at that hour college gates slammed shut and the only way home was past a humorless guard. To avoid him, and subsequent punishment, latenight revelers engaged in a dubious sport.

"Night-climbing," wrote Sylvia Plath while she studied at Cambridge in 1956, is "a secret and hazardous occupation. At every strategic

Coats of many colors at Cambridge: Clad in the scarlet robe of a doctor, renowned Argentinian writer Jorge Luis Borges is escorted to the Senate House to receive an honorary degree. Cream-colored trousers—with grass-stained knees—are the traditional garb of cricket players. To pedal beside the Cam— and perchance to encounter some cattle grazing on Sheep's Green—casual attire is recommended. To collect donations for the local fire department, anything goes.

184

climbing point the belated undergraduate finds ingenious revolving spikes, metallic teeth, and thorny tangles of wire. The only alternative to success, it would seem, is the rather unpleasant fate of being impaled until dawn on spears of rusty iron."

The best of the nocturnal climbers were no doubt members of Cambridge's Alpine Club, whose motto was: "Though there's doorway behind thee and window before, go straight at the wall."

The club and the curfew are now defunct, but students still honor tradition by scaling college walls to reach their rooms in the dead of night.

For those who prefer less strenuous activity, strolling around Cambridge provides equal pleasures. The colleges with their chapels present a delightful mix of every kind of English style—from Norman to Tudor, Georgian to Victorian, to jarringly modern. All of this is set in a necklace of meadowland, fen, and river where cows graze, punts drift, and rowing eights dash.

During term time the city is pumped full of life. Organ music thunders from an open chapel door as an undergraduate practices a fugue; choir members march in procession to King's College Chapel for evensong in their white Eton collars, black gowns, and top hats. The streets seethe with two-wheeled life—a brigade of bikes is always at your back.

For moments of relaxation, the River Cam offers more leisurely transport. It is a placid river, neither wide nor deep, and in the winter it may freeze solid (in 1947 and 1962-63, piano recitals were held on it). But in warmer months you can rent a punt or canoe and make your way along the Backs—where the river meanders past the backs of several colleges in a curving course through green lawns and gardens, and under graceful footbridges.

Here more than anywhere you are likely to discover what sets Cambridge apart—that marvelous alchemy between the works of man and nature that can evoke a pang of nostalgia in any English soul.

PETER CROOKSTON

May Week, which comes after exams in mid-June, is a time for merrymaking at Cambridge. Several colleges stage elaborate May Balls; students set off in formal evening attire (opposite) and dance and celebrate until the wee hours. Then it's off in a punt (left) for the traditional trip to Grantchester—two miles up the Cam—for breakfast.

Essence of Essex—and of rural England—the village of Thaxted thrived in the 14th and 15th centuries, made prosperous by wool merchants and the cutlery trade that centered here. The grandeur of its 14th-century parish church testifies to the wealth of the town's tradesmen. Nearby, a windmill built in 1804 is a relative newcomer by regional standards. Legions of windmills served to drain the Fens until they were replaced by more reliable steam engines and today's powerful electric pumps.

If, however, you prefer the real thing, you can visit the Duxford Airfield, a branch of the Imperial War Museum near Cambridge, where aircraft of all ages are on show.

From Cambridge we took our boat to Littleport, famous for the hunger riots of 1816, when farm workers' wages fell to nine shillings a week and families starved because they could not afford bread. Soon we entered the Little Ouse and journeyed into a part of the Fens renowned for its storytelling, especially at the Ship Inn, where Mark Twain once recuperated after a serious illness.

As we explored the Little Ouse and the River Wissey we found many friendly, well-stocked riverside pubs, where we could eat anything from a simple bar snack to a five-course evening meal—a far cry from 1816. The Plough Inn, at Fen Ditton on the River Cam, served one of my favorites—the "Big Daddy," a large roll of garlic bread filled with bacon, kidneys, and mushrooms. After a cold day afloat we found a quiet, comfortable hotel in Clayhythe, where we warmed ourselves by the log fire.

The next day we moored upstream from the Ship Inn. After supper we went for a walk along the edge of the fields. We could not get over the silence. It forced us to listen, and to look up at the stars. We were the only people alive on earth. We stood there, mesmerized, until the distant croak of a pheasant broke the spell, and a wild duck's invisible flight whirred across the darkened field.

In the morning the sound of tractors woke me. I dressed and once again climbed the flood bank, to discover a perfect example of modern crop rotation. To the right were 30 acres of winter-sown barley, emerald green. To the left were 25 acres, ebony black, in which men were planting potatoes. I commented to one of the men on the marvelous picture the land created. "I just can't get over the blackness of it."

"Black? That's not black, that's brown," he said. "If you want to see black fens you should go over to Feltwell. Now that *is* black."

Much of this land is now below sea level. The peat soil has been shrinking ever since the Fens were drained. At

Holme Fen an iron post driven like a nail into the ground in 1851 has already recorded more than 14 feet of subsidence since nearby Whittlesey Mere was drained that year. The shrinkage is caused by natural decomposition as well as by the draining of the water. And by the wind. Fen soil is dry and light in spring, and when strong winds blow, great dust storms may sweep across the fields. These are called Fen blows, and they are feared by every farmer who has just planted his sugar-beet seed, for a Fen blow takes with it not only the soil but the seeds and fertilizer as well. I have driven through such a storm at midday, barely able to see even with my headlights full on. Roadside ditches that were three feet deep in the morning would be level with the road by the end of the day.

High-arching bridges in the ancient inland port of Godmanchester, Cambridgeshire, show respect for the flood record of the River Great Ouse. Projects like the New Bedford channel help control the river's flow and ease the devastation of tidal surges like the one that inundated 6,000 acres in 1953.

Sadly, our journey by boat was over too soon, and we returned home to Peterborough. Nathaniel Hawthorne visited this city in the 19th century and admired the cathedral so much that he stayed for a couple of days. In his *English Notebooks of 1857* Hawthorne recalled how, passing through the Norman gateway into the Minster Precincts, he gazed in wonder at one of the finest examples of ecclesiastical architecture in Europe—the cathedral's Early English triple-arched west front.

Outside the cloistered atmosphere of the cathedral is a thriving, expanding city. Where the shops of the old city once stood, a huge new shopping center, Queensgate, now attracts bargain hunters from all over Britain and the Continent. Queensgate illustrates the kinds of changes that are transforming the whole of East Anglia. In 50 years the area may be totally different from the East Anglia I have described, just as today it is very different from the way it was 50 years ago.

Finally, there is a place of pilgrimage I must mention, where Nicholas Ferrar once lived. This son of wealthy parents, educated at Cambridge University, member of Parliament, turned away from his promising career in 1625 and adopted the life of a religious recluse. He moved to the remote, almost forgotten village of Little Gidding, where he and his family established a Christian retreat. It has been an oasis of peace for troubled travelers ever since. Charles I sought refuge here during the political upheavals of the 17th century, and T. S. Eliot commemorated it in his poem "Little Gidding." In spite of modern change, what Eliot said about Ferrar's tiny church, hidden away in this corner of Cambridgeshire, can, I think, still be said of much of East Anglia:

> *If you came this way,*
> *Taking any route, starting from anywhere,*
> *At any time or at any season,*
> *It would always be the same: you would have to put off*
> *Sense and notion. . . .*
> *Here, the intersection of the timeless moment*
> *Is England and nowhere. Never and always.*

By Bryn Frank
Photographs by Annie Griffiths

The Midlands

I am still giddy, dizzied with the hammering of presses, the clatter of engines, and the whirling of wheels; my head aches with the multiplicity of infernal noises, and my eyes with the light of infernal fires,—I may add, my heart also, at the sight of so many human beings employed in infernal occupations. . . .

ROBERT SOUTHEY, 1807

Shropshire foundry worker removes hardened dross from a container called a bogie.

ere of a Sunday morning
love and I would lie,
ee the coloured counties,
d hear the larks so high
out us in the sky.

OUSMAN, 1896

Fields of yellow rape flowers brighten meadows near Hereford.

The first impression I received of it was a town whose inhabitants spend a great portion of their lives leaning over old oak galleries, smoking and chatting and watching life go by below them in the streets. . . . The main streets of Chester give you the impression that a huge galleon has come to anchor there with easy, leisurely passengers leaning on the deck rails.

H. V. MORTON, *In Search of England*, 1927

Behind magpie facades on Chester's Eastgate Street run the Rows, balconied shopping arcades.

An April shower has given the landscape a spring clean. Shafts of sun slice through bruised clouds; wheeling gulls pursue a red tractor over a verdant field. Even at a hundred miles an hour these images are etched sharply within the frame of the train window. Bound for London I gaze out at the Nottinghamshire countryside.

As I follow the meanderings of the muddy River Trent, a companion leafs through a ragged copy of the Wolverhampton *Express & Star* that someone has left behind. "Why do they call Wolverhampton the heart of the Black Country?" he asks.

I turn from watching a solitary angler silhouetted against the sky. "It's because of the pall of black smoke from factory chimneys around Smethwick, Dudley, Wolverhampton, West Bromwich—that sort of place."

"But it says here," he persists, struggling to liberate a British Rail fruit pie from its cardboard wrapping, "that the Black Country is disappearing by the hour; that only old people really remember it for what it was."

I stand corrected. Our train, smooth as silk at top speed, whizzes past a medieval church with a big Victorian house close by—the vicarage, probably. In this part of Nottinghamshire the landscape is predominantly green, and farm buildings mainly red brick—a nice contrast. Dusk gathers as we speed through the darkening countryside.

My companion speaks again. "There's also something very interesting here about fox hunting."

"Oh yes," I reply. "It's a permanent fixture in the Midlands. You don't have to like it, but you can't ignore it. Actually it's quite romantic." I warm to it. "You know the sort of thing—winter sun rising over barren fields, powerful horses and rolling farmland, stirrup cups"—the brandy cocktails traditionally drunk before the hunt.

I turn back to my window to savor the parting day. Beneath high-voltage power lines, rust-colored cattle graze. There is a red brick pub and a beer garden with white tables and chairs. For a while we travel beside a canal with rows of green and yellow narrowboats moored along its banks. It is an intriguing landscape—the bit-in-between scorned by country folk and city dwellers alike: a little too urban, a little too cluttered, to qualify as true countryside. It starts to appeal immensely.

"That's not what it's got here," he says. "According to this, quite a few Leicestershire fox hunts are now having to be canceled because of saboteurs who sound hunting horns and put aniseed down to confuse the hounds." He grins. "It rather looks as if you're a bit out of touch."

I decide he is right. Even as we have been talking, as I've watched Nottinghamshire glide by, I have decided to take a more leisurely trip northward, to renew my acquaintance with the Midlands. Here at England's core, in the areas around Birmingham, Coventry, and Stoke-on-Trent, the Industrial Revolution of the late 18th and early 19th centuries took a firm grip and a great toll. Here the pursuit of coal scarred limestone hills, turned sparkling rivers into cesspits, consigned children to subterranean depths to "devil"—fetch and carry—for coal miners. And here the potteries and the iron foundries sprouted over the coal mines that provided them with fuel for growth.

But in the counties that surround this industrial core is a different Midlands—the England of D. H. Lawrence at his most romantic, in *Sons and Lovers* and *Women in Love*; of the young Samuel Johnson, who called his native Lichfield a "city of philosophers"; of A. E. Housman, whose verses tell of melancholy village lads in love. The England of gold-colored stone churches and mansions, of red brick that glows with an inner fire in the evening sun.

I inform my companion of my travel plans. He is not impressed. "The Midlands? Rather you than me," he replies.

His words ring in my ears as I drive into Towcester, just inside the Northamptonshire border, a couple of days later. Assaulted by the clamor of six-wheeler trucks roaring past, I turn with relief off the main road and strike out across the Northamptonshire countryside.

Say "Northamptonshire" to most outsiders and they conjure up pictures of shoes and shoe factories. King John

Crucible of the Industrial Revolution, the Midlands earned a gritty reputation when smoke belched from 18th-century coal-fueled factories in Birmingham and the sooty Black Country. Now electricity powers West Midlands plants that produce everything from chocolate to automobiles. At the heart of the British motorway system, Birmingham's Gravelly Hill interchange—a maze of tangled concrete nicknamed Spaghetti Junction—provides a speedy escape to the countryside. The surrounding eight counties offer a different Midlands—of pleasant rural drives and myriad small-town delights.

bought a pair of Northampton boots for ninepence in the 13th century, and since the Civil War in the 17th century, the British Army has been shod mainly by Northamptonshire. During World War II the county produced more than 150 varieties of boots and shoes for the men and women of the armed forces. There is a museum in Northampton, the county town, which boasts a remarkable collection of footwear, including ballet slippers worn by Nijinsky and Margot Fonteyn, and a set of boots made for an elephant that scaled the Alps in 1959 (part of a British Alpine Expedition reenactment of Hannibal's original crossing). Only since the 1970s has the industry declined, due partly to an influx of imported goods.

But there is more to Northamptonshire than shoes. Tiny villages rub shoulders with rambling estates. Yellow flowers of rape blanket pale green farmland. I cannot believe that I am only 50 miles from London, or that this scenery belongs to the much maligned Midlands.

Every town here has its own claim to fame. Take the village of Sibbertoft. The River Welland rises from a spring on the grounds of the vicarage, but legend says that its true source is in the cellar of the house, which would not stay dry until drainage pipes were installed.

Ecton is the home of the Franklins—blacksmiths for generations when, in the 1680s, the family emigrated to America, where Benjamin was born in 1706.

Oundle is the quintessential Northamptonshire town—something straight out of Dickens. Cottages and shops along New Street stand perilously close to the road; the juggernauts that rumble down the narrow street pose a constant threat to their quaint facades. An open gate reveals a walled garden; a hidden alleyway promises a shortcut to a sun-drenched vegetable patch. It is almost 6 p.m. when I arrive here, and as shops close and traffic dwindles, the late afternoon sun bathes the town's buildings with warmth, a rhapsody in silver-gray and golden stone.

In the bar at the Talbot Hotel I eavesdrop on a conversation between hunt followers and the wife of a local Master of Foxhounds. They are discussing how the fox's guile

compensates for its strong scent—how many a fox, knowing its territory, will put a river or stream between itself and the hounds, killing the scent that would normally keep the dogs in hot pursuit all day long.

I listen for reports to confirm my train companion's words—reports of hunts canceled and hunt saboteurs horsewhipped for their mischief. I hear nothing of the sort. Although there is a broad-based antihunt movement in Britain, the sport appears to be alive and well in the Midlands. Everyone follows the hunt; it is as common a topic of conversation as the weather.

Corby is quintessential too, but in a different way. Here is Northamptonshire's industrial face. The Romans mined the local iron ore almost 2,000 years ago—from its oxides the Northamptonshire stone gets its characteristic gold hue. The early 1930s saw the boom of Corby's steel industry, but now the steelworks are gone, replaced by unemployment and bitterness. There is still pride, though, among the mainly expatriate Scottish population, drawn here some 50 years ago by a combination of high wages and a rural setting. They will remind you at the drop of a tam-o'-shanter that Corby is regaining its industrial vitality. More than 200 new factories have been built since 1980.

After Corby, Leicestershire's undulating countryside offers a change of scenery. As I drive from village to village I see church spires everywhere.

The church at Twycross contains some of the finest stained-glass windows in the world. Originally the windows, with their uncommonly beautiful blue backgrounds, were among those that graced the walls of several churches in France, including Sainte-Chapelle, the Gothic shrine that St. Louis built in Paris to house the crown of thorns. During the French Revolution many of these windows were dismantled for safety; some were sent to England, and a few found their way to Twycross as a gift from King William IV. In 1945, when the French decided they wanted the Twycross windows back, they offered half a million pounds to redeem them. But the townspeople resisted, and the magnificent stained glass—some of the oldest in

A grocery in Bakewell, Derbyshire (opposite), offers more than it advertises—even a selection of unskinned rabbits (by law, skinned animals must be wrapped in plastic or displayed indoors). Strict rules govern the dairy industry too; dairymen once kept cows in their yards and dispatched milkmaids to customers. Now national dairy firms have cornered the market on deliveries, depositing 30 million pints of milk daily on doorsteps like the one in Derbyshire's Buxton (left). Sheep, raised for wool and meat, are also big business; two men enjoy the bidding at an auction in Bakewell (above).

201

England—remained in their modest little church.

The windows in Melton Mowbray shed light on a different subject—this busy, tightly knit town seems particularly well endowed with butcher shops. I am lured to one by a window display of black puddings and succulent sausages. The town is also the home of pork-pies and Stilton cheese. From David Young, a pork-pie manufacturer, I learn that the famous cheese is partly responsible for the delectable flavor of the equally renowned pies. For each 15-pound cheese (the final product is about 8 inches wide and 9 inches high) 17 gallons of milk must be curdled. Once the curds are scooped out for the cheese, the remaining whey is fed to the pigs. Their diet, says David, is what makes the flavor of the pigs' meat so distinctive.

We pass a queue of people waiting patiently for the day's pork-pies. "Give the world a taste of something good, especially if it is what they remember from childhood," David says, "and they will beat a path to your door."

You can buy less celebrated, but no less tasty, pies in the open-air market at Leicester, a city with a cosmopolitan, sometimes even exotic, atmosphere. In the 700-year-old market, teenage Indian boys peddle umbrellas, rugs, gilt saris. Most young Indian women choose modern western fashions for work in the city-center offices—you can see them strolling along sidewalks in jeans and boots. They go home, though, to traditional religious and cultural values. Many still wed husbands chosen by their parents, although modern custom allows either the bride or the groom to refuse to marry if the choice is unacceptable.

Patrick Ward

Sporting life in Leicestershire runs the gamut from riotous "bottle kicking" to formal fox hunting. On Easter Monday the hardy folk of Hallaton and Medbourne kick small kegs of beer—and each other—toward boundaries a mile apart, then drink together to the victors. All pomp and propriety, the scarlet-coated Huntsman leads hounds to the start of the Quorn Hunt; spectators will follow the field in cars and on foot. A knight at Belvoir Castle cavorts by a quintain; his task will be to lance a ring without hitting the shield, or a ball and chain on the quintain's opposite arm will pivot around and clout him.

OVERLEAF: *Workers resurface the 250-foot-wide reflector dish of the Jodrell Bank radio telescope in Cheshire. Radio signals from space bounce from dish to collector (where the photographer perched). The signals are amplified, then translated into images by a digital computer.*

203

In Leicester, a city of almost 300,000, one of every five persons is Indian. At a Leicester shop (opposite), women inspect gold-embroidered saris. Indian women usually wear saris draped traditionally; English-women often have the six-yard lengths of cotton and silk tailored into Western fashions.

Traditional social and religious customs prevail among first generation Indian immigrants, who flocked to Britain's industrial cities in search of jobs after World War II. The second generation, influenced by Western educations and life-styles, may rebel against old ways, but many rituals remain sacred. A Hindu couple (right) enters happily into a prear-ranged marriage; they exchange flower garlands that symbolize mutual acceptance.

Nottinghamshire tradition blends history, literature, and legend. D. H. Lawrence was born here in Eastwood, a coal-blackened mining town dropped into a quiet, green landscape. This wonderfully incongruous juxtaposition of scenery is typical of the area. Not 200 feet from Lawrence's birthplace, now a museum, is a view that embraces as bu-colic a setting as ever there was—patches of pastureland defined by hedgerows, dotted with cottages and cattle. And in the distance loom slag heaps, the tops of mine pits and coal shafts. Such striking contrasts lent *Sons and Lovers*, one of Lawrence's early novels, its setting.

Nottingham, rising phoenix-like out of the blight left by the Industrial Revolution, affords similar contrasts. Yates's Wine Lodge, at the heart of the city, is garish and ornate, although I find the interior intriguing—something like a cross between a Victorian music hall and a railway station. Around the corner, the classically elegant Theatre Royal stands like a palace, bathed at night in floodlight.

And, of course, there is Nottingham Castle, built as a fortress in 1068 by William the Conqueror, destroyed once during the Civil War, and again by an angry mob in 1831, and finally transformed into a museum and art gallery in the late 19th century. Carved partly from the rock on which the castle stands, Ye Olde Trip to Jerusalem inn claims to date back to the Crusades.

Other claims have the legendary Robin Hood scaling the very same rock to reach Nottingham Castle. Visitors to the castle seem undaunted by the absence of actual evi-dence of Robin's existence; there is, after all, a reassuring statue of him just outside the walls. And from time to time, as if to prove that the legend lives on, posters about town announce dances for "Robins and Marians."

True believers can look further for clues in Sherwood Forest, which stretches north from Nottingham. There was more to it in the 12th century, when the forest extend-ed for 20 miles to cover a fifth of the county, but enough still remains to satisfy willing imaginations: Robin and Marian were wed at Edwinstowe in the church of St. Mary; an ancient oak tree nearby, (Continued on page 212)

Annie Griffiths (both)

Backcountry Idylls on Canals from Another Era

Meandering for almost 80 miles through the countryside, past field and hedgerow and picturesque village, the Oxford Canal provides vistas that make it one of England's most popular boating canals.

Canals such as this served as the highways of the Industrial Revolution—avenues of commerce that carried farm products and factory goods to market cheaply and reliably. At the peak of trade in the 1840s, a network of some 4,000 miles of canals and navigable rivers linked the burgeoning cities of England's industrial center with the four great estuaries formed by the Mersey, Severn, Trent, and Thames. All told, some 35 million tons of cargo were floated along these waterways each year.

Then came the railways, and with them the gradual decline of the canals. By the end of World War II commercial traffic on most of the canals had decreased dramatically, choked off by competition and by shallow channels and narrow locks inadequate for modern requirements. Many canals were abandoned or kept open only for drainage.

But boaters and conservationists, recognizing the canal system's potential for recreation and renewed commerce, banded together after the war to form the Inland Waterways Association. Volunteer work parties began to undo the ravages of neglect, repairing lock gates and dredging weed-choked channels. About 2,500 miles of canals are now navigable, and each year offer pleasure and relaxation to millions of boaters and fishermen.

Hundreds of recreational outfitters stand ready to rent

A flotilla on the Oxford Canal (opposite) lies moored below the old lockkeeper's house close to the village of Napton on the Hill. A narrowboat (left) squeezes its seven feet of beam through the Foxton Locks on the Grand Union Canal.

Annie Griffiths (both)

anything from punts and skiffs for an afternoon outing to fully equipped cabin cruisers for an extended vacation.

One of the most popular rental cruisers is the narrowboat, a long, thin craft modeled after the colorfully painted wooden vessels that once hauled raw materials such as coal, sand, clay, and wood pulp, and finished products such as pottery and paper. Some of the old narrowboats still function commercially.

Narrowboats converted to pleasure cruising are far outnumbered by modern, diesel-powered counterparts; these sturdy, steel-hulled craft chug along at 4 mph (the maximum allowable speed on most of the canals). Such boats are frequently seen moored near a wayside pub or inn, cruising through a picture-book village bowered with trees, or rising inside a lock while the crew manipulates the gates.

Although the Romans built Britain's earliest canals—one of them, the Fossdyke, connects the Rivers Trent and Witham at Lincoln—canal construction didn't come into its own until the 18th century, with the opening of the Bridgewater Canal. The ten-mile waterway, completed in 1761, was built to haul coal from the third Duke of Bridgewater's mines at Worsley to the textile mills around Manchester. It included an aqueduct to carry barges across the River Irwell and was hailed at the time as "the greatest artificial curiosity in the world," comparable to "the noblest work of the Romans." The instant success of the Bridgewater Canal touched off a spate of canal building that flourished undiminished until almost the middle of the 19th century.

James Brindley, who supervised the construction of the Bridgewater Canal, achieved even greater success with the 93-mile Grand Trunk (or Trent and Mersey) Canal linking England's east and west coasts via a series of 76 locks and 5 tunnels.

Today the work of Brindley and other canal builders lives on in the restoration of their works to former glory.

EDWARD LANOUETTE

Bridging the centuries, an aqueduct carries leisurely traffic over a modern highway on a 150-year-old section of the Shropshire Union Canal near Nantwich (left, upper). A canal boat (lower) re-creates the 19th century; even the water can bears the painted rose decorations favored by old-time boatmen and their families.

Selected Canals
of Britain and Ireland

—— Canals
—— Other navigable
    waterways

Once bustling with commercial traffic, 3,000 miles of canals and navigable waterways now serve a growing armada of pleasure craft. Most canals thread through England's midsection, but other areas have them too. Along Devon's 11-mile Grand Western Canal, horse-drawn boats prevail (left). Scotland's Caledonian Canal connects two coasts. While Ireland's Grand Canal remains open, the River Shannon is by far more popular with boaters.

Patrick Ward

211

known as the Major Oak, sheltered Robin's band when they met. Will Scarlet is said to be buried in the churchyard at Blidworth; the evil King John had a hunting lodge in nearby Old Clipstone. In Fountain Dale, Robin Hood first met Friar Tuck; the stream in which Robin received his dunking is there still.

Southwell—a secluded cathedral town as blissfully peaceful as Nottingham is abuzz—stands near the edge of Sherwood Forest. At the celebrated Saracen's Head I enjoy a breakfast of porridge and kippers, and also learn from the waitress how to make jugged hare.

"It's easy," she says. "You hang the hare for a day, use the blood to thicken the gravy, and add a spoonful of vinegar to stop it clotting."

Across from the inn is Southwell Minster, a cathedral built by the Normans between the 12th and 14th centuries and known for the exquisitely realistic carvings of leaves, flowers, and animals that adorn the capitals atop the chapter-house columns. No one knows who the sculptor was, but a face full of humor peers through the stone foliage; it might have been his—it wears the master mason's cap.

Many have sought the tranquillity of Southwell. Thomas Cardinal Wolsey spent troubled times here before he died in 1530, no doubt reflecting on the political problems that plagued him; Charles I was here just before the Civil War began in 1642, and again in 1646 after surrendering to the Scots. The only person who seems to have disliked Southwell's solitude was George Gordon, the flamboyant Lord Byron. "I wander about hating every thing I behold," he wrote. Byron wished that this "region of dullness itself" would be "swallowed up by an earthquake."

Lord Byron was happier with the lively atmosphere at nearby Newstead Abbey, an estate purchased by his family in 1540 after Henry VIII's Dissolution of the Monasteries, which transferred the lands of the monasteries to the crown and, after that, to anyone who could afford them.

Lord Byron spent several years at Newstead in the house adjoining the abbey, surrounded by more than 300 acres of lakes and gardens. The poet flooded the monks' mortuary

to make a bathing pool for himself and his dog, Boatswain, and described his evening activities thus: "We were a company of some seven or eight, with an occasional neighbor or so for visitors, and used to sit up late in our friars' dresses, drinking burgundy, claret, champagne, and what not, out of the skull-cup, and all sorts of glasses, and buffooning all round the house, in our conventual garments." Today the abbey belongs to the city of Nottingham, and many of the Byron family treasures are on display there.

I change my course and head south to the West Midlands, industrial heart of England. I book a hotel room in Coventry with an expansive, rather nondescript view—concrete roadways, low-rise office blocks, housing developments in the distance. But here and there I can pick out the spires and towers of churches that sketchily recall the city's skyline before the morning of November 15, 1940, when a Luftwaffe raid left Coventry in smoldering ruins. From the Mediterranean came H.M.S. *Coventry's* poignant message: "Express sympathy with citizens in their adversity, but assure them that the ship will endeavor to repay." Replied the mayor of Coventry: "We have had a hard knock but are in good hearts. Will play our part on land as your brave lads are playing their parts at sea."

Coventry's main attraction is its cathedral. Most of the original structure was leveled by bombs; its blackened ruins form an entryway to the new cathedral, built from pink-gray sandstone. The new nave, lit by a bank of slanted stained-glass windows, glows gold in the sunlight. Graham Sutherland's "Christ in Glory" hangs behind the altar; ten

"The sand of Coventry binds itself into stone which can be built halfway to the sky," wrote John Ruskin in the 1800s. Indeed, after Coventry's Cathedral Church of St. Michael burned in a 1940 Luftwaffe raid, the spire and outer walls still stood. At one end of the ruined nave (opposite)—

now linked to the new cathedral —a restored effigy of Bishop Yeatman-Biggs cradles a model of the church as it was.

An artist shades stained glass with iron oxide at the John Hardman Studios in Birmingham. A pattern book (below), one of more than ten, contains the studio's original designs.

men took almost three years to weave this, the world's largest tapestry, which weighs nearly a ton. Outside, on the original altar, a cross made from charred timbers stands before the inscription, "Father Forgive."

Before leaving Coventry I dine in a Chinese restaurant where I hear three beefy youths in T-shirts discussing Lady Godiva. Her statue graces Broadgate and her story is still told by residents and visitors alike. Godiva, the wife of Leofric, Earl of Mercia, "went prancing about Coventry with no clothes on," says one of the trio, to dissuade her husband from overtaxing the citizens. In contemporary revivals of the original 11th-century parade, Godiva rides her horse through town in a body stocking—an improvement at least on the Victorians, who dressed her up in petticoats. Three statues commemorate the "Peeping Tom" who dared to look at her. One is on the first floor of the Hotel Leofric, one is above a shop on Hertford Street, and the third is on a clock overlooking the town's main square. When a revolving Lady Godiva passes in front of the clock's face, Peeping Tom jumps up.

Birmingham, just down the road, is Britain's largest city after London. It is an industrial metropolis where small factories and small houses crouch back-to-back, and high-rise flats overlook wasteland due for redevelopment. The city center's modern wedding-cake architecture and painstakingly restored Victoriana have never really come to terms with motorways and multistory car parks.

Generally unromantic and matter-of-fact, Birmingham nevertheless has a few surprises—more miles of canals than

Domino rows of suburban duplexes are home to tens of thousands who crowd into Birmingham on workdays. A few savor the rain-washed churchyard at St. Philip's Cathedral (right). The 1980s saw the gravestones removed and pathways widened to accommodate pedestrians in the only large open space at the heart of Birmingham. Residents still call themselves Brummies, from "Brummagem"—a nickname for the manufacturing city that refers to its 19th-century reputation for cheap or inferior products. Brummies are proud of their industrial heritage, despite the name's connotations.

Venice has, some of the best Victorian pubs in England, and, at nearby leafy Edgbaston, one of the handsomest cricket grounds in the country.

Driving northwest from Birmingham I am in the heart of the Black Country—roughly 10 miles by 12, with Wolverhampton and Walsall in the north, Stourbridge and Halesowen in the south, and Dudley in the center. By 1850 the region, once predominantly green, had become the most densely populated and economically prosperous part of the Midlands; it was also blackened with heaps of waste from primitive iron-smelting methods.

Today, the area is in a state of flux. New, neat, small garment and plastics factories have sprung up; the old smokestack industries have died. Amid broken-down machinery, beneath the girders of decrepit warehouses long open to the sky, lupines, dog daisies, and nettles grow. Some of the forgotten factories, their harsh outlines softened by nature's touch, are almost picturesque.

I stop in Dudley at the Glynne Arms—a pub built over an abandoned mine. The ground has settled over the old mine shaft, giving the place its local nickname, the "Crooked House." I chat with an off-duty train driver who recalls that during World War II, Black Country manufacturers were encouraged to let their chimneys smoke a little more than usual to confuse enemy bombers. But now, he says, people do not identify with the place. "Nobody ever admits they come from the Black Country. They always tell you the Black Country starts just down the road."

Farther north, in Longton, I enter the once dark and mysterious world of the Potteries where, for more than 300 years, craftspeople in the small towns of north Staffordshire have produced the fine sculptured ceramics and tablewares of Wedgwood, Minton, Spode, Copeland, and Royal Doulton, sought by collectors everywhere.

A few decades ago more than 2,000 bottle kilns littered the Potteries like huge masonry flagons. J. B. Priestley described them as "peeping above the house-tops on every side, looking as if giant biblical characters, after a search for oil or wine, had popped them there, among the dwarf

streets." To me, the delicate china that emerged from those giant black kilns seems like the flowers that grow over battlefields.

The real business of making pots still goes on today, but most of the old kilns have been torn down. Electricity and gas have replaced coal fires, and the blanket of smoke that once hovered above the Potteries is gone.

Staffordshire's bottle kilns may have disappeared, but its coal mines have not. I visit the Chatterley Whitfield Mining Museum, where you can explore a mine no longer in operation. My guide, a long-retired coal miner, takes me down to the coal face, where the tiny beams from our safety helmets only emphasize the total blackness around us. I begin to understand the miners' traditional solidarity. This is a different and alien world.

My guide tells vivid stories. "My grandfather worked down the pit from the age of 12 to 50, when he died of what today they would call silicosis. The pit ponies, they were looked after better than the boys. We sometimes had to use explosives to shift the coal, and what we used we had to pay for—it came off our wages."

Beyond Staffordshire and the Potteries lie Derbyshire and the 540-square-mile Peak District National Park, the most beguiling and least populated section of the Midlands. If here you spot a diversion sign marked "scenic route," follow it. The landscape is unpredictable. You will drive on a switchback along a steep cliff where stunted trees jut up like the last surviving wisps on a balding head, then suddenly emerge before (Continued on page 224)

Ronald Reagan character jugs wait with an assortment of other Royal Doulton figures for a trip to the kiln at the factory in Stoke-on-Trent. The finished figures derive their beauty from a tradition of painstaking handwork, exhibited by several Midlands industries. Steady hands fill etched traceries on a Minton dinner plate with 22-karat gold, and paint the wisp-thin stripes on a Rolls-Royce hubcap. The creation of one Rolls-Royce requires so much hand labor that the main factory in Cheshire has produced fewer cars in 80 years than General Motors plants do in one week.

217

Stately Homes: Palaces for Living

The great house sprawls amid the Derbyshire hills, its rambling wings and galleries partly screened by venerable oaks and lime trees. Below the house glides the River Derwent, once an unruly stream prone to flooding but long since tamed. The house is Chatsworth, a showpiece among the stately homes open to the public in Britain and Ireland.

"Not a palace . . . not a museum, but a house," insists its chatelaine, the current Duchess of Devonshire, "a place for people to live in."

Some place! Its 1.3-acre roof shelters 1.7 million cubic feet of space—enough to hold 365 two-bedroom cottages. Its walls enclose 175 rooms, including 21 kitchens and workshops, 24 baths, 17 staircases, and more than 3,400 feet of corridors. "Children can roller-skate for miles without going out of doors," notes the Duchess in her engaging history of the house, but "it is a terrible place to house train a puppy."

While many of the rooms are of normal size, 51 of them "are very big indeed," she adds. The Great Dining-Room, for example, could swallow 8 houses; the Sculpture Gallery 14.

Keeping such a house in proper order requires a staff of almost a hundred—from a head butler and housekeeper to platoons of gardeners, handymen, and housemaids (7,808 windowpanes to keep sparkling, 2,084 light bulbs to attend to).

Chatsworth's many treasures, accumulated over four centuries, put all but the biggest museums to shame: Rare books and manuscripts; paintings by Rembrandt, Van Dyck, Reynolds, Sargent and

Chatsworth, also known as the Palace of the Peak for its location in the Peak District of Derbyshire, presides over a languorous River Derwent and a stone bridge built by James Paine in 1762.

Fred Maroon

a host of others; sculptures by renowned 19th-century artists; wall and ceiling murals; tapestries and other furnishings by some of the world's most skilled artisans.

Chatsworth as it exists today is a far cry from the ungainly Elizabethan manor begun in 1552 by Sir William Cavendish, treasurer to King Henry VIII, and his formidable wife, Bess of Hardwick. Succeeding generations all but obliterated the original structure (which five times held Mary Queen of Scots as an unwilling houseguest), rebuilding until, as the Duchess writes, Chatsworth "fits its landscape exactly."

Land provided the financial basis for Chatsworth and many other estates—either in rents or agriculture. The Dissolution of the Monasteries under Henry VIII saw the rise of estates such as Woburn Abbey and Beaulieu. Later, the Industrial Revolution and the spread of Britain's colonial empire created new wealth and renewed construction. But since World War II many homes have fallen victim to taxes and inflation.

Thousands of acres have been sold to make ends meet. Family heirlooms have been consigned to the auction block. Many houses have been demolished, others

Fred Maroon (also opposite). Below: Annie Griffiths

Chatsworth's cavernous rooms and well-kept grounds each year draw more than a quarter million paying visitors, making it one of Britain's most heavily visited stately homes.

Scenes from the life of Julius Caesar enliven the walls of the Painted Hall (above), a reception room bigger than 10 small houses. The Library (opposite) holds only a portion of the 50,000 books and manuscripts collected by the Dukes of Devonshire. Outside, gardeners tend the estate's 1,100 acres of lawns, gardens, and parkland, which also include fountains and an artificial waterfall.

221

deeded to the government or to charitable trusts. Hundreds now open their doors to paying visitors—and some have even turned spacious lawns into safari parks and circuses.

But to the Duchess of Devonshire and the hundreds of thousands of sightseers who tour Chatsworth each year, the house still carries an aura of enchantment. Beyond this realm "the unknown world may be ugly and badly arranged, but within the magic boundary all is well."

So it is, too, with the multitude of other manors, mansions, and palaces on public display. Every one is unique —Longleat House with its incomparable gardens; Sir Winston Churchill's birthplace, awesome Blenheim Palace, built to celebrate Britain's military might; Woburn Abbey with its trove of furniture and paintings.

In 1938 playwright Noel Coward wrote:

The Stately homes of
England
How beautiful they stand,
To prove the upper classes
Have still the upper hand.

Time and taxes may have broken the grip of a lot of "upper hands," but many of their houses remain—monuments to a tradition of wealth and power.

EDWARD LANOUETTE

Selected Stately Homes of Britain and Ireland
Hundreds of manors, historic houses, and palaces regularly welcome paying visitors as a way to help defray upkeep costs. Their architectural styles range from the fortified keeps and corbeled towers of Blair Castle and Scone Palace in Scotland to the more classical lines of Westport House in Ireland and the splendor of English Baroque in Blenheim Palace (right). Fanlike hand guides (opposite) helped 19th-century guests to recognize paintings and other landmarks in the rooms at Holkham Hall in Norfolk.

Dan Dry. Right: Courtesy of Viscount Coke D.L.

223

Agriculture thrives in counties surrounding the industrial heart of the Midlands. A Shropshire lass treats a pet goat to a snack; cows graze on watercolor slopes near Eyam in Derbyshire's Peak District National Park. The gentle terrain here belies Eyam's valiant confrontation with death: In 1665-1666, more than 80 percent of the 350 villagers perished from plague that came from London in a box of cloth for the town tailor. The stout-hearted citizens followed the example of their rector, William Mompesson, and quarantined themselves within the village to keep the scourge from spreading.

a panoramic view—rugged moors of heather and peat or a landscape of grass and bleached limestone, where distant grazing sheep look like chunks broken off rock walls.

Bakewell nestles in a dip among the moors, and in rough weather it is a relief to find refuge here from the windswept bracken and the peat bogs. The town is almost indecently pretty. On a cold, windy day The Old Original Bakewell Pudding Shop is warm and cozy, filled with tempting pasties and pies and, of course, Bakewell puddings. A Saturday girl in a starched white apron says the puddings originated when a local cook misunderstood a recipe for strawberry tarts, spreading the egg mixture on top of the jam instead of putting it in the pastry.

Just across the border in Cheshire, I have a preview of the county's famous half-timbered Tudor houses, with their patterns of pitch-darkened timbers and white plaster. It is called "magpie" architecture, after the chattering black-and-white bird, although the crosspieces of the original half-timbered structures were the natural gray-brown colors of the wood. The Victorians, dissatisfied with these hues, painted the beams black. Little Moreton Hall, near Congleton, looks like a flock of magpies. The house was built more than 400 years ago and has long since then been out of touch with perfect symmetry.

More modest versions of Little Moreton Hall, old and new, are everywhere in Cheshire, where, after days closeted with accountants or bank managers, manufacturers from Manchester steer their Rolls-Royces, turning soundlessly up leafy drives toward splendid Tudor homes.

Chester, the county town, is the only city in England with its enclosing ramparts intact. The Romans built the original walls, which were embellished during the Middle Ages with a series of new towers and gates. A two-mile walkway atop the walls offers on one side a bird's-eye view of the town's exuberant black-and-white hodgepodge of half-timbered architecture, and on the other side a prospect of woods and distant hills.

The early bloom of spring in the countryside draws me on to Shropshire and to Bridgnorth, the northern terminus

A coracle and its maker drift on the River Severn beneath the graceful arc of Shropshire's Iron Bridge. Relics from the Celtic past, willow-and-canvas coracles are still used for fishing, then carried home with the day's catch. To eliminate hazardous ferry trips across the deep, unpredictable Severn, engineers erected the world's first iron bridge here—a Midlands monument to the industrial age. Cast at the foundry in Coalbrookdale, the bridge's great ribs—380 tons of iron—were pieced together between 1779 and 1781 with the same joints carpenters use to build wood furniture. The bridge designer did not understand bolts and rivets well enough to use them for so large a metal structure. The central section spans 100 feet, curving above the river, said one British journalist, in "miraculous elegance, for a first essay, as if the world's first flight had been in a Spitfire."

of the Severn Valley Railway's popular steam-engine train run. Small boys from five to seventy, fancying themselves engineers for a day, examine the locomotive's greasy pistons. Conductors wearing charcoal-colored serge suits doff their peaked caps, heavy with gold braid; red carnations brighten their lapels. At each flower-decked station they glance at fob watches; silver whistles glisten and trills pierce the air. The train chugs off self-importantly.

Rail travel along the River Severn offers views unavailable from the highway. The river curves languorously to the east of the track, gleaming like polished pewter in the sunshine. The Welsh border lies to the west; the country along this boundary is called the Welsh Marches. Belying its closeness to the industrial Midlands, it is windswept, lonely terrain with tree-clad hills that look easy enough to climb; in actuality the going is rough. Stout boots and healthy lungs are a necessity.

My train ride ends in Bewdley. I head for Broadway—south and east across the Vale of Evesham. Here, the county of Hereford and Worcester dips into the Cotswolds and grabs the best plum of all. For Broadway, a village of honey-colored old stone buildings, is a Cotswold classic—perhaps the most famous of all the little towns that lure charabancs and Sunday drivers on afternoon jaunts from London, Birmingham, and Coventry. This is the kind of place where you would expect to see not real people, but life-size models wearing smocks and chewing straws.

Just east of Broadway, on the high escarpment that overlooks the Vale of Evesham, I pick out flat Midlands accents among picnickers. On a very clear day the Brummies among them can see the skyline of their native Birmingham. Their pride in the city is manifest. For an outsider, though, Birmingham is an acquired taste; so is the Midlands as a whole. Here is England's ugly duckling—not born great, but grown into its own special beauty. The Midlands hides its light, but just half an hour of any skeptic's time will give the lie to its reputation for slag-heap mediocrity. My companion on the train ("rather you than me," indeed!) might be surprised.

227

By Frank Entwisle
Photographs by Ian Berry,
Magnum

The North Country

T he ground it selfe for the most part rough,
& hard to be manured, seemeth to have hardened
the inhabitants, whom the Scots their neighbours
also made more fierce and hardy . . .

WILLIAM CAMDEN, 1610

In Northumbria, Hadrian's Wall crosses Cuddy's Crag, less than 20 miles from today's Scottish border.

Coketown . . . was a town of machinery and tall chimneys, out of which interminable serpents of smoke trailed themselves for ever and ever, and never got uncoiled.

It had . . . vast piles of building full of windows where there was a rattling and a trembling all day long, and where the piston of the steam-engine worked monotonously up and down, like the head of an elephant in a state of melancholy madness.

CHARLES DICKENS, *Hard Times*, 1854

Ranks of millworkers' chimneys muster before a now dormant smokestack in Bradford, West Yorkshire.

When we were lads and wore long shorts and wiped our noses on our jersey sleeves, we lived in Sunderland, a bleak northeast coast borough of 180,000 souls, which called itself the greatest shipbuilding town on earth. Shipyards lined the steep banks of the narrow River Wear. There were launchings every week or two. And our smoky days were filled with the roar of riveting and our nights with gunfire, and some mornings when we crossed the big steel bridge to go to school one of those new ships lay in midstream with only a mast or crumpled funnel above water, sunk by the *Luftwaffe*.

Six miles north was another industrial river, the Tyne. The nearest Tyneside town was Shields. And between Sunderland and Shields, among the colliery winding towers and black pit villages, there was a swamp to which we went with ha'penny fishing nets on bamboo sticks to dredge for sticklebacks and tadpoles.

It was there we met the boys of Shields, who spoke with so different an accent that we pitched them in the ponds on the reasonable grounds that they must be Scotchies. I never discovered what strange race of urchins they thought *we* were (perhaps some breed of Southerner which—as both sides would have at once agreed—was a pretty contemptible thing to be) but they were equally intent on giving us a ducking too, and sometimes they succeeded.

The point of this joyful reminiscence is to show how two northern English populations, sharing the same industrial culture, the same everyday experiences—separated by but six grubby miles—could have different vowels and even a varying fund of words. A lane can be a "lonnen" (lovely word!) in Northumberland, a "snicket" in Yorkshire, a "vennel" in Durham, and a "loaning" in Cumbria, the sounds mysteriously expressing the texture of each county.

So who *are* Northerners, these English who feel so different from other English . . . suspecting that in the South a softer, more effete, more predatory England has fattened upon northern inventiveness, upon northern sweat in

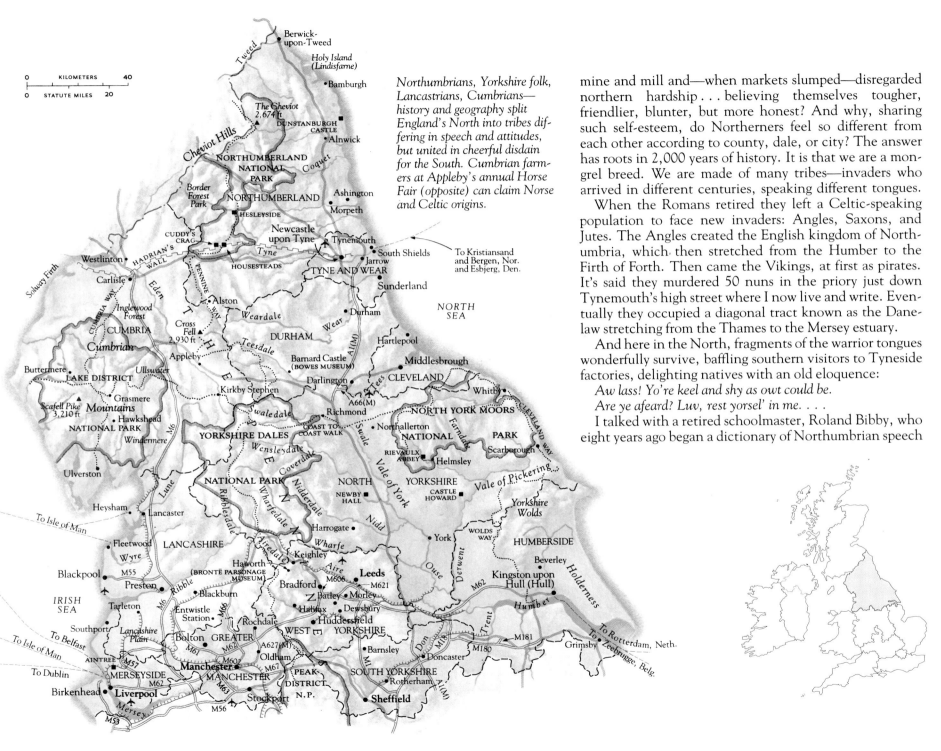

Northumbrians, Yorkshire folk, Lancastrians, Cumbrians—history and geography split England's North into tribes differing in speech and attitudes, but united in cheerful disdain for the South. Cumbrian farmers at Appleby's annual Horse Fair (opposite) can claim Norse and Celtic origins.

mine and mill and—when markets slumped—disregarded northern hardship . . . believing themselves tougher, friendlier, blunter, but more honest? And why, sharing such self-esteem, do Northerners feel so different from each other according to county, dale, or city? The answer has roots in 2,000 years of history. It is that we are a mongrel breed. We are made of many tribes—invaders who arrived in different centuries, speaking different tongues.

When the Romans retired they left a Celtic-speaking population to face new invaders: Angles, Saxons, and Jutes. The Angles created the English kingdom of Northumbria, which then stretched from the Humber to the Firth of Forth. Then came the Vikings, at first as pirates. It's said they murdered 50 nuns in the priory just down Tynemouth's high street where I now live and write. Eventually they occupied a diagonal tract known as the Danelaw stretching from the Thames to the Mersey estuary.

And here in the North, fragments of the warrior tongues wonderfully survive, baffling southern visitors to Tyneside factories, delighting natives with an old eloquence:

Aw lass! Yo're keel and shy as owt could be.

Are ye afeard? Luv, rest yorsel' in me. . . .

I talked with a retired schoolmaster, Roland Bibby, who eight years ago began a dictionary of Northumbrian speech

and uses such delightful words as "clish-ma-claver" (gossip) and "bowdykite" (scoundrel). I mentioned my tadpoling days. He suggested the urchins of Tyne and of Wear fell out of sorts and into ponds because the Viking influence on language stopped short of the Tyne by six miles.

Six miles! An old quarrel precisely but unconsciously recalled a thousand years later.

When people speak of Northumbria today they usually mean the old counties of Northumberland and Durham and the new metropolitan counties of Cleveland and Tyne & Wear. But when they speak of Northumbrians they properly refer only to the inhabitants of Northumberland. Of English counties it is one of the largest, most sparsely populated, and least known to other Englishmen.

But this rumpled counterpane of greens and golds between the Tyne and Tweed is to me the fairest. North from the chimney stacks of Tyneside it emerges, becomes a lush farming countryside with the appearance of well-tended parkland until, growing wilder by little river, lake, and crag, it searches for the border up bare Cheviot valleys.

A gentle line of mounds the Cheviots look. But listen to their names. Black Hag's Rig and Windy Gyle. Bloody-bush Edge and Yearning Law, High Bleakhope, Yeavering Bell . . . and listen also to the curlew's lonely cry, immeasurably old and knowing, the sentry of the Cheviots, signaling your intrusion across the emerald wastes.

The peace that now inhabits Northumberland is a newcomer; across those fells Scots and English once waged war and banditry. It is a land of fortresses—more castles than

The bride bares a garter at a wedding in Manchester, the great Industrial Revolution cotton center whose fortunes rose and declined with the industry's. Completion of the Manchester Ship Canal in 1894 turned the landlocked city into an ocean port and opened it to other commerce.

Quiet fishing boats in Whitby belie the North Yorkshire town's lively past as a major coal and whaling port. A revival began in 1955 when a dock strike shut down nearby Hull.

At Newcastle upon Tyne a pigeon fancier exercises his flock above the river, a shipbuilding artery since the mid-1800s.

234

anywhere in England. Bamburgh like a colossal ship stranded among coastal dunes, still inhabited. Dunstanburgh, a gaunt, romantic clifftop ruin. Berwick-upon-Tweed, itself a fortress town, embraced by ramparts—now Scottish, now English, its nationality changed 13 times.

There are fortified houses known as bastels. Vicars lived in little forts called vicars' peles, with room for cattle below when the raiders came, and space upstairs for all the villagers—the air raid shelters of their time.

But the rustling and raiding was not all one way. Nor were its participants all riffraff. Four great local families—Charltons, Dodds, Robsons, Milburns—harried Scots till the 18th century. There's a mansion called Hesleyside in a wooded valley. A Charlton lives there still—gentleman farmer, gentle man, justice of the peace. On his wall hangs a pardon from Queen Anne bidding an ancestor cease banditry. In his pantry Major Charlton keeps a spur in memory of wild days. When food was low the Charlton women served it on a platter. The signal meant "Take horse, ride north—and bring us back some good Scotch beef."

"Sweet Hesleyside!" It became the title of a melody played on the Northumbrian pipes, a softer, more melodious instrument than the Scottish kind. Its breath comes from bellows squeezed beneath the arm, so a man may sing or argue with a Scotchie, and still play on.

I motored through Border Forest Park, Europe's largest man-made forest—160,000 acres of strategic woodland. Ten thousand years ago the hills were wooded. Settlers cleared them and their sheep devoured the seedlings. The soil soured. Then, in World War I, the U-boat blockade almost strangled Britain. Cut off from Scandinavian timber, coalfields ran out of props to shore the workings. It was resolved that industry must nevermore be so imperiled. Reforestation brought new villages and commerce. And now that pit props are made of steel, Britain exports softwoods from the once bare hills.

I came to Alnwick (pronounced AN-nick, population 7,300), a fine stone town guarded by stone lions on bridge and pillar and the county's grandest stronghold, Alnwick

235

Amid the Cumbrian Mountains of the Lake District, Hawkshead village takes its name from a 10th-century Viking raider named Haukr who established a settlement here: Haukr-Sætr. In Cumbria words from the Old Norse abound—a mountain is a "fell," a waterfall a "force," a stream a "beck," and a valley a "dale"—the legacy of post-Viking Scandinavian farmers who came from Scotland or Ireland and cleared the land.

Angles settled Northumbria, across the Pennines. A delivery boy there (opposite) sports a T-shirt boosting his hometown, Alnwick, whose castle bespeaks the region's history of warfare with the Scots. The castle belongs to the Duke of Northumberland, descendant of Shakespeare's Harry Hotspur— "he that kills . . . some six or seven dozen of Scots at a breakfast, washes his hands, and says to his wife, 'Fie upon this quiet life! I want work.'"

Castle, home of the Duke of Northumberland. There stone sentries still gaze north from battlements to deceive invading Scots. I wandered across the estate and came to a tower on a hill. Below me was a ruined monastery. Beyond, the sea.

In 1982 Britain sent a task force to the far end of the earth to succor the inhabitants of what amounted to an English village. Other claimants had renamed the Falklands' Port Stanley "Puerto Argentina." Her Majesty's Ship *Sheffield* was sunk (alas, also Argentina's *General Belgrano*). The British force's entire complement of troop-carrying helicopters had gone down in a Tyne-built freighter called *Atlantic Conveyor*. A woman then came to this lonely place —daughter of seawise forefathers, mother of one sailor in the South Atlantic. She looked across the hills toward the sea. I met a man who saw her there. He said she was wracked with anxiety. Her name was Elizabeth Windsor. She was Queen of England.

Newcastle upon Tyne, July, two years later: Inert hulk of blue-painted metal—longer than the gardenless terraces of workers' houses, higher than their churches—slanting down toward the water. Not yet alive. Not yet a ship.

Slowly at first that sultry afternoon a crowd began to muster amongst the chains and dunnage of the yard. Buses disgorged more. Traffic halted. All over Tyneside, from town after town, husbands and wives, children in their Sunday best, grandpas who knew their port from starboard, now gathered about the great box of steel, looking up.

I was on a high stack of oil-soaked timbers. A boy stood at my side. We looked down on a confetti of summer shirts and dresses. He and I had stood thus at bleak pierhead many a freezing dawn to watch some grey vessel emerging from the fog. No flags among us Tynesiders. Only a mysterious ancestral awe. A kind of love.

I, but not the boy, had seen many launches, never without a tightening of the throat. The local vicar said a prayer. A short speech. The words Falklands and South Atlantic reached us. A woman wearing a red hat swung a beribboned bottle and said, "I name this ship *Atlantic Conveyor*

". . . May God go with her and all who sail in her."

A new hull, an old name. The steel box moved, gained speed, struck water and made a kind of curtsy. A great wave ran across the river. Eleven hundred tons of drag-chain, arranged in mounds along the ways, squirmed, leapt, sent up an obscuring cloud of purple rust, and disappeared. A brass band played "The Blaydon Races," which is the tribal anthem of Tyneside. ". . . the lasses lost their crinolines and the veils that hide their faces./Aa got two black eyes and a broken nose gannen to Blaydon Races."

The box had gone. The big tugs moved in and swung her. She was not a pretty vessel. But she was now a ship.

The boy said, "The whole landscape has changed, Dad!" Then—"All ships are beautiful, aren't they, Dad?" I knew then he knew what I knew.

To fully comprehend Tynesiders you have to know about their ships, their pride in building them. And town-scapes that change with a burst bottle of champagne. That and their coal.

Coal made the Tynesider. During the 18th and 19th centuries Scots, Cornish, Irish, and Midlanders swelled the towns and villages along the lower reaches of the River Tyne to build ships, dig coal, and load the ships with coal to fuel London and the Empire. The members of this new tribe, for some reason now forgotten, christened themselves Geordies—an affectionate equivalent of George. I recall that when they celebrated the silver jubilee of George V in 1935 they painted huge wall slogans in their shabby streets reading "Good Old Geordie King!"

Fair days in the North Country erupt with maiden dunkings and puppet shows at Alnwick, and the jingling, jouncing rhythms of Morris dancers at Hawkshead. Such festivities trace their origins to pagan antiquity, when spring and summer rites honored fertility gods and warded off evil spirits.

Their native Tyneside accent survives—a lovely sing-song way of talking. And the songs they sing are 19th century, industrial, self-deprecating, with working class heroes no one else can fathom.

She-ee-ees . . . a big lass an' a bonny lass an' she likes hor beer,
An' they caal hor Cushy Butterfield an' I wish she was heor. . . .

At first they lived hugger-mugger in twisting alleyways that plunged by step and landing to Newcastle's sustaining quaysides. Houses piled on top of houses, Victorian upon medieval, thicket of reeking chimney stacks outclimbing forest of domestic flues, producing the most spectacular industrial landscape in the North—perhaps on earth. If there was beauty it was in the play of light in coal smoke, the aurora borealis of the 19th century. If there was warmth it was in hundreds of pubs and gin palaces—the Hydraulic Crane, the Forge & Hammer, the Blastfurnace, the Brass Man, the Mechanics' Arms, the Gun. . . .

Then on the plateau above they did an amazing thing. They built one of the most elegant city centers in Britain. Style, classical. Rhetoric, restrained. Mood, gregarious. The broad curve of Grey Street descends toward the wharves without the pomposity of Haussmann's Paris or—to my northern senses—the dandyism of Georgian Bath.

And in the middle of town the stone-vaulted alleys of the Grainger Market offer the nearest thing in England to the bazaars of Isfahan. A woman called me "tulip" there the other day when I was buying tomatoes from her stall. Northerners call even strangers "luv," but only Geordies dispense such warm extravagance as "tulip."

The county of Tyne & Wear, of which Newcastle is the commercial capital, contains over a million people. It consists, essentially, of many villages overrun by the juggernaut of the Industrial Revolution, with barely a green paddock to denote passage from one into another. Kind writers call it dismal. Such a town is Jarrow.

Jarrow still haunts England's conscience. In the 1930s slump its proud shipbuilding yard was closed. Sooty grass

Dan McCoy, Black Star

241

grew on the slipways. A whole community became workless. Tuberculosis, diphtheria, and scarlet fever scythed through the terraced rows. The men of Jarrow—decent men, not mendicants or revolutionaries—marched, feet blistered, heads up, bellies thin, to their Parliament 300 miles away to ask for work. A nation was moved to sympathy and helpless shame. The Great Jarrow March! . . . appeased, rewarded in the end not by compassion but by war.

I went to Jarrow. It still suffers—unemployment once more 21 percent, empty quays. There I came upon a little valley, rimmed with oil-storage tanks and a thin froth of cherry blossom. Below was a dirty stream and a little church—fragment of the monastery where the Venerable Bede lived when this was fair and open country.

Bede was more than a historian. Some say he was the first Englishman, by which they mean his writings formed the English consciousness. Here in this desolate patch—a great center of European culture in his lifetime—he popularized in 725 the chronology we use today . . . B.C. and A.D. Here, in a sense, our time began.

Miles of municipal housing dwindle south from Tyne & Wear to merge with County Durham. Old railway tracks, new power lines lace land and sky. Houses thin out as the Great North Road cleaves south, land rising westward till it becomes the Pennines. Long horizons. No peaks, few people. A wilderness of heather pierced here and there by lead-mine chimneys long forsaken.

Eastward, the land tilts toward the sea, beaches oozing colliery effluent as if the county bleeds. Land strewn with grim villages—straight rows, fatigued chapels, dismal shops. The race that inhabits this territory is, by and large, the mining race. And by and large they are dear, kindly people with bright firesides and tea for strangers, their trade unions born in Methodism. In this huge coalfield I stood above one mine where 200 men had died entombed in January 1862. Some of those "men" were ten years old.

But in this same coalfield is little Durham City, one of the most glorious sights in Europe. It stands alongside the London-Edinburgh railway. (Continued on page 250)

The billowing landscape of the Yorkshire Dales has borne the tides of history since Ice Age hunters. Now visitors come in droves to walk these gentle hills and to enjoy the pastoral scenes described by author-veterinarian James Herriot. Water-soluble limestone underlies much of the area, imparting lush emerald hues to the vegetation.

Gypsy families from Yorkshire and other parts of Britain and Ireland attend the Appleby Horse Fair. A gypsy trader (above) displays his wares.

243

Through the Snickets, Ginnels, and Alleyways of Ancient York

As you walk along York's medieval walls, your steps echo those of Romans, Anglo-Saxons, Vikings, Normans, and others who manned the city's successive fortifications.

When you reach Micklegate Bar ("bar" is the medieval name for a fortified gate) you share a view once accorded such unfortunates as Richard, Duke of York, beheaded in 1460 in the Wars of the Roses. His head was stuck on a post above the bar so that, as Queen Margaret observes in Shakespeare's *Henry VI*: "York may overlook the town of York."

The city's multilayered story began in A.D. 71, after the Roman conquest of southern England, when legionaries established a fortress here—Eburacum—which later became a provincial capital. Preservation work in 1961 beneath York Minster, the city's cathedral, uncovered remains of command headquarters, including a 22-foot stone column, now re-erected nearby.

The remains of Eoforwic—

York's name when it became the seventh-century capital of Anglo-Saxon Northumbria—are few besides a splendid helmet on display at the Castle Museum. But York was a center of monastic learning; an altar in the Minster's crypt commemorates the Christian baptism in 627 of warrior king Edwin in a church thought to have stood on this site.

The Vikings captured York—which they called Jorvik—in 866. Their two centuries of dominance here yielded an archaeological bonanza at Coppergate.

At the Jorvik Viking Centre, automatic "time cars"

St. Mary's Abbey ruins form a backdrop for the York Mystery Plays, a religious pageant performed at the York Festival held every four years. At left, medieval city walls snake toward York Minster's twin-towered west front. Locals call the stone tracery design in its great window the Heart of Yorkshire.

whisk you back to the world of the Vikings. You glide past lifelike figures of Thorfast the bone carver and Svein the cobbler amid the mix of sights, sounds, and smells of Jorvik in 948. In the crowded thatched timber houses, children swap riddles, and housewives gossip over their chores; on the banks of the Foss, seamen unload a cargo of herring and German wine.

The Norman Conquest severed York's Scandinavian links, but its Viking heritage lives on in street names ending in "gate" from *gata*, the Old Norse word for street.

High and Low Petergate and Stonegate follow the Roman routes. At one corner a statue of Minerva, Goddess of

York is best explored on foot. You can take a conducted tour to get your bearings; there's even a ghost tour. A two-mile circuit of the medieval walls offers a panorama of the city— and a convenient approach to its excellent historical museums.

Those descending at Monk Bar pass half-timbered St. William's College, where a restaurant serves medieval banquets (far right) by arrangement. The overhanging houses of the Shambles (opposite) make the most of a narrow space.

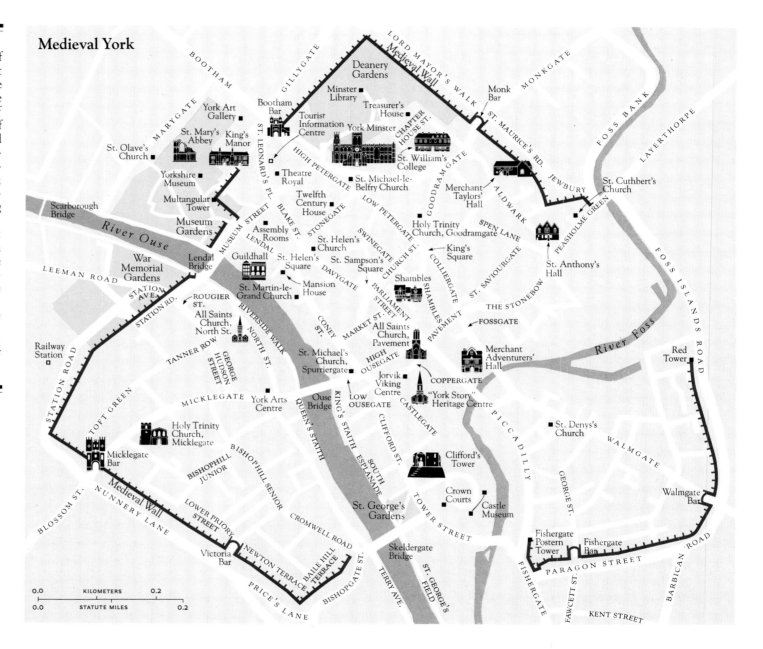

Medieval York

Wisdom, denotes a former bookbinders' alley. On Stonegate a red devil recalls "printers' devils"—boys who carried type—and a plaque states that Guy Fawkes's parents lived "hereabouts."

Around these, other medieval streets meander, joined frequently by old foot passages. The cobbled Shambles—where meat hooks still hang—was the butchers' street. In 1586 a saintly butcher's wife named Margaret Clitherow was executed, "pressed" to death under a door piled with stones, for hiding Jesuit priests—a grim case of religious intolerance.

Even grimmer was the massacre of some 150 Jews in 1190. They fled to a Norman keep on the site of Clifford's Tower. There, besieged by a mob, many committed suicide; the rest were murdered.

Most street names of medieval York have a meaning: Ousegate and Fossgate lead to the rivers that made York an important port. Whip-ma-whop-ma-gate—York's longest name and its shortest street—may derive from "a medieval expression of scorn meaning roughly Call-that-a-street-you-must-be-joking,"

Ian Berry, Magnum (both)

247

declares Mark W. Jones in his *A Walk around the Snickelways of York.* A snickelway, he explains, is a combined snicket, ginnel, and alleyway—all narrow passageways best negotiated on foot.

On Fossgate stands a mellow half-timbered hall that belonged to the rich Merchant Adventurers' trade guild. Colorful banners adorn its great hall. The guilds performed the York Mystery Plays on double-decker pageant wagons that were drawn around town, each guild acting out a different Bible story. The name "mystery" may come from a medieval word for mastery, or craft.

Wherever you wander in York's medieval maze, you can orient yourself by the towers of majestic York Minster. Built between 1220 and 1472, the Minster is the largest Gothic cathedral in England. "Minster" comes from the Latin *monasterium*, a center of Christian teaching. As

Contenders for a June 1984 York Festival cycling trophy streak past the Minster's south front at speeds up to 40 mph. In July, fire damaged this transept but spared most of the rest of the cathedral. Restoration may cost three million pounds.

mother church of the northern province of the Church of
England, it is outranked in
importance only by Canterbury Cathedral.

The Minster's medieval
stained glass glows like rich
mosaic. Master glazier John
Thornton of Coventry created the east window, the size of
a tennis court, in just three
years—for a fee of 56 pounds.
Other windows display glass
painting from every period
since the 13th century. Individual glazed areas of glass are
called "lights." The cathedral
soars in airy spaciousness, lit
by its glorious windows.

As you stand in the nave,
organ chords swell up to the
vault, where a painted carving depicts the Apostles gazing at the soles of Christ's feet
as He disappears into heaven.
At noon the deep voice of
Great Peter tolls the hour—
high above Anglo-Saxon Edwin's altar and the sleeping
ruins of a Roman fortress.

MARY B. DICKINSON

*Festival events include medieval
dancing and exhibits in the
Minster nave, cleared of chairs
for the occasion. Statues of
William II (far right); his
father, the Conqueror; and 13
successors grace the 15th-
century choir screen at rear.*

249

I've seen northbound passengers at their port and Stilton put down their glasses when that spectacle is fleetingly framed in the window of a dining car, then just as suddenly withdrawn: below, the grey slate roofs of a wholesome town, streets, bus station, stone bridge, church tower. Then up behind, mounted on a wooded cliff, castle and cathedral—growing from the pitman's county, rooted in the city, inhabiting the sky and dwarfing all. The travelers return wordless to the reality of Stilton. Indeed what *could* they say but "Gosh!"

For Northumbrians traveling the other way, the first halt south of the Tees brings awareness of arrival in a foreign district—and not just in England's broadest shire (which Yorkshire is), not only in territory where Viking words survive, not merely in a province where men revere the cult of cricket as medievals honored chivalry. Out of Northumbria, where the heart is worn conspicuously upon the sleeve, one has entered cannier climes.

A dour chap leaned against the bar at the Black Swan in Helmsley. Helmsley is a grey-stone, red-roofed market town near the lovely ruins of Rievaulx Abbey in the North York Moors. I asked him the way to Farndale, a steep valley which, for a few spring weeks, bursts into a golden miracle of wild daffodils.

He eyed me beneath the peak of his flat cap and then said, "If tha does owt fur nowt, allus do it fur thissen—If you do anything for nothing, always do it for yourself," a Yorkshire proverb. Nevertheless he gave me meticulous directions and didn't charge. He winked at the barmaid and raised his glass. "Here's to me," he said, "and me wife's husband." The girl refilled my glass at his expense.

Yorkshiremen appear to relish a reputation for parsimony and bluntness. They also call themselves "Yorkshire tykes." My dictionary says a tyke is a "cur" or "low fellow." It is all, I do suppose, some solemn Viking joke.

Yorkshire is now three counties—North, West, and South—and most of Humberside, too. North Yorkshire is England's biggest county. Yorkshiremen can be proud of their great shire. If history had taken a different turn—if

North Sea oil refineries and petrochemical plants, such as this one at Middlesbrough, have helped offset the decline in coal, steel, and shipbuilding, the northeast's traditional industries. Sheffield, the South Yorkshire steel center long famous for cutlery (above), is trying to attract electronics and microchip firms to bolster its economy. A spinner in Darwen, Lancashire, still has work (left) but thousands of other northwest textile jobs have disappeared since 1950. In contrast to the present, the 19th-century mills, factories, and mines of England's North produced the goods that made today's world, among them the first steam turbine and first public railway.

Alfred the Great had not tamed the Danes and united much of England—Yorkshire would have made a splendid little kingdom. It has everything.

The Vale of York is richly fertile. Yorkshire has coal. It once had iron; the cutlers of Sheffield have made knives, swords, and tools for centuries. It has York itself, where Romans walked, where Vikings ruled, where medieval walls still embrace great churches and splendid taverns. England's highest cliffs defend the Yorkshire coast. It has medicinal spas—at Scarborough, England's first seaside resort, and at Harrogate with its great Victorian hotels.

And of course Yorkshire has wool—the first source of England's riches—with hardy Swaledale sheep on which to grow it, fast lime-free streams in which to full it, a score of mill towns in which to turn it into cloth, Leeds to make garments with it, Hull to ship it.

This splendid little kingdom could have had no finer port than Hull (rebuilt since the Blitz of World War II and part of Humberside since 1974). Nearby, the world's longest single-span suspension bridge leaps the Humber into what Northerners think of as the beginning of the South.

From Helmsley I motored northwest to see the first of the world's 70 Richmonds, a humpetty old stone town. There I climbed the castle keep above the hurtling River Swale to survey the corrugation of green dales that sweep down toward the Vale of York. I wandered from Swaledale to Coverdale to Wharfedale. In Wensleydale I bought the famous cheese. And in a tree-studded amphitheater of grand limestone cliffs I found the little spring that starts the River Aire and runs down to Airedale. Then I lost count of dales. Some say there are 565, others 581.

The small wool town of Haworth is just over 50 miles from York. It might as well be a thousand. The mill in the valley bottom is now a biscuit factory. The Yorkshire Penny Bank has become a tourist bureau. There's no denying the film-set drama of the steep, stone-paved main street that toils up between gapless housefronts stained dark by Pennine rain. But the shops where the Brontë sisters used to buy their soap and candles have twee names like the

Stable Door, the Copper Kettle, and Spook Books. I stayed at the Black Bull, where Branwell Brontë boozed away his talent. Day-trippers had come in by the busload, swamping the little bar, playing transistor radios, their numbers eroding what at least some of them had come to find.

Up in the treeless hills one morning before breakfast, looking for Wuthering Heights, I heard my first cuckoo of the year. Swift as the passing of a storm cloud the dun landscape turned from brown to green. Six funereal magpies took off beside me and disappeared. The sun broke through. It touched the chimney of a defunct mill far down below, making it a blade of gold. The fells echoed a host of cuckoos. It was summer.

I returned to Haworth, packed, and took a taxi. Should one regret the passing of a way of life, albeit a hard one?

Well . . . down the Worth Valley of West Yorkshire I came to Keighley (pronounced KEETH-ley). Twenty years ago great choirs filled its splendid Protestant chapels. On my way to meet Ian Dewhirst, author and historian, I passed an ornate building—"Keighley Cycling Club" incised in stone high above the street. It dates from 1896, grand days when cycling across the fells was a mass pursuit of millworkers, disciples of a godly brand of socialism.

I will not cease from Mental Fight,
Nor shall my Sword sleep in my hand,
Till we have built Jerusalem,
In England's green & pleasant Land,

the poet Blake had written. And by gum they sang it—on moor top and in pitch-pine pew! Dear innocents.

The grand facade of the Walker Art Gallery (right) dates from Liverpool's 19th-century heyday as a world port. Irish immigrants arrived in the 1840s; the Roman Catholic Cathedral, with its sculpted door (left), attests to their numbers. Although the decline of its port brought hard times, Liverpool's spirit blooms—along the Mersey River, where gardens and exhibition halls (above, left) replace decaying dockland, and in the music of the city's favorite sons, the Beatles.

PAGES 254-255: A horse and rider take a spill at Liverpool's Grand National Steeplechase.

I talked with Ian in England's first Carnegie Library, built when mills were roaring and the great banks along Keighley's North Street changed golden sovereigns. "A sad town now," he said. "Utterly depressed. Apathetic. Petty crime. Vandalism rife. In the 1930s we had poverty. But we had the chapels. And civic pride. Local government reorganization in 1974 took the heart out of this proud borough. Turned us into a suburb of Bradford."

Bradford—once the wool capital of the world—is itself trying to survive. A few years ago this place of Blake's "dark satanic mills" declared a rebirth. It announced that it would be a tourist center, and the rest of Britain smiled.

But when I turned up at the railroad station, a uniformed chauffeur was waiting with a civic limousine. Bradford wanted to show me what people from America, Africa, and Europe—businessmen, historians, architecture students—come here to see. Mills built like Florentine palaces, only bigger. Warehouses like Romanesque cathedrals. And a Congregational church—grand semicircular portico, giant Corinthian columns—that would have enhanced a street in Rome. Something stupendous happened here in the last century. Nothing like it anywhere.

Bradford may well rise again.

I took a train to Lancashire across the Pennines. Leeds, Batley, Dewsbury, Huddersfield . . . green hills netted in a mesh of dry-stone walls built by Herculeans . . . mills as big as Cunard liners, then Manchester, Entwistle Station, Blackburn—England's land of cotton.

Here, on the west side of the Pennines, grew the Lancastrian tribe. The rain beat in from the Atlantic and filled the valley streams that drove the waterwheels that powered the mills that made the cotton cloth that once garbed half the world. When water was turned to steam for driving looms and spindles, the crofters—descendants of Norseman and Celt—who had eked out a moorland living by handweaving in their cottages, clattered down into the new mill towns that were exploding in the valley.

They were thrifty. Some saved their wages and invested in the mills. Some bought looms at five pounds apiece and

became mill owners. They were inventive. Men tinkered in backyards and made devices—the spinning jenny, the flying shuttle, the water frame, the self-acting mule—multiplying output not just of cotton but of Yorkshire wool.

They were—they are—humorous in a lugubrious, painstaking way. The slow Lancashire dialect with its abbreviated definite article—"Thurs trouble at t'mill"—sounds vastly comical to other Englishmen. Who can say whether it echoes the accents of the Celts and the old Norsemen who landed on its sands so long ago?

They were idealists. The industry was cut off from its raw material during the American Civil War. There was a cotton famine, hardship, and starvation. Lancashire and its newspapers still supported the Yankees and campaigned against southern slavery.

In the 1830s Lancashire cotton made up half the exports of the world's greatest trading nation. By 1910 seventy per cent of the world's exported cotton goods came from Lancashire. All India wore Lancashire cotton. And the fashionable of Europe and America sported her finest fabrics.

But the cotton story is even sadder than the woolen story. Between 1912 and 1964 foreign competition brought 667 million weaving looms to a stop forever. By the late sixties Britain was importing from Asia almost as much cotton cloth as she had once sent to India alone.

The village of Manchester used the world's first steam-powered mill, became a town, then—linked by canal to Liverpool—became an inland port and one of Britain's great cities. "What Manchester does today," they said, "the world will do tomorrow." Manchester made the world's first digital computer. In Manchester in 1913 Ernest Rutherford described the nucleus of the atom.

Lancashire is another victim of the Local Government Act; in 1974 it lost Manchester and its suburbs, which became the county of Greater Manchester, and it lost Liverpool, that rumbustious, cosmopolitan city which swelled when the Irish arrived as refugees from the potato famine of the 1840s. (In 1847 alone, 300,000 landed—more than the city's native population.) (Continued on page 264)

Sun, fun, and whimsy enliven Blackpool, a brash Victorian resort on the Irish Sea. Each year the seven-mile-long beach attracts some eight million vacationers and day-trippers, mostly from the industrial cities of the North. The sunbather opposite relaxes near one of three amusement-laden piers jutting out to sea. A bench (above) provides entertainment to footsore holidaymakers near the beachfront promenade, here decorated with teapot streetlamps. Among Blackpool's attractions are an Eiffel-like tower; a "Golden Mile" of rides, arcades, and other amusements; and the autumn Illuminations, five miles of dazzling colored lights.

The Lake District: Fells and Dales and Walks in the Ever Changing Light

Ian Berry, Magnum (both)

Every year up in Wasdale, under Scafell's looming bulk, they hold a Liars' Contest: One year the runner-up said, "I been up on Scafell when t' mist was so thick I took me stick, an' I stook it in t' mist, and it stood up. An' then I took me jacket off and I hung me jacket on it. It was that thick." And the winner said, "I believe you."

The whole story may be a lie, too, but that's in the spirit of the thing. And it's certainly no lie that mist often shrouds Scafell Pike, the Lake District's highest peak—and most other fells, as mountains here are known.

Yet the region draws throngs of visitors. In summer up to a thousand a day flock through the Lake District National Park's information center at Brockhole. Motorists jam the roads and walkers swarm over the fells. Why do so many venture so willingly—often on foot—into England's chanciest climate?

For one thing, this is England's most dramatic moun-tain scenery. The mountains may not sound high—Scafell Pike rises only 3,210 feet—but they *look* high, jutting steeply from little more than sea level, with cloud-piercing sunbeams playing over peaks and lakes and dales.

Indeed, that play of light and shadow encouraged poet William Wordsworth (1770-1850) to live here, and many visit his various homes, such as Dove Cottage at Grasmere.

Wordsworth was one of the Lake District's first conservationists, winning a campaign to stop the new rail line from going beyond Windermere.

His "host of golden daffo-

Still as a dream, Buttermere's surface mirrors a Lakeland "fell," from the Old Norse for "mountain." Picnickers dine in the shadow of a dry-stone wall west of Windermere (opposite). Trademark of the Cumbrian countryside, most walls were built during the 18th and 19th century land "enclosure."

258

Ian Berry, Magnum

dils" may seem sentimental today, but Wordsworth was a literary rebel. Before his time, poets looked to the classics for inspiration. Wordsworth and his fellow romantics began to examine the countryside instead; they alerted us to the mystical beauty of lakes and forests and rivers:

> *Soft as a cloud is yon blue*
>   *Ridge—the Mere*
> *Seems firm as solid crystal,*
>   *breathless, clear,*
> *And motionless; and, to the*
>   *gazer's eye,*
> *Deeper than ocean, in the*
>   *immensity*
> *Of its vague mountains and*
>   *unreal sky!*

Wordsworth would be glad to know that motorboats today are banned from most of his crystal lakes. Cars, however, are not banned, and you can tour the district that way, driving along the shores or

England's vest-pocket Colorado, the Lake District National Park is only 30 miles wide, yet includes a dozen major lakes, the highest English mountains, and scores of footpaths. The park operates ten information centers; one, at Brockhole, has a small museum. Park residents pursue traditional livelihoods, such as raising these Swaledale-Herdwick crossbred sheep.

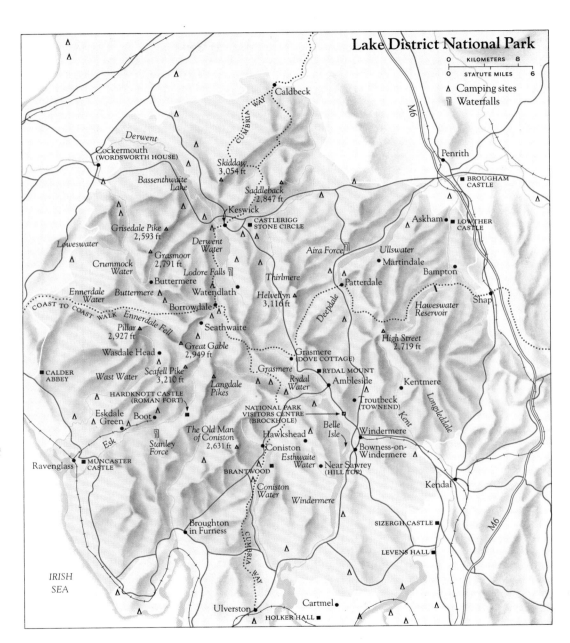

Lake District National Park

up steep, one-lane roads over passes clad in bracken and dripping with waterfalls.

But the best way to see Lakeland is on foot, along with the cheerful English, young and old, who tromp earnestly about the countryside undeterred by the occasional drizzle.

In 1984 the park initiated day-long "Discovery Walks," guided by local experts. They're an excellent way to learn about such things as the centuries-old greenstone slate roofs you see, or about the traditional devices invented to ease the walker's way: Stonewall squeezer stiles, slits too narrow for sheep but wide enough for not-too-portly humans; clapper bridges, slabs of slate laid over streams; and kissing gates, which swing one way within a tight pocket of fence to allow walkers, but not livestock, through singly (and which also allow one person to trap another in mid-

Lakeland scenery draws so many walkers that queues may form to climb some summits. Even when weather is fine below, as here on Buttermere, sudden fogs can close in fell tops and call for map and compass. A telephone recording updates fell-top weather twice daily.

Ian Berry, Magnum

gate to work his or her will).

You can also try a walk on your own, maybe near Martindale at Ullswater. From a small chapel you head up a narrow dale road, lined with trees and dry-stone walls, past slate-roofed buildings sweetly redolent of hay and manure.

There is an ineffable coziness to the English countryside, to its comfortably tidy lanes and footpaths with their stiles and signs and cottages and gates and little bridges.

Maybe it's because this is Beatrix Potter country—she lived over in Near Sawrey. If you speak English, chances are good you grew up with her *Peter Rabbit*—or with Lofting's *Doctor Dolittle* or Grahame's *The Wind in the Willows*, or other stories set in scenery like this. That could be why, no matter how distant your native land, an English country walk creates a sense of déjà vu, as if you have stepped back into a bedtime story. It is a landscape that snuggles you in its lap.

But continue up the valley, and farm lane becomes mountain footpath. The storybook scenes give way to hills of grass and heather topped by raw rock outcrops. This is open, windswept drama, more Scottish than English, where alpine moors unencumbered by tree or wall stretch the eyes. Top the ridge crest, and you can see the sun slanting through clouds into Deepdale below.

Near the base of the ridge you come across another artifact of this wild-yet-tamed landscape: a wrought-iron bench built into the slope. Generations of fell walkers must have rested a while on it; it bears the insignia "1897 VR"—Victoria Regina. Join them, and enjoy the view.

JONATHAN B. TOURTELLOT

Jim Brandenburg

Selected Footpaths of Britain and Ireland
Long-distance footpaths account for only a fraction of Britain's elaborate 120,000-mile network of public walkways. Some follow rights-of-way centuries old. Ramblers can stop in at the many hostels, bed-and-breakfasts, and cozy pubs along the route. In the north a footpath probes rugged Scottish realms on the Island of Skye (left). The Irish Republic plans to add more long-distance paths to its two. Everywhere, walkers must follow the "country code," showing consideration for the farmers whose land they are permitted to cross.

Ah Liverpool!

She spreads along the Mersey's north shore with her seven miles of noble docks and warehouses now almost empty.

By all that's logical her canyons of banks and shipping offices and insurance buildings and colonnaded public buildings, her multitude of statues to 19th-century statesmen, philanthropists, and traders, her gorgeously Gothic pubs, her great art galleries, her concert halls should be but a sad monument to a departed empire.

But despite crippling unemployment, Liverpool still lives and throbs and sings and laughs—laughing mostly at her own adversities. Liverpudlians refer to themselves as Scousers after a kind of poor man's broth (lobscouse) concocted by immigrant seamen from the Baltic.

Her Chinese (and Irish), lascars (and Irish), Caribbeans (and Irish), Africans, Arabs, native English (and Irish) speak with an accent unlike any other in the British Isles, and they use it with a wit and humor which was echoed in the Beatles' music of the 1960s.

Liverpool is by English standards a modern city—which is to say Victorian—her sprawl ungoverned by the medieval focal points of church, castle, ford, or market. It just happened. And it happened all at once.

Liverpudlians are perhaps Britain's newest tribe. And while they survive so will the energy and humor of a very Dickensian and yet very Irish and rebellious city.

Ah Liverpool!

The M6 Motorway climbs north out of Lancashire's teeming mill towns, Pennine crags on one hand, Lake District peaks over to the west. This side of the Pennines is steeper and less somber than the eastern flanks in Durham, Northumberland, and Yorkshire. The rain-bearing Atlantic winds strike hard, but somehow soften the slopes, bringing color—brilliant greens and tawny browns—to the Cumbrian landscape, making lush valleys and nourishing small villages and towns of unique beauty.

When the Anglian invaders moved into Northumbria, they absorbed some of the native Britons, but the rest retreated with their Celtic tongue toward Cumbria and

the Lakes. In Northumbria few towns bear Celtic place-names, but here they survive: Penrith (chief ford), Carlisle (a "caer" is a fortress), Glencoyne (reedy glen).

Is there a fairer town in all the North than Kirkby Stephen? Ruskin described a nearby view as "one of the loveliest in England and therefore the world." Is there a stranger place than Alston, perched on a Pennine hump? Its streets—mostly dogleg alleys—show no names or numbers. How else do you fool marauding Scots?

I pushed on north and came at last to the Roman frontier, where the Emperor Hadrian's Wall sweeps across northern England from Solway to the Tyne—the far rim of the old Mediterranean world. I turned homeward, following the route of the legions and their auxiliaries who came to this wild territory from all quarters of the empire. The wall marches across the Pennines using crag and tarn as bastion and moat. Ruined forts, milecastles, barracks, granaries, temples, offices, and bathhouses (the Roman equivalent of the English pub) litter the land. Sculpted heads of emperors and godlings, the refuse of an army of 2,000 years ago, are found in field and ditch—graffiti, jewelry and combs, children's toys and workmen's tools.

At the gateway of the great Roman hill station now called Housesteads, the marks of chariot wheels are cut deep into the pavement—the same gauge, incidentally, chosen by George Stephenson for Britain's railways.

I climbed up the wall at a place called Cuddy's Crag and looked across the wastes into the land of Pict and Scot, as many a sentry, far from Rome, must have done before me.

Leaving the wall, I turned south toward the 12 counties of 13.5 million Northerners, ravaged once more by unemployment, riven by a great miners' strike. I bought a newspaper; a Manchester University professor had written that the tension between North and South had roots in medieval history. Northerners had a deep distrust for the South, he affirmed—a sense that they were part of an unregarded, marginal world that the South exploited. True—but it implies a sense of inferiority. And that's a feeling that Northerners, of whichever tribe, do not possess.

Hawking and hounding, sports of ancient lineage, still find favor in the North. At Newby Hall in North Yorkshire, a falconer prepares to launch a hawk eagle in a demonstration of its hunting prowess.

In the Cumbrian town of Grasmere, eager hounds spring away at the start of an event called hound trailing, following a course scented with aniseed. The race may have roots in the days when keen-nosed "sleuth" dogs tracked raiders from across England's borders.

Ian Berry, Magnum (both)

Of Tax Havens, Come-overs, and the TT: Surviving on the Isle of Man

In his farmhouse parlor Sir Charles Kerruish, Speaker of the House of Keys in Tynwald—the Isle of Man's parliament—is telling me what it means to be Manx. We are cautious, he says. Survivors. Outside, a pair of sheep watch us curiously through the window. They are not the rare four-horned Manx Loaghtans, but English Swaledales —and that, in a way, is the issue: Can this island's unique "Manxness" survive Britain's overwhelming influence?

When you land on the Isle of Man—of Manannan Mac Lir, Celtic god of the sea— you have left England, left the United Kingdom, in fact. Man is a self-governing crown dependency, with its own currency, passport, and laws.

The island certainly has a Celtic feel—cloudy, windy, hilly, sparsely peopled, and as green as Ireland. Its deep past, from 4,000 to 1,000 years ago, crops up everywhere— Neolithic monuments, pagan Celtic round houses, tiny sixth-century Christian Celt-

ic chapels called keeills.

Around A.D. 798 the Norse arrived. In 979 they established the parliament, Tynwald. "It has survived for a thousand years," says Sir Charles. "Tynwald is the world's only Norse form of government operating in the original manner."

The opening ceremony on Tynwald Day in July reflects the Celtic-Norse mix, he says. "You'll find rather pagan actions. We still recognize Manannan. On the path between the church and the hill we have rushes strewn as an offering to the sea-god. People wear a little spray of ragwort to ward off evil spells. Even the bishop takes out a bit of insurance."

But almost half the island's

A rowboat in Douglas Bay and nets piled on a Ramsey quay attest to Manx seafood delicacies, such as small scallops— "queenies"—and kippered herring made without additives.

65,000 people are not Manx but mainland British, many retired. These are the "come-overs," and the Manx government wants 10,000 more of them to boost the economy, even at the cost of reducing native Manx to a minority.

A kind of cultural suicide? Not according to Sir Charles: "New residents may be more enthusiastic about preserving Manx culture than the Manx themselves." Some of them join organizations like Friends of Peel Castle. This surf-lashed fortress dates from Viking times. David Freke, a University of Liverpool archaeologist, is excavating here, hoping to discover how native Manx culture fared under the four centuries of Viking rule: What survived, what was assimilated?

He showed me his major 1984 find, the tenth-century grave of "the Norse pagan lady." Its location in a Christian cemetery inside the castle could signify a transition

Hub of the Irish Sea, the 32-mile-long Isle of Man has gained thereby a resilient mix of Celtic, Norse, and English. "Whichever way you throw me, I stand," the Manx translate the motto under their three-legged national emblem. Sweep of green (opposite) near Castletown typifies Manx countryside. Trees grow in hedgerows and in deep, mysterious glens, suited to the half belief in fairies that survives here.

Isle of Man

period from Nordic beliefs to Christian. She was a woman of means; the items buried with her included well-made tools, a brooch, and a necklace of amber and glass beads.

Modern Manx seek wealth by using their autonomy to pass lenient tax laws. Like the Channel Islands, Man has achieved considerable success as a financial center. Relaxed laws also lure visitors who come to gamble in the public casinos. In June, the government closes roads for the world-renowned TT (Tourist Trophy) motorcycle races, which draw thousands of fans.

Government help has preserved antique narrow-gauge rail systems—steam trains, an electric railway, and the open horse-trams that ply Douglas's Victorian seaside promenade, a resort built for Lancashire's millworkers. Visitors can also see the waterwheel at Laxey;

Summer comes in with a roar when the Manx turn their tranquil island into a motorcycle racetrack for June's two-week-long Tourist Trophy races. Native Manx tend to favor the TT, which brings in revenue, but the growing population of "come-overs" have doubts, especially those who bought cottages on the TT route.

this marvelous 72-foot-high bit of Victorian technology, looking a bit like a Ferris wheel in a horse trough, once powered the drainage pumps of Laxey's zinc, silver lead, and copper mines.

Preservation efforts extend to the tailless Manx cats, most of which are now bred in a cattery in Douglas. Taillessness is a mutation that does not always breed true; some Manxes have normal tails, some short tails (stumpies), and some none (rumpies).

The island is laced with footpaths like the one I took one sunny afternoon south of Peel. A gale blasted in off the Irish Sea and over the moorland. From clifftops almost 300 feet high I gazed down on gulls circling above the seething breakers.

This open, remote countryside is distinctive, but like the Manx themselves, it is just a *little* distinctive. David Freke told me, "The Isle of Man has always been just big enough to maintain its own identity, but too small not to be influenced by the countries around it."

From atop Snaefell, the island's only real mountain, you can sometimes see all four of those countries—England, Wales, Scotland, Ireland— yet you stand in none. The Manx, cautiously, survive.

JONATHAN B. TOURTELLOT

By Norman Lewis
Photographs by Linda Bartlett

Wales

So it must have been after the birth of the
    simple light
In the first, spinning place, the spellbound horses
    walking warm
        Out of the whinnying green stable
            On to the fields of praise.

DYLAN THOMAS, 1946

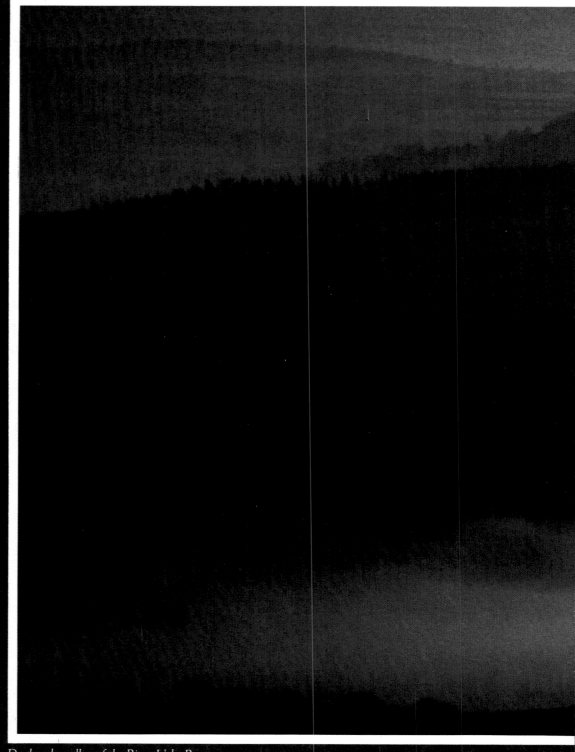

Daybreak, valley of the River Usk, Powys

Bright town, tossed by waves of time to a hill,
Leaning Ark of the world, dense-windowed, perched
High on the slope of morning,
Taking fire from the kindling East. . . .

Prouder cities rise through the haze of time,
Yet, unenvious, all men have found is here.
Here is the loitering marvel
Feeding artists with all they know.

VERNON WATKINS, "Ode to Swansea," 1959

A grand and mysterious past surrounds Wales. It is a land where myths are woven into the fabric of people's daily lives—where legends come not from the dim Celtic past but rather from "a good while ago, say in my great-grandfather's days." This is the way we felt as children in Carmarthen about one of the most compelling of all Welsh myths, even though the story is set in the 12th century. It tells of an encounter between a human and a fairy, and we believed it happened near a village only 30 miles away.

A young shepherd from Myddfai, Carmarthenshire (now part of the county of Dyfed), kept watch over his sheep one day as they grazed by Llyn y Fan Fach, a lake near Black Mountain. Suddenly, a beautiful girl rose from the water. The shepherd was smitten, and asked for her hand. The girl agreed to marry him on one condition: If he struck her three times without cause, however lightly, she would return at once to the lake.

The shepherd agreed and the two were wed. They produced either one or three sons, depending upon variations of the legend. But, down the years, he heedlessly tapped her once, twice, and, inevitably, a third time. She vanished into the lake and the shepherd followed her.

But the Lady of the Lake returned, the legend says, to teach her son Rhiwallon to heal sickness with medicinal herbs. He became a physician, and the father of three physicians. There is a medieval manuscript containing Rhiwallon's prescriptions for long life. He advised his patients to go supperless to bed and, to drive away sorrow, take an occasional dose of saffron in milk. With the latter recommendation came a word of caution—too much saffron might cause death from excessive joy.

Here the legend oddly veers into reality, for until the middle of the 19th century, many physicians of the region claimed descent from Rhiwallon. I even found evidence that suggests his medical advice was followed with a degree of success when, during a visit to Myddfai in the wooded hills of western Wales, Owen Buffett, landlord of an

Farrell Grehan. Pages 274-275: Linda Bartlett, Folio, Inc.

ancient inn called the Tafarn Yr Arad, showed me around.

The average life expectancy in England in the 18th century was about 40 years. But when Owen unlocked the church to show me memorial inscriptions on its wall, I found that one of the famous Myddfai physicians of that century, David Jones, died at the age of 61. On the floor we found several tombs from the mid-17th century; here lay people who had lived to be 70, 76, 85, 90, and 91. Inscriptions in the graveyard outside the church showed that many of Myddfai's inhabitants survived into extreme old age, even by the standards of our own time.

Wales's legends and history begin to merge in the fifth century A.D., when Rome withdrew her legions from the Celtic lands. For the next two centuries, the Welsh were ruled by warring native princes, and by 600 were faced with invasions by neighboring Anglo-Saxons, whose word *wallas*—foreigners—gave the Welsh their English name. (Their own name for Wales, *Cymru*, means "the land of fellow countrymen.") The Welsh managed to stave off the Anglo-Saxon attacks, and by the 11th century had forged a rudimentary state.

Then a Norman, William the Conqueror, overpowered England and sent his lords into Wales. The Welsh princes united to fight the new invaders, but their revolts came to an end in 1282 with the death of Llywelyn ap Gruffydd, last of the native princes. For over a hundred years there were no major rebellions. Then, in 1400, a new prince named Owain Glyndŵr rose to lead his people in a long struggle, but this, too, ended in defeat for the Welsh.

Welsh faces reflect strength born from struggle against an infertile, mountainous terrain, deeply etched by ravines and wild rivers—and against centuries of invaders who swept over the English border. Hope for Welsh sovereignty died in 1536 when Henry VIII united Wales and England, but a distinct national character lives on. It is expressed by an eloquent people whose language is uniquely suited to music and verse. And it is manifested, said Welsh playwright and patriot Saunders Lewis, "in a generous spirit of love for civilization and tradition and the best things of mankind."

277

Hope for independence was revived one last time in 1485 when the Welsh hailed compatriot Henry Tudor's victory over Richard III at Bosworth Field—legend says Lord Stanley crowned his Welsh stepson King Henry VII of England on the battlefield that day. Henry put the red dragon of Wales on his coat of arms and named his first-born Arthur in honor of the legendary Celtic king. But Arthur died and Henry VIII took the throne. In 1536 he abolished Wales as a nation with a law that prohibited any-one who spoke the Welsh language from holding "any manner office or fees within this realm of England."

The proclamation did little good. Welsh history and traditions—along with climate, mountainous landscape, and, above all, the national temperament—make Wales as different from the rest of the British Isles as any nation on the European Continent. Wales is really a small country, less than 170 miles long and averaging about 70 miles across, with a population of just under three million.

You can walk the lanes and footpaths of this empty countryside for hours without seeing another human be-ing, yet stone monuments everywhere give evidence of teeming activity among an ancient population with primi-tive engineering equipment and considerable skill.

According to legend, some of the stone monuments in Wales show signs of life. The Stone of Sacrifice near Pen-maenmawr has been heard to groan; the Fish Stone near Crickhowell seen to swim; Llia's Stone near Ystradfellte in Powys drinks from a nearby river. Carreg Lleidr, the Robber's Stone in Anglesey, uproots itself. Others will

Poet in a land of poets, Dylan Thomas spent his last years in the Boat House, a cottage on the River Taf in Laugharne. The Welsh poet spoke no Welsh, but captured its seduc-tive cadence in verse recalled by an abandoned hobbyhorse:
With wild sea fillies and
  soaking bridles
With salty colts and gales in
  their limbs
All the horses of his haul of
  miracles
Gallop through the arched,
  green farms,
Trot and gallop with gulls
  upon them
And thunderbolts in their
  manes.

do mischief to anyone who digs beneath them for treasure.

King Arthur is said to watch over Snowdon, the highest mountain in England and Wales. Here sleep the Knights of the Round Table, awaiting Arthur's call to fight the Saxons—still the Welsh name for the English. Scholars now believe that the legendary King Arthur evolved from a sixth-century Celtic warrior who had no Knights of the Round Table and led no search for the Holy Grail—myths that trace to 12th-century writings. Some claim that he came from the West Country and that his grave lay at Glastonbury. But Wales claims much of his legend.

Welsh tradition says that Arthur's wizard, Merlin, lies in a grave far to the north, off the Lleyn Peninsula on Bardsey Island, with such "precious curiosities" as a veil that makes its wearer invisible, a chair that can carry a person anywhere, and a vessel that will provide any liquor desired. But the citizens of Carmarthen believe Merlin was born there in the fifth century and buried in a cave on Merlin's Hill just outside the town.

Merlin is said to have prophesied that Carmarthen would one day be submerged permanently by the floodwaters that have often inundated the area. At the bottom of the road where I lived as a child, there was an ancient oak tree that bore the inscription: "When Merlin's Tree shall tumble down,/Then shall fall Carmarthen Town." To the horror of many townspeople, the tree was taken down recently to make way for a road. Although the town built a wall to alleviate the flooding problem, those who opposed the uprooting confidently await the cataclysm.

Arthurian tradition also thrives in Cardiff, a Roman outpost that became the principal city of Wales. They say in Cardiff, as if Camelot were yesterday, that from here Lancelot took ship to escape Arthur's wrath when the king discovered Lancelot's dalliance with Queen Guinevere.

Cardiff has been the capital of Wales only since 1955, when its official status was declared by Queen Elizabeth II. It is a cosmopolitan city; its 280,000 inhabitants are devoted to education and the arts. There are probably fewer bingo halls in Cardiff than in any British city of comparable

A reflective mood, reflected in the window of Dylan Thomas's writing shed. His wife, Caitlin, said the poet retreated here each afternoon to "bang into intensive scribbling, muttering, whispering, intoning, bellowing and juggling of words." In this room he wrote most of Under Milk Wood, *an earthy comedy of Welsh manners. Quite the performer, Thomas adapted his own manners to the role of a heavy-drinking, poverty-stricken rebel, which increased his popularity in America. He died of an alcohol overdose in New York at age 39. A simple cross marks his grave in the churchyard at Laugharne.*

size, and more choirs, debating clubs, and drama groups. Almost everyone is engaged in self-education of some sort.

A good thing, too, for Cardiff is a city of no great architectural distinction except, perhaps, for Cardiff Castle—a lavishly restored medieval fortress. Concrete and drab Victorian terraces abound. Said one local poet (poets abound as well), "It gives you the creeps, doesn't it, boyo? But at least there's nothing here to take your mind off your work."

Modern Cardiff was built with the bituminous and steam coal wrested from the valleys of south Wales, and at Pontypridd, only ten miles northwest of Cardiff's crowded streets, there is a brusque change of scene. The operation of 60 collieries here in the Rhondda Valley turned an entrancing green landscape to grisly wasteland.

The advent of the Industrial Revolution brought a coal-mining population of over 160,000 to join the slightly more than 500 farmers who were once the sole inhabitants of this valley. But now some seams are nearly exhausted and others too unprofitable to work, and the population here is down to about 81,000. Unemployment is high and can only increase as more pits cease operation.

A 65-year-old retired miner who cut his first coal at 14 said, "We went down the mine because we had to, and everybody who could find some way of getting out did. I only had one boy to bring up, so I spent everything I had to make a lawyer of him, and he flew away like a bird. Where there were two or three boys in a family there was no hope of raising the cash. The ones who had to stay on are trapped here. There's no future for them."

There have been attempts to restore the Rhondda Valley to its former state. New companies here are struggling for economic viability, and 45 small factories provide several hundred jobs. There are plans for a heritage museum. Grassland sprawls where pithead machinery and slag heaps once loomed, and there is talk of tourists and a winter sport center. But many are pessimistic—it generally snows here only two winters out of three.

Less than 30 miles northeast of Cardiff, in a village named Chepstow, you can leave behind the forlorn valleys

of industrial south Wales and find a relic of the Welsh past—Offa's Dyke, a wide earthen bank with a ditch running beside it. The Dyke is named for the Anglo-Saxon monarch who built the earthwork around 784 to mark the boundary between Wales and his kingdom of Mercia. The line of the Dyke extends 149 miles along rivers, across steep hill country, and through the perpetual twilight of dense woods. Though not an official border, the Dyke marks much of the division between England and Wales. Most place-names to the east of the Dyke are English, to the west, Welsh. At Llanymynech in northern Wales, both the line of the Dyke and the legal border run down the middle of the main street and split a hotel, whose landlord pays both Welsh and English taxes.

About 80 fragmented miles of the earthwork still exist; most of it can be explored from Offa's Dyke Path, a 168-mile footpath along Wales's eastern frontier. Mystery surrounds the construction of the Dyke. How did such a tiny kingdom—Mercia's population probably did not exceed 200,000—build it, excavating the ditch in some places to a depth of ten feet? How many able-bodied men labored through their adult lives to complete it?

These same questions had occurred to a self-educated historian I met in a Chepstow pub.

"When I was a lad," he said, "the local farmer took on 15 or 20 of us to help him fill in a hundred yards of the Dyke that ran through his land. We worked ten hours a day or more for a month, then gave up. It would have taken a couple of years to finish the job!"

Tucked between Chepstow and Monmouth, along one of the more accessible sections of Offa's Dyke, is Tintern. The 12th-century Tintern Abbey is first sighted from the road cut into the hillside above the town; the majestic gray buildings stand out against a feathery spruce and larch background. On fine mornings and evenings, sashes of mist rise from the River Wye to give the view a ghostly quality. The river is of the clearest emerald green, its banks shorn as close as a lawn by grazing sheep. You may see an occasional angler, but otherwise humans intrude hardly at

In sport, song, and ceremony, the Welsh unite to preserve their culture. The Welsh rugby game has been described as democratic, witty, resourceful, courageous, and full of panache. To inspire the players, enthusiastic fans up to 60,000 strong sing hymns or the Welsh national anthem—in perfect unison.

In equally high-spirited harmony, members of the Pontardulais Male Choir raise toasts and voices at an impromptu post-rehearsal gathering. They compete, and often win, at the Royal National Eisteddfod, an annual festival of Welsh arts. At the 1982 Eisteddfod, young girls dance before the robed Gorsedd of Bards in a ceremony invented to conjure ancient druidic ritual. Robe colors indicate position within the Gorsedd: green for the novitiate order, blue for the more skilled, and white for the exalted Bards of the Druidic Order—those who have made important contributions to Welsh literature, music, art, or scholarship.

Linda Bartlett, Folio, Inc.

Farrell Grehan

all. Aside from a few small, trim villages, there is something of a no-man's-land along this border, and you will not see many isolated houses.

The Welsh counties that border England make a defiant and sometimes stubborn assertion of their nationality. Most public notices and some street signs are in Welsh. Sometimes English translations are supplied, but even when they are not, the English-speaking visitor will have little difficulty, for the ancient Celtic language of Wales has been modified over the centuries by a steady infiltration of English words. Many familiar articles, particularly those of modern invention, have only slightly Welshified names: bicycle becomes *beic*; paper, *papur*; train, *trên*; saucepan, *sosban*; traffic, *traffig*. The most familiar and heartening sign in any Welsh town is *Croeso!* (Welcome!). *Dim Parcio* (No Parking) signs are everywhere, but in the relaxed and permissive Welsh border country, violations are ignored more often than not.

Food, like language, is a matter of national pride along the border. Laverbread—boiled, chopped-up seaweed that tastes rather like spinach—is mixed with oatmeal and fashioned into cakes that are fried in bacon fat. Many gourmets believe Welsh mountain lamb to be the best in the world. It is frequently roasted in honey, although Chepstow offers its own specialty in the form of "lamb Casgwent"—lamb cutlets grilled with thyme and black treacle. The flavor takes some getting used to.

So does some Welsh tea. Sometime around 1900, my grandfather, David Warren Lewis of Carmarthen, bought a cargo of tea from a ship that had sunk in Swansea Bay. He rinsed the tea, bought a pony and trap, and traveled around to all of the farms in the area doing his best to persuade the farmers—who until that time had drunk nothing but enormous quantities of milk—to take up tea.

In this he was largely successful. The fact that my grandfather's tea leaves retained a slight saltiness from their dunking in the bay made no difference to the newly initiated, for they had no standards to go by. In some country households (my own included) it is still customary to add a few grains of salt to the pot.

Tenby, about 30 miles southwest of Carmarthen, is my favorite seaside town in the whole of the British Isles. So many English have settled in this area that it long has been called "little England beyond Wales." The English imported all their freer attitudes toward life's pleasures, which makes Tenby a colorful place compared with most Welsh resorts. Streets start as staid Georgian terraces, but take on a more festive appearance with every few steps toward the

A shallow sea of machine-made waves lulls swimmers at the Swansea Leisure Centre—an eight-million-dollar facility built to revitalize the city's dead industrial area. A more controversial use of Welsh land began during the Industrial Revolution, when the British government first dammed high valleys in the Cambrian Mountains— flooding villages—in order to provide booming English cities with water. Beneath the still surface of Llyn Celyn Reservoir (opposite) lie the remains of Capel Celyn. In times of drought, the town's ruined chapel, school, and houses rise above the water line.

sea. Here an arcaded facade, there an Italian-style loggia squeezed in between ersatz Gothic houses. Pointed Venetian windows are favored, and a balcony might be roofed with an onion-shaped dome. At the end of such streets, the town spills out onto superb beaches.

Tenby, within its well-preserved medieval walls, is scented with brine and make-believe. One looks out from the town's highest points on a walled harbor full of pleasure boats painted in a rainbow of colors; on the debris of a Norman castle; on a 19th-century chapel set at the sea's edge.

In 1948, hoping to find a secluded place in which to work, I rented an extraordinary building called St. Catherine's Fort in Tenby. For a rental of six pounds a week, I perched on a steep rock some hundred yards offshore and inhabited 4 main bedrooms, 16 turret rooms, and a banquet hall with a life-size marble statue of Queen Victoria and a disjointed suit of armor. Hollowed out in the depths of rock beneath my castle was a powder magazine that once contained 444 barrels of gunpowder.

This remarkable fortress, completed in 1870, was built by Lord Palmerston to defend Milford Haven and the naval dockyards at Pembroke against French attack. In 1907, the government sold the abandoned fort to a private buyer for £500; in subsequent years it changed hands many times.

Installed there, I soon realized why previous occupants had left. At low tide I could walk or wade to shore to do my errands, but forgetting the time and the incoming tide, I was more than once compelled to swim back to the fort.

My rooms were lit by oil lamps, my water came from a cistern that collected rain and several primitive forms of life. Every square yard of the island and much of the fort itself were appropriated in the summer by nesting gulls that started up a tremendous clamor shortly after three o'clock every morning. The powder magazine had been colonized by giant black rats that scurried up and down the stone steps on their way to attack the gulls, or on their way back with the ghastly trophies of their raids.

Worst of all, the fort's inevitable reputation for being haunted ruled out domestic help, and tradespeople refused

A Svengali gaze and alert crouch characterize the Border collie, whose instinctive sheep sense makes it invaluable in a land with more than eight million sheep. At the Welsh National Sheep Dog Trials (right), a collie herds five sheep—a packet—across open fields, then waits to head off runaways as the shepherd pens the animals.

Small farms live on despite government incentives to merge such marginally profitable holdings. The Jones family has farmed near Llanuwchllyn, Gwynedd, since 1640; Simon Jones cradles a Welsh mountain ewe as it is shorn (right, below). His nephew, John, and sons, Simon and Arwyn, gather spring lambs in pens (opposite) where they receive the farm's traditional notched earmark and painted wool mark.

PAGES 288-289: *Hedgerow patterns beside Aberdaron Bay, at the tip of the Lleyn Peninsula, have replaced ancient divisions of this farmland—some of the oldest in Wales.*

Farrell Grehan. Below: Linda Bartlett, Photo Researchers

Linda Bartlett, Folio, Inc. (also pages 288-289)

to deliver supplies. Here I lived in majestic isolation for an interminable spring, summer, and autumn until loneliness took its toll and I withdrew. I have yet to return.

There is no better starting point than Tenby for an exploration of Pembrokeshire Coast National Park. Follow the coastline up to St. David's Head and you will find cliff scenery and wildlife as beautiful as any in western Europe—seals, seabirds, myriad butterflies, and, if you are lucky, a peregrine falcon.

Near the tip of the peninsula is the village of St. David's; its cathedral was the destination for countless pilgrims during the Middle Ages. A few miles inland from the magnificent coastline you can see the rounded slopes of Preseli Mountain, where the colossal bluestones of Stonehenge were quarried some 4,000 years ago. More than 80 stones weighing up to four tons each were transported, probably on sledges, rafts, and small boats, to the famous site—perhaps as many as 180 miles by the shortest route.

I have childhood memories of the coracle men from Carmarthen, carrying their featherweight boats on their backs down to the River Tywi, where they put down their nets for salmon. Welsh coracles are almost all gone now, but I heard that they were still in use on the River Teifi near Cilgerran in Pembrokeshire (now part of Dyfed)—an hour's drive from St. David's. This would be my next stop.

In Cilgerran I discovered a cult of the coracle, presided over by Mrs. Anita Clayton and her pretty 24-year-old daughter, Pascalé. Coracles have not changed much in design for thousands of years, and the people of Cilgerran are purists. In their only concession to modern materials, they substitute pitch-sealed calico for the skins that once were stretched over the framework.

The construction of a coracle is often a communal enterprise: One specialist cuts and strips lengths of hazel and willow, a second prepares the calico, a third assembles the boat and adds an edging of plaited hazel. A finished coracle weighs from 20 to 30 pounds, depending upon the size of its owner, for whom it is custom-built. The easily maneuvered craft is flattened at the front and rounded at the rear; the

287

occupant sits facing the front and leans over the bow to paddle forward with a figure-eight stroke.

Seventeen coracles are still used by licensed fishermen in Cilgerran, although their salmon catches are declining, as they have in recent years in many rivers of southern Britain. Some townspeople, like Mrs. Clayton, Pascalé, and their friends, simply use the coracles to take a turn on the river every Sunday.

"In summer we have races," said Pascalé. "But usually all we do is paddle a couple of hundred yards up the river and back. Still, I can't imagine life without a coracle."

As I made my way from south Wales to north Wales, I noticed a difference in travelers' accommodations. South Wales, deprived of its revenues from coal, derives its major income from manufacturing, with tourism a useful sideline. North Wales relies more and more on a huge influx of seasonal visitors and caters to them with exemplary efficiency. The country is dotted with first-class hotels, and numerous farmhouses offer hospitality as well. I strongly recommend the farmhouses because they provide a closer view of the working lives of ordinary Welsh people and serve up truly Welsh food that cannot be found in hotels.

North Wales offers the visitor a chance to explore castles, slate caverns, textile and woolen mills. Both sea and river fishing are superb. And, of course, there is Snowdon.

Snowdon is spectacular when it first comes into view, wrapped in its habitual turban of clouds. A single glance tells you that this mountain is unlike any other—its breathtaking precipices and stark, savage scenery contrast with meadows full of flowers and browsing cows below. Its high valleys preserve lost worlds that have survived for thousands of years: Tree trunks and branches shrouded in cooling lichens and ferns; orchids wedged into rock niches; exotic darting dragonflies; a bird called the dipper that plunges into a racing stream, swims underwater with its wings for 20 feet or more, then bursts from the water with an insect clamped in its bill.

Explore the slopes of Cader Idris at the back of Dolgellau and you will find rare species *(Continued on page 298)*

Farrell Grehan. Left: Linda Bartlett, Folio, Inc.

Welsh workers face unemployment in a changing labor market. Coal miners—Dai Coomes (opposite) among them—have lost their jobs as collieries close in the Rhondda Valley. In Blaenau Ffestiniog (above), grey with slate and the rainiest weather in Wales, children scale mountains of rubble from defunct slate mines. Only a few dozen Penclawdd villagers race the tide to rake up cockles (right) where hundreds of cocklers once plied the trade.

Linda Bartlett, Photo Researchers

291

Castles: The Romance and the Reality

It was not easy to enter a medieval castle uninvited—especially in Wales, where castle technology reached a peak. If the castle had no moat, and if invaders survived the arrows, spears, and rocks raining down from the battlements, they could try tunneling under the massive walls or climbing them with a scaling ladder. They could hurl boulders and flaming missiles over the walls with an outsize catapult. They could use a battering ram to crumple a wall or smash through the gate, a castle's most vulnerable spot.

But getting past one wall might only put the invaders in an outer court, with a second wall to conquer. And if that were done, defenders could often hold out in the central tower—the keep.

Better to lay siege—prevent supplies from reaching the castle—and await a surrender, biding the time by finding and poisoning the springs that fed the castle's well. And hoping that reinforcements would not arrive to rescue the besieged castle.

During the last part of the 13th century, Edward I built a series of 17 castles in Wales to aid his campaign against the Welsh. (These castles —Conwy, Harlech, Caernarfon, and others—featured massive twin-towered gatehouses instead of central keeps.) The feisty Welsh responded by erecting their own fortresses. This arms race in stone left the Welsh countryside studded with castles.

Though castles were effective defenses, as domiciles they left much to be desired. Often all the residents—the lord, his family, and all his knights, soldiers, and serfs—

Massive, eight-towered Conwy Castle and its walled garrison town are one of 17 military bases established in Wales by 13th-century English king Edward I. Edward himself was briefly besieged here by Welsh forces; reinforcements hastened to his rescue.

Farrell Grehan

lived in one large room, the great hall. Windows were few, since they weaken walls. Fireplaces, braziers, torches, and candles provided scant heat and light. Plumbing was a rarity. Latrines—along with residents—became malodorous, a problem exacerbated by lack of ventilation. Altogether, life in a castle was dank, dark, dirty, and stone cold.

The earliest fortresses, dating from prehistoric times, were simple affairs, hilltops defended by a surrounding ditch or a stone or earthen wall. The Iron Age brought larger, more complex hillforts. The multiple ramparts of Maiden Castle in Dorset, still visible, enclosed 47 acres. But earthworks proved no match for the Romans.

With the Romans came a greater use of stone, particularly for walls around towns

"The pleasantest spot in Wales" wrote 12th-century scholar Gerald de Barri about Manorbier Castle, his birthplace. The present owners live in a modern house within the castle walls. Young knights (right, upper) defend the great hall. In the archers' gallery (right), sunlight dapples the shelter where bowmen once stood to shoot through narrow windows.

Robert W. Madden, National Geographic Staff (all)

and military camps. But it was the Normans who built England's first true castles. Early Norman castles were usually made of wood and earth, and mostly on a "motte and bailey" plan: a central mound (motte), topped with a stronghold (the keep) and circled by a wall. The enclosed area was called the bailey.

Strengthening their conquest, the Normans built new and more lasting concentric castles, with stone keeps surrounded by two stone walls fortified by round or rectangular towers. Norman castles were royal military bases; each warrior lord maintained a force to control the area and expand the invasion.

The Normans also built Ireland's oldest castles. Superb Carrickfergus, begun in 1180 and well preserved today, was probably the first true castle in Ireland.

A garrison town was usually built next to each castle, but the castle itself had to be sufficiently self-supporting to survive a siege. Each one con-

A high-rise office building now dwarfs the ruins of 14th-century Swansea Castle, one of the last castles built in Wales. It served as a debtor's prison in the 18th century.

tained not only living areas but also stables, workshops, gardens, storerooms, and a chapel. In times of peace as well as in war, castles served as economic, administrative, and social centers for a feudal society.

Government centralization and the end of feudalism—probably even more than the introduction of explosives—gradually made castles obsolete. A few noble families still live in them, but their small armies consist of household servants. Some castles, like fabulous Warwick, for nine centuries home of the earls of Warwick, have had to open their doors to the public to meet expenses. Of course, there are still castles—Windsor, for example—for royalty.

But it is the grim ruins—like 14th-century Tantallon in Scotland—that give the best idea of what medieval castles were all about. Superbly sited on a rugged headland, Tantallon was well protected by cliffs on three sides and a massive gatehouse and wall on the fourth. Tantallon survived several sieges in the warfare between the Scots and the English. But in 1651, after a 12-day cannon bombardment, Tantallon fell to the English, its days as an impregnable fortress ended.

SHIRLEY L. SCOTT

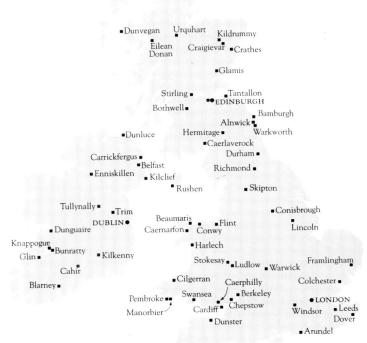

Selected Castles
of Britain and Ireland

From fairytale St. Michael's Mount off Cornwall to the dramatic ruins of Urquhart on the banks of Loch Ness, hundreds of castles—some now converted into hotels—transport visitors to the age of knights, dungeons, and drawbridges.

Windsor, the royal family's country home, is perhaps the most popular. Order of the Garter ceremonies take place in the splendid St. George's Hall here (right, upper). A carving in the chapel depicts St. George and the dragon.

297

of alpine flowers that have survived since the Ice Age. From the top of Bwlch y Groes pass, north of Machynlleth, spreads a vast panorama of ancient mountains—gnarled and bitten-down volcanic outcrops dating to the Ordovician period, which began some 500 million years ago.

The Snowdon Mountain Railway, the only working rack-and-pinion railway in Britain, chugs at five miles per hour to Yr Wyddfa, Snowdon's highest peak. From 3,559 feet up you can survey the breathtaking scenery of Snowdonia National Park—green-mantled slopes and deep gorges with holiday chalets tucked into likely niches—and, at the same time, see working timber plantations and farms with stone-walled fields. Writer George Borrow, who tramped through "Wild Wales" in the 19th century, said it is only in Snowdonia, with its "mountains, lakes, cataracts and groves," that "Nature shows herself in her most grand and beautiful forms."

This idyllic environment is overshadowed by impending disaster, for the ecosystem of Snowdonia is bound to the diminishing population of native broad-leaved trees, particularly the oak. Only 2.5 percent of the nearly 800 square miles of Snowdonia's ancient oak forests remain.

The natural process of change is irreversible. Grazing sheep crop the oak seedlings as soon as they appear, preventing regeneration of the forests. Oaks that survive the sheep are threatened by rhododendrons, which surround and stifle the trees. Imported from the eastern Mediterranean and the Himalayas for Victorian gardens, these shrubs have escaped into the mountains. Encouraged by a climate milder and damper than their native one, they grow in great profusion—tens of thousands spreading great purple quilts of blossoms. Their deep, strong roots compete with the young oaks; their dense shade deprives the delicate oak saplings of sunlight. And moisture runoff from the rhododendrons is slightly toxic.

The oaks will eventually lose the battle. David Bellamy, a leading British environmentalist, warns, "For the oaks, this is the end of the road. Now it is no longer a question of whether, but when they will cease to exist." With the

Donkey rides by the bay at Llandudno brighten holidays for British youngsters. Wales's largest vacation resort, Llandudno stretches along a two-mile sweep of beach on the Irish Sea. The town was built at the turn of the 20th century with Victorian elegance and expansiveness in mind: Hotels and guesthouses line broad boulevards and the spacious promenade along the beach. Accused of wasting land with overly wide avenues, one town planner rejoined that in a hundred years people would complain that the streets were too narrow. He was wrong—even by today's standards, Llandudno's boulevards are considered lavish.

eventual loss of the trees, the character of the region must change. Evergreens will replace the oaks and little will grow in the deep shade they create.

Seaside resorts line the northern shore of Wales. One of them, Llandudno, should not be missed. Strict local authorities keep control over the town's appearance. "You can paint your place any color you like," a Llandudno hotelier told me, "so long as it's white or cream."

Everything here is spotless. Armies of cleaners work in the streets morning and night. Shops along the principal avenues have canopies of uniform Regency design, supported by fine wrought-iron pillars—the Llandudno Woolworth's must be the smartest anywhere. Elderly people sit in peaceful rows on comfortable esplanade chairs, gazing at gentle sand dunes where, it is said, Lewis Carroll once strolled with young Alice Liddell, transformed by his imagination into Alice in Wonderland.

I stopped to chat with a woman who said, "I've been coming to Llandudno for 30 years, and if anything, it gets steadily better." She gestured toward the museum-piece of a pier, and beyond toward a sweep of unspoiled cliffs. "Just look at that scenery. They say it's quiet, but I expect heaven is too. I shan't object if heaven is like this."

The island of Anglesey lies off the northwest tip of Wales, across the narrow Menai Strait. A spindly but elegant suspension bridge leaves the mainland at Bangor. After the wide vistas of Snowdonia, Anglesey is Wales in miniature—narrow, deeply hedged lanes and tiny hamlets. The seashore, with its innumerable sandy inlets and secret coves, is never far away.

The mild breath of the Gulf Stream wafts over Anglesey; the harsh winters of Snowdonia seem far away, though the mountain is clearly visible across the Menai Strait. Palms grow here in sheltered spots. Anglesey is sometimes enveloped in mist of a special, translucent quality. It distorts distances, and navigators must be cautious along the shore.

Moat-girded Beaumaris Castle, a gigantic storybook fortress on Anglesey's southern shore, dominates Beaumaris —a frolicsome, painted little town like a snippet of Tenby

In the soft light of a foggy autumn morning, Llanddewi-werth-y-Rhyd—Church of St. David near the Ford—stands on a hill where its namesake once stood. St. David, patron saint of Wales, is said to have selected this Llanwrtyd site for a church in A.D. 519, and one has occupied the spot ever since. Vicar here from 1738 to 1763, the Reverend Theophilus Evans drank from Llanwrtyd's reputedly poisonous sulfur springs, curing himself of a "radicated scurvy, of many years' continuance and very near a leprosy." The vicar's testimonial established the village as one of several "wells," or spas, in central Wales, where ancient igneous outcrops give rise to mineral springs.

Like this water forcing its way to the surface, Wales's formidable past pushes into the present. Dead heroes like St. David coexist with the living. On this hill, the biblical phrase remembered by Dylan Thomas in one of his most famous poems seems especially apt: "And death shall have no dominion."

at its best. Also popular is Beaumaris's carefully preserved Victorian jail. An entertaining, if somewhat macabre, tour snakes past its punishment cell, chamber for the condemned, and along a walkway to the gallows.

Anglesey, farthest refuge from Wales's oft-invaded border, sheltered generations of beleaguered Welshmen. Here the last of the Druids gathered before their massacre by the Romans. They worshiped the spirits of sacred groves and lakes; ancient swords, shields, and spears used to conciliate these spirits have been recovered since.

At the prehistoric tomb of Barclodiad y Gawres (the giantess's apronful) near the western shore of the island, I encountered the Anglesey mist. The sun burned through in patches, illuminating fragments of landscape, suspending them in the void until the fog blotted them out again. I was within a few feet of the burial mound before it suddenly loomed into view—a great smooth hump of turf. I followed the 20-foot passage cut into the mound when it was excavated in 1953. In the dim light of the burial chamber at the end of the passage, I could make out the intertwining Celtic designs on five of the great stones.

Back outside, a party of schoolboys stumbled into sight. They had arrived here quite by accident, and were full of astonishment.

"What on earth is that?" asked one as they peered up the passageway.

"The tomb of one of our ancestors," I told him.

"A bit lonely, isn't it?" said another, looking around apprehensively.

At that moment the mist parted like a great curtain to display the tremendous panorama of the sea, transparent over a sandy bottom and darkening toward the horizon. A serration of red cliffs ran northward, all the way to Holy Island off the west coast of Anglesey. Gannets dove for fish through the last of the morning's vapor, which blew like swansdown from the wave tops. I could see the birds' streamlined shapes gliding under the surface.

The boys began to grin. Barclodiad y Gawres, dark and gloomy only moments ago, had become a cheerful place.

By Clifford Hanley
Photographs by Nathan Benn

The Scottish Lowlands

The happiest lot on earth is to be born a Scotsman. You must pay for it in many ways. . . . You have to learn the Paraphrases and the Shorter Catechism; you generally take to drink; your youth . . . is a time of louder war against society, of more outcry and tears and turmoil, than if you had been born, for instance, in England. But somehow life is warmer and closer; the hearth burns more redly; the lights of home shine softer on the rainy street. . . .

ROBERT LOUIS STEVENSON, 1883

May Day dawn beckons young revelers to Arthur's Seat in Edinburgh.

cots, wha hae wi' Wallace bled,
ts, wham Bruce has aften led;
come to your gory bed,
        Or to victorie.

ERT BURNS, 1794

Scots in Glasgow cheer on the team at a football game against England.

*T*hey are of great renown and compelling
interest, and they are charged with rare beauty,
so much so that critical analysis is stilled and
description tends to dwell upon their undoubted
poetic quality.

STEWART CRUDEN, HER MAJESTY'S INSPECTOR OF ANCIENT
MONUMENTS FOR SCOTLAND, *The Scottish Castle*, 1960

It rains in the Scottish Lowlands, but don't go away. The reports, like the one of Mark Twain's death, are greatly exaggerated. As I write, the Scottish Lowlands are dancing under blue skies—have been for a month or so—while golf competitions in the south of England are being rained out.

What the rain does, as in Ireland, is nourish the land. If you travel through Scotland by train, you get the impression of a continuous green golf course interrupted sporadically by human settlements. Where the golf course recedes, you see everything from lush alluvial plains to grim mountains to bleak moors—and a lot of rivers. Quite a varied piece of real estate for a country that is only about 150 miles wide at its widest point.

This diverse land nurtured a remarkable people. The original Scots, who seem to have been there since the Ice Age, were called Picts, or painted people, by Roman invaders. The breed was modified by subsequent arrivals. Britons came from Wales, Scotti from Ireland, Angles from Europe. They came thinking the land was rich and rewarding; they were wrong, but settled here anyway. Vikings from Norway came with the same idea, but were eventually driven away by the stubborn residents. The Picts and Scots, who united to fight off the Norsemen, formed the basis of the future Scottish nation.

Although in theory a single kingdom by the 13th century, Scotland had gradually separated into two distinct parts, the Highlands and the Lowlands. The Highlanders were Celts, with their own Celtic language, Gaelic. In the Lowlands, the rich ethnic mixture spoke English, but Scots-English. This is not a provincial form of English-English, but a tongue that developed on its own from similar roots. I find it richer and saltier than the London variety, but it is, I fear, practically opaque to other English-speaking peoples. What an Englishman would call a sickening, lopsided little chap, a Lowlander would call a scunnersome, shilpit wee bauchle. The Scot, in other words, is altogether a different animal.

From the start, England wanted to own Scotland. In 1296 Edward I of England, the Hammer of the Scots, claimed sovereignty over Scotland, removed from Scone Palace the Stone of Destiny on which Scottish kings were crowned, and installed it in Westminster Abbey. From then on the two countries were almost constantly at war. In 1603 King James of Scotland succeeded to both thrones (the Union of the Crowns, they called it); even then the quarreling continued for nearly 150 years.

My first sight of Scotland's largest city, Glasgow, was my first sight of anything, and I fell in love with it. I am prejudiced, and I aim to stay that way.

Glasgow was one of the cradles of the Industrial Revolution, and as such was never a pretty city. Toilers pouring in from rural areas to work in the iron and steel and shipbuilding industries squeezed into grimy tenements, some with only one toilet for several families. These living conditions helped to mold the nature of today's Glaswegians. They are resilient and wry—cheerful fatalists, convinced that life is basically a joke.

That Glaswegians are an extremely friendly lot stands on plenty of independent testimony. I gave a ride to a Cockney student who lives in Aberdeen and likes it so much there that she will never go back to London. But she hitchhikes constantly to Glasgow because, she said, it's a town where you won't be without a friend.

If you're a man, don't be alarmed in this odd place if you find your name has changed to Jimmy. Jimmy used to be the generic name for bartenders, but now it applies to

Industry and education flourish in the Scottish Lowlands. In the small area between the River Clyde and the Firths of Forth and Tay, live three out of every four Scots, including this auburn-haired art student in Glasgow (opposite).

South of this central valley lie the Southern Uplands, noted for wool and whisky. Trout-filled streams lace the Border area; far to the north the Grampian range rises, threshold of the Highlands. Narrow valleys (glens) and deep lakes (lochs) furrow the region.

309

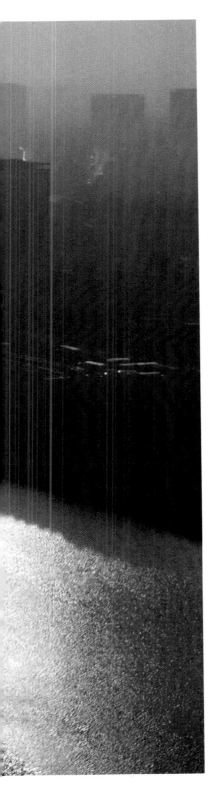

every male. The other day a young fellow yelled to me across the street, "Hey, you're Cliff Hanley, aren't you, Jimmy?" A stranger who reaches Jimmy status may take it that he has become an insider.

Glasgow's river, the Clyde, achieved great shipbuilding fame, but looking back now the very idea seems crazy. The stream is so shallow it had to be dredged all the time, and you can nearly spit from bank to bank. The oceangoing giants had to be launched with thousands of tons of drag-chains trailing behind to prevent them from shooting across the channel and ploughing up the main street on the other side. The *Queen Mary* and the two *Queen Elizabeths* were built here. The noise of the riveters was perfectly hellish, but they were proud of it and wrote songs about it.

During the industrial boom the city crouched under a dome of sooty smoke half a mile high. But in the late 1950s soot was banned—domestic open coal fires prohibited—and now, weather permitting, you can see the sky.

Glaswegians developed a mania for scouring grime off the inner city's Victorian tenements to reveal the almost luminous cream and pink sandstone underneath. Many of the buildings have been remodeled since the 1960s to create bigger apartments with novelties like hot water and baths. The bourgeois houses, which were always fairly opulent, still line old streets, along with a lot of impressive public buildings. Britain's late poet laureate, Sir John Betjeman, called Glasgow the greatest Victorian city in the world, and rightly so, I think.

With heavy industry gone, the River Clyde has been

Glasgow's murky skies recall a time when the city was a titan of the Industrial Revolution. Now giant cranes stand mostly idle along the River Clyde, marking shipyards that before World War I turned out a third of the world's steamships.

At the Scott-Lithgow yard (left), which dates back to 1711, prosperity returns temporarily as workers assemble a drill rig destined for North Sea oil exploration.

Vandalism takes its toll at an empty housing project (above, left). Such buildings await either renovation or destruction in the Gorbals district, a once notorious Glasgow slum.

spruced up for the use of the citizens. Tree-lined walkways and a new trade center grace its landscaped banks. The water is getting so clean that in 1984 salmon were sighted; they provoked great excitement all over town.

Glasgow's Art Gallery and Museum in Kelvingrove Park boasts one of the best art collections in Britain outside London. It also basks in the glow of broad-based community support. Much of the money to build the red sandstone Victorian palace that houses the collection came from private donations and public funds. So did a substantial part of the purchase price of Salvador Dali's "Christ of St. John of the Cross." The gallery director bought it with discretionary funds in the 1950s and some of the city councillors went white with rage at the extravagance. So the director set out a collection box. Glasgow's citizens, who weren't enraged at all, came out and queued up in great numbers, donating their pennies to see the thing.

A stone's throw from Kelvingrove Park is one of the nicest bars in Britain, the Stirling Castle. So popular are its food and drink that the owner, Davie Main, had to open another pub across the street, which he called the Overflow. The Overflow immediately got crowded, but life is dull without a bit of jostling.

I also enjoy the Saracen's Head, or Sarry Heid to the natives. It is named after a famous inn, now demolished, that was visited by such literary notables as Dr. Samuel Johnson, William Wordsworth, and Samuel Coleridge. It is just a nice, scruffy old boozer, as pubs are called locally. But be cautious with the cider on tap. Deceptively powerful stuff. The Saracen's Head is in the Barrows neighborhood, a sprawling market of open-air and covered stalls that comes to life every weekend with the cheery ruckus of hucksters and canned music. It is what guidebooks call "flavorsome."

So is Wilson's Pub in Byres Road. It's a working-class watering hole so the talk can be salty, but since most of it is in the incomprehensible Glasgow dialect, this isn't a problem. You may hear something like: "Wherrurry annat?" "Erry urr ower err annat." This means: "Where are they and that?" "There they are, over there and that."

Portal to the past in a modern setting, the entry to an English castle stands beneath the gaze of a bronze by Rodin (opposite). Statue, doorway, and some 8,000 other objects—the Burrell Collection—were deeded to Glasgow in 1944 by Sir William Burrell, a shipping magnate who amassed his fortune buying and selling entire merchant fleets. A new custom-built gallery, opened in 1983, houses the collection.

Students at the Glasgow School of Art (right) pursue their muse in a turn-of-the-century building designed by Scottish architect Charles Rennie Mackintosh. His pioneering art-nouveau style influenced generations of artists—and is reflected in this chair he designed.

The Fine Art
of Making
the Water of Life

One of the very few words that Gaelic has given to English is whisky. The Gaels called it *uisge beatha*, or the water of life. They pronounced it *ooska va*—and the English turned the *ooska* into whisky. (The Irish spell it whiskey, claim to have invented it, and make it almost the same way the Scots do.)

Distilling began as a cottage industry. Wherever there was a surplus supply of barley, stills were set up, often in the open air, to convert the grain into an ardent spirit that became more of a currency than gold or silver. An Act of Parliament in 1823 made it more profitable and less unpredictable to take out a license and distill legally. Illicit distillers graduated to respectability and proceeded to perform openly what they had for so long and so expertly accomplished beyond the law.

There is a continuity about the making of whisky. The still may now be fired by oil or gas, the barley malted not by hand but by machine, the shining brass wheels replaced by electronic buttons, but the alchemy and traditional skill that convert a porridgy mash into the water of life remain unchanged. Visit a distillery today and you will see the same processes whisky makers took pains to hide from the excise men two centuries ago.

The formula for making Scotland's greatest export is simple enough. You steep ripe barley grains (right) in water and allow them to germinate. This releases an enzyme that helps convert barley starch into fermentable sugar. Then you dry the green malt over a peat fire in a distillery kiln. Scottish kilns, unlike Irish, expose the malt to the peat smoke, giving Scotch whisky its distinctive smoky quality.

Old kilns have a pagodalike tower (opposite, lower left). The malt is mixed with water in a process called mashing and fermented with yeast. The liquid is then distilled twice in onion-shaped, hand-beaten copper stills (opposite, upper) until the condensed spirit runs clear. Years of aging in oak casks will mature and smooth the spirit.

There are many imponderables in the alchemy. A great deal depends on the quality of the barley, the heaviness or lightness of its malting, the composition of the water in its flow over granite and peat, the shape of the still, and the skill of the man in the stillhouse. By monitoring the alcoholic strength of the liquid as it runs through a "spirit safe" (lower right), he decides when to begin and when to cease collecting the condensation from the still.

But what makes Highland Park and Scapa, two Orkney Islands whiskies, so noticeably different? And why should the eight distilleries on the island of Islay—often sharing their barley sources, their peating formula, and even their water supply—produce such dissimilar malts?

Old hands will tell you that the time of year when a whisky is made can have a marked effect on its development, or that the position of the barrel in the warehouse may subtly influence the maturing spirit.

Even so, the essence of a special Scotch comes in the final step, when men with educated noses decide which whiskies to blend into one.

DEREK COOPER

Jim Brandenburg (all)

In a rite of Scotch whisky making, David Howie, master blender of John Dewar & Sons in Perth, "noses" one of up to 40 different whiskies that may be used to create one blended whisky. Blenders use their trained noses to assess the quality, not the taste, of Scotch. Ears muffled against the bang-ing of stave and hoop, workers at a cooperage in Glasgow repair whisky barrels. Used American barrels find new jobs in Scotland and Ireland because U. S. bourbon must age in new barrels only.

(Annat—and that—is thrown in from simple generosity.)

Glasgow has the advantage of being a city that is easy to escape from—you can make pleasant excursions in every direction. Loch Lomond lies only 20 miles to the northwest, with its sprinkling of little islands and its backdrop of mountains. The banks and braes are bonny indeed, and ever changing, too. Loch Lomond never looks the same on successive days—sometimes clear and smooth as glass, sometimes dark and stormy. The road along the west side of the loch is twisty but good and is dotted with nice wee hamlets like Luss and Tarbet.

If you drive directly north from Glasgow, you come to the Trossachs, a scenic area that Sir Walter Scott put on the map when he wrote *The Lady of the Lake* in 1810. Scott described this wooded gorge, stretching from Loch Achray to Loch Katrine, as "so wondrous wild the whole might seem the scenery of a fairy dream." Two craggy mountains, Ben An and Ben Venue, tower over a rocky valley where hazel, oak, rowan, and birch grow. You feel like reciting poetry as you go along. These days a tour usually starts from the village of Aberfoyle, which provided the setting for *Rob Roy*, Scott's novel about Rob Roy MacGregor, a real-life 18th-century Robin Hood.

The River Clyde is another way out of Glasgow. Heading downstream, you pass Dumbarton Rock, a geological accident that soars up from the north bank. From a small castle on top, Scots once kept a lookout for marauding Vikings. I travel downriver on the *Waverley*, the world's last survivor of a huge seagoing paddler fleet. The sun shines in a blue sky. My heart lifts as the beautiful old boat, cradled by rolling hills, churns down the narrow river toward its estuary, the Firth of Clyde, where the river broadens into a stretch of tidal water dotted with islands and small coastal resorts. The wind and the light there change all the time—it's a yachtsman's paradise.

To portside is the coast of Ayrshire, now part of Strathclyde. I like Ayrshire. Lush farmland, nice beaches, some really cracking golf courses. And, of course, the home of Scotland's national poet, Robert Burns. He was born the

son of a poor farmer near the town of Ayr and grew up to dazzle his contemporaries with verse that has been translated into every language from Russian to Danish to Czech.

Around his birthday, January 25, Burns Suppers are held all over the world. Nobody does this for Shakespeare. Burns lovers say the reason is that Burns spoke to ordinary people with ordinary heartaches. He accumulated plenty of grist for his poetic mill—Burns loved more women than can be recited. At one Burns Supper—well supplied, as tradition demands, with Scotch—I heard an orator underscore the poet's popularity by asking, "Do any of you deliberately go out and get drunk on Shakespeare's birthday?" to which a wee man replied, "Aye, probably."

I traveled to several towns that Burns once frequented. Twenty miles south of Glasgow is Kilmarnock, where his poems were first published. The public park here has a monument with a small museum inside. The poet farmed near a pretty little hamlet named Mauchline. The town of Ayr, which he praised for its "honest men and bonnie lasses," is a lovely holiday resort, and a little farther south is the village of Alloway where Burns was born in his family's thatched cottage. The building has been preserved, and nearby is the Brig o' Doon, over which Burns's hero, Tam o' Shanter, galloped on his horse Meg to escape a horde of screaming witches:

> Now do thy speedy utmost, Meg,
> And win the key-stane o' the brig;
> There at them thou thy tail may toss,
> A running stream they darena cross.

Culzean Castle, seat of a clan named Kennedy since the 15th century, keeps a seaside vigil near the town of Ayr. Rebuilt around an ancient tower in the 18th century, Culzean has been restored and opened to visitors.

Gaunt walls of Melrose Abbey (right, above) recall centuries of Border wars, when English invaders sacked and pillaged the Lowlands. Later years of turmoil are romanticized in the novels of Sir Walter Scott, who helped restore parts of the abbey, and whose bronze death mask (right) resides in his nearby home, Abbotsford House.

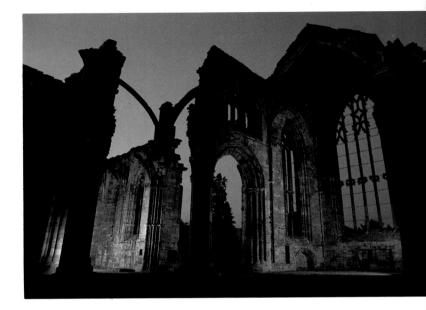

The poet died—at the age of 37—in Dumfries. The town has its share of memorabilia, including an impressive memorial to Scotland's bard. But I always enjoy Dumfries just for itself. It's a lively market town built of the local red sandstone. A few 18th-century buildings still stand, and there's an attractive waterfront area with a medieval stone bridge over the River Nith. There is quite a variety of taverns; several of them, of course, claim to have been connected with the great man.

Another part of lowland Scotland, the Borders, is memorialized by Sir Walter Scott. The violent history of the area unfolds in the author's romantic poems and novels. Abortive Roman invasions throughout the first and second centuries were followed by 1,400 years of English attacks, border skirmishes, and family feuds. The centuries of conflict left a sad trail of ruined castles, towers, and abbeys.

Traveling in the Borders today—through the gentle, undulating landscape—it's hard to imagine those times of savagery. Nowadays, the most violent encounter you're likely to witness is seven-a-side rugby football. It's rather an out-of-this-world sort of place, where you lose all sense of time. Near Melrose you can visit Abbotsford House, the dream home that Scott built for himself during the early 1800s. His great-great-great-granddaughters, Jean and Patricia, live there today and preserve some of the rooms just as they were when he died in 1832. His vast collection of rare books and historical relics are still there to be seen.

Scott is buried in nearby Dryburgh Abbey. His great-grandfather owned the abbey lands around 1700, but later generations lost possession, retaining only the right to "stretch their bones" there. The ruins of three other magnificent medieval abbeys stand close by—Jedburgh, Kelso, and Melrose. The last, founded as a Cistercian monastery in 1136, was nearly destroyed by the English in the 16th century, and local vandals carried off abbey stones to build private houses. But vandalism was routine in the Borders country where, apart from official warfare, the regional sports were reiving and cattle rustling.

With a history as turbulent as Scotland's, you expect all

Knee deep in a crimson tide, workers at a mill in Selkirk begin to combine a rainbow of colors (left) to produce variegated yarns. Some will be woven into cloth that carries Scotland's name far beyond its borders.

At Hawick (above), bolts of cloth are cleaned and dried in a cloth-finishing factory. Cashmere-sweater capital of the world, Hawick has 25 knitwear firms that export goods to some 40 countries.

Throughout Scotland's borderland towns and cities, woolen mills today produce knitted goods and tweeds second only to Scotch whisky in dollar-earning capacity—bringing in about 200 million dollars a year.

its castles to be grim, fortified bulwarks. In fact, many—such as Culzean in Ayrshire—were built after the turbulence, and are simply grandiose country houses. But not Stirling Castle. When you see it towering above the River Forth northwest of Edinburgh, it's difficult to suppress a delightful twinge of terror. There was a medieval castle here first, but the Scots dismantled it in the 14th century to keep the English from moving in. They started building this one in the 15th century and kept at it for a couple of hundred years. When it was done, Stirling Castle meant business—war business. Highland regiments trained inside its hefty walls until 1963.

The Stirling area has seen more than its share of history. Scotland's great freedom fighter, William Wallace, ousted the English from the castle at the Battle of Stirling Bridge in 1297. An enormously high tower on a nearby hill commemorates him, and when you drive through the district you get the feeling it will be in your sight forever. I've always liked Wallace. He fought for more than loot and glory; the glory didn't last long for him anyway. The English captured him a few years after the famous battle and gave him a trial of sorts, after which he was hanged, drawn, and quartered. He was only in his thirties.

At Bannockburn, on the outskirts of Stirling, Robert the Bruce finally won Scotland's Wars of Independence in 1314, beating off England's imperial ambitions. But in 1603, when Scottish King James VI was also crowned James I of England, he moved the court to London.

Thereafter, Scotland retained its parliamentary independence until 1707, when a piece of political chicanery, the Act of Union, bloodlessly absorbed it—an event still quite widely regretted here. Bonnie Prince Charlie tried in vain to reclaim the Scottish crown, and was finally defeated at Culloden in 1746. Scotland has remained England's junior partner ever since.

History is everywhere in Scotland, and as you walk around the capital city of Edinburgh, you can feel it seeping up through your bootsoles. All the buildings along the Royal Mile, from (Continued on page 330)

Edinburgh's Strip of History: The Royal Mile

They stare at you from the walls of the Picture Gallery at Holyroodhouse Palace— 89 Scottish kings from Fergus (A.D. 330) to James VII (1685)—vying for attention, smugly contemplating their glorious and gory reigns. Here in the palace the past is compressed, the natural sequence of events foreshortened until celebration follows tragedy with disrespectful swiftness.

Holyroodhouse Palace stands at the lower end of Edinburgh's Royal Mile; at the upper end of the sloping ridge Edinburgh Castle looms atop a massive volcanic plug called Castle Rock. The mile-long ridge itself, carved by Ice Age glaciers, slices through the heart of Edinburgh, and its story was for centuries the story of the Scottish nation. Fortresses on Castle Rock have dominated the surrounding countryside since the sixth century. Pictish princesses stashed away for safety were perhaps the rock's first royal residents. Then came a stream of challengers who would raze one structure and raise another on the site.

In 1057, Malcolm Canmore killed his father's murderer, Macbeth, and became king. Around his stronghold on Castle Rock, the city of Edinburgh grew. Canmore's son David I built Holyrood Abbey at the opposite end of the Royal Mile, encouraging the spread of anglicized clergy in Scotland. In 1329 King Robert the Bruce granted Edinburgh a royal charter, and in the mid-1400s it replaced Perth as Scotland's capital.

For nearly six centuries after Canmore occupied Edinburgh Castle, it remained a coveted target—and several times a residence—for English invaders. Each time the

Castle Rock (far right) and the Gothic rooftops of Old Town Edinburgh rise to meet the dusky sky. Behind them runs the historic Royal Mile; in the foreground stands the National Gallery of Scotland.

Adam Woolfitt, Susan Griggs. Below: Nathan Benn

Select regiments and bands of the Military Tattoo, spotlighted above in a stirring rendition of "Auld Lang Syne," parade nightly during the annual Edinburgh International Festival.

In the 18th century bagpiping was outlawed for a time by the English, who believed the music helped inspire the rebellion of 1745. Today the Army School of Piping (right) instructs students within the walls of Edinburgh Castle.

Scots staged daring raids to recapture the fortress. Sir Thomas Randolph, Earl of Moray, and 30 stalwart followers scaled the rock in the dead of night to take the castle in 1313.

Some 30 years later Sir William Douglas, Knight of Liddesdale, led a band of Scots disguised as merchants up to the castle gates and convinced the English governor that their sacks of rocks contained edibles from England. As the gates swung open the Scots cried, "A Douglas! A Douglas!" They threw down their bundles to hold back the gates and charged inside.

For some, the castle was not a prize, but a prison. The Duke of Albany's celebrated escape from David's Tower in 1479 still horrifies: After plying his guards with potent wine he murdered the lot and piled them onto the open hearth to roast in their armor. By the time they were discovered, he was on his way to France.

Mary Queen of Scots occupied Edinburgh Castle in the next century. The center of controversy from infancy, she dominates the city's past. When she was two, King Henry VIII sought to wed her to his son, Edward, so that Henry could rule her kingdom from England. The Scots

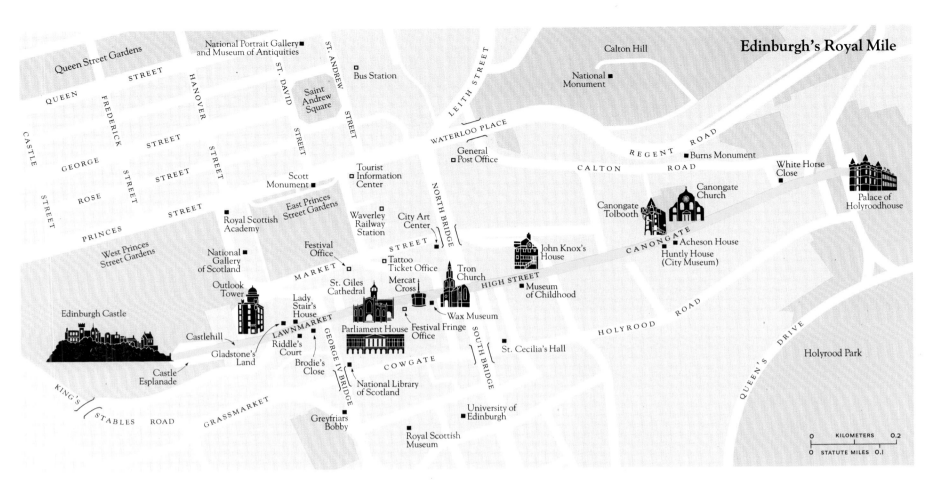

Edinburgh's Royal Mile

Stretching from castle to palace, three streets fuse along a ridge to form Edinburgh's Royal Mile, the backbone of Scottish history. Castlehill spills into Lawnmarket, where traders used to sell fine linens. High Street passes Tron Church, site of the old tron, or weighing beam, to which merchants were nailed by their ears if their goods were incorrectly marked. Down the road, Canongate Tolbooth's landmark clock ticked away the sentences of those imprisoned within its walls.

Enclosed courtyards such as White Horse Close (left) line the Royal Mile; such compact clusters of housing made efficient use of a valuable commodity in the 17th century—living space. Children play before the inn, now restored, which hosted the officers of Bonnie Prince Charlie's army when he occupied Edinburgh in 1745.

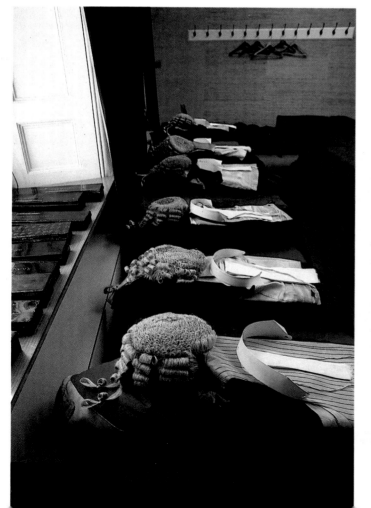

326

Nathan Benn (all)

refused, packed Mary off to France, and the jilted Henry twice reduced their capital to rubble.

In the castle you can visit the cramped bedchamber where Mary, returned from France and married to the foppish Lord Darnley, gave birth in 1566 to James, who would become king of both Scotland and England at the Union of the Crowns in 1603.

As the English and the Scots fought for possession of the castle, the city of Edinburgh filled with people. For 250 years the Flodden Wall, hastily constructed following James IV's massive defeat at Flodden Field in 1513, defined the boundaries for safe city living, and within its confines Edinburgh's population squeezed into ever more cramped quarters. Tenement rose behind tall tenement, sometimes up to 14 stories. From these heights residents emptied their chamberpots directly onto the streets below, alerting pedestrians with the shout, "gardyloo!"—a garbled version of the French *garde à l'eau,* meaning "mind the water."

Today the city is somewhat more picturesque. You can visit Outlook Tower and take a bird's-eye tour via its rotating camera obscura, a reflecting periscope that scans the tangle of streets around it and casts views onto a round, horizontal screen inside. Guides point out "closes," courtyards sealed by gates at night, which indent the street fronts. "Wynds," narrow lanes, twist between open shops called "lands." You can see Brodie's Close, where the deacon who inspired Robert Louis Stevenson's *Dr. Jekyll and Mr. Hyde* lived by day and lurked by night.

Not far from the tower is Mercat Cross, where Bonnie Prince Charlie declared his father King James VIII of Scotland. Many who gathered there that September of 1745 believed his claim justified. Holyroodhouse Palace hosted a ball for the short-

Defenders of Scots law confer over tea in Parliament House. The Scottish system remains cloaked in traditional wigs and robes (opposite, below), but has been renowned since the 16th century for its liberal stance on divorce, and for its unusual verdict, "not proven," sometimes translated as "not guilty, but don't do it again." The Right Honourable the Lord Emslie (opposite, above), the highest court judge, poses before a 300-year-old portrait of his similarly garbed predecessor.

lived court. But the inhabitants of Edinburgh Castle were loyal to the house of Hanover, and fired a cannon at the palace. They missed, and the wayward cannonball is still embedded in a house along Castlehill.

Parliament House, where the Scottish government met until the Act of Union in 1707, today holds Scotland's highest civil and criminal courts. Beneath the ceiling's arched timbers, solicitors and advocates engage in Scots law which, based more on the Roman system than the English, relies on principle rather than precedent to resolve a case.

Across Parliament Square, St. Giles Cathedral displays its distinctive 15th-century crown tower, an airy cap supported by eight flying buttresses. Inside, the Colours of the Scottish regiments hang in the still air where the Protestant reformer John Knox daily pitted church against state, roaring fiery sermons against the young Catholic Queen Mary.

Where High Street merges into Canongate, a line of S's embedded in the pavement marks the ancient limits of sanctuary extended by Holyrood Abbey until 1880. Debtors were often seen running toward the line with creditors in hot pursuit, as bystanders

wagered on the outcome.

One mile from the castle esplanade are the gates of Holyroodhouse Palace—the ironwork as intricate as the twisted family tree of those who have claimed residence there. Beyond, sprawling gardens engulf the ruins of Holyrood Abbey; from the foundations of its guesthouse rose the palace. The graceful spaciousness of its design set the style for the 18th-century Georgian "New Town" that spread to the north.

Symmetrical and soothing, the palace and its grounds seem a sedate end to the Royal Mile and its turbulent history. But murders took place here, too, and shifts of power which wrought havoc in the lives of Edinburghers. They believe there are ghosts beneath the Royal Mile, and maybe there are. Everywhere in Edinburgh there is a bit of history—like "a lyric," wrote Charlotte Brontë, "brief, bright, clear, and vital as a flash of lightning."

MARY LUDERS

Nathan Benn (both)

Edinburgh elite (left) gather at the Palace of Holyroodhouse, at the foot of the Royal Mile. Robin Hill, assistant city curator for Edinburgh, reconstructs a bit of local history (right).

Edinburgh Castle down to Holyroodhouse Palace, have wonderful stories to tell. Holyroodhouse Palace is the present Queen's official home in Edinburgh. If the royals are not at home, there is a guided tour of the palace and grounds that is well worth taking.

Edinburgh has a feeling of excitement that never fails me. For a start, it looks good. Few cities have streets like the Royal Mile, with a mountain at one end topped by a real castle. Edinburgh Castle's massive fortifications, rebuilt several times, are a potent reminder of its violent history. The Scottish National War Memorial here, with its long Gallery of Honour dedicated to the 12 Scottish regiments, is quite beautiful—but also infinitely sad, recalling young men who were killed before they could taste the sweetness of life. It has been called "a cry in stone."

From the castle you can look down on Princes Street, part of Edinburgh's Georgian "New Town," conceived as a unified city plan back in 1767. The streets and squares have the grace and space of a Henry James novel. In particular, the north side of Charlotte Square, designed by Scottish-born architect Robert Adam, is considered a gem of Georgian terrace architecture.

Sir Walter Scott grew up in Edinburgh, a lawyer before he turned to literature. Indeed, Scott the romantic was quite willing to display lawyerly discernment if a certain tale is to be believed. Around 1820, two smooth-talking brothers, the Sobieski Stuarts, claimed to be grandsons of Bonnie Prince Charlie. They said that they had discovered (in a Cadiz monastery, of all places) a book containing the lost patterns of the Scottish clan tartans, outlawed after Charlie's failed rebellion in 1745. Scott dismissed the tale as nonsense. He knew there never had been any special family tartans. But everybody else believed it. They went wild for clan tartans. So now we have them, and visitors can track down their own plaids and buy their own kilts. Tartans or no tartans, Scott has his statue in the Victorian Gothic Scott Monument, towering above Princes Street.

Edinburgh's big contribution on the international level, of course, is the Edinburgh International Festival—a

Massive columns of Edinburgh's intended "Parthenon," begun in 1822 as a memorial to the dead of the Napoleonic Wars, stand above the city as a reminder of war's futility. The monument was left unfinished when funds ran out.

A young Edinburgher takes a cigarette break (above).

330

celebration of music and drama which takes place for three weeks during August and September. Even more interesting, perhaps, is the simultaneous Fringe Festival, of grassroots origin. It is now the biggest festival of its kind in the world. Tiny companies and hopeful amateurs perform everywhere in the city, in any room bigger than a kitchen.

The city is well supplied with culture the rest of the year too—at the National Gallery of Scotland, the Royal Scottish Academy, and the Scottish National Portrait Gallery. And the National Museum of Antiquities provides a fascinating picture of Scottish life from the Bronze Age to the present, together with glimpses of famous Scots through a collection of their personal belongings.

Parallel to Princes Street is Rose Street, which may have more bars per yard than any other street in the world. Currently there are some twenty bars and restaurants within four blocks. Young men still attempt a lunatic rite of passage, downing a drink in every single one of them. Don't.

One other brief warning about Edinburgh. There's an old field gun on the castle esplanade, which is fired at one o'clock every day except Sunday. I was strolling with a young lady who had served with the British Army in Northern Ireland; the gun went off at the appointed moment, and an instant later I found her flat on her face in a shop doorway. Brace yourselves.

There is a long-standing mock hostility between Glasgow and Edinburgh. Glaswegians think their eastern neighbors a rather cold crowd, and claim that when a guest in Edinburgh is welcomed with "Come in, you'll be

The Jubilee Course at St. Andrews, sandscaped, some claim, by the devil himself, has confounded pro and duffer alike since it was built in honor of Queen Victoria's Diamond Jubilee in 1897. The course is actually one of four owned by the town. More than 350 other courses dot the Scottish countryside, elevating the game to a national sport—or mania.

At the University of St. Andrews, caps and gowns are graduation garb (above, left). But gowns are worn on other occasions too, and signal academic class. The higher the class, the farther off the shoulders the gown hangs.

Twilight's glow illuminates the walls of Blair Castle, seat of Earls and Dukes of Atholl for more than seven centuries. The castle's strategic location in central Scotland often made it a target for invading armies.

Rebuilt and extensively remodeled since the last siege in 1746, Blair Castle today is the home of George Iain Murray, tenth Duke of Atholl. The only man in the British Isles legally empowered to maintain a standing army, the Duke poses here in the entry hall with a brace of Atholl Highlanders. His ancestor, the second Duke (opposite), commands a staircase built in 1756, together with an ornate stucco ceiling.

hungry," it isn't an opinion, it's a guarantee.

As for the Edinburghers, they are not as demonstrative as their Glasgow neighbors and they admit it cheerfully. In truth, they regard Glaswegians with a kind of puzzled amusement, like adults regarding the antics of crazed adolescents (they may be right). Anyway, it does seem to take longer to get to know the Edinburghers, though they are awfully nice when you do.

Edinburgh was the home of the first golf association. Scotland invented golf (no matter what anyone else tells you), along with steam power, anesthesia, logarithms, modern philosophy, capitalist economics, and a lot of other things. Golf was created, no doubt, with the intention of driving other nations crazy.

Payment for the honor is exacted, though, by Scotland's stern Presbyterian God, who sees behind bushes and notes every furtive, uncounted stroke. There is a story about a Presbyterian minister far from home on vacation alone, who sneaked out for a solo round on the Sabbath. God saw, and gave him a hole-in-one at the long third.

"That's hardly a punishment," St. Peter complained.

"No? Whom can he tell?"

Anyway, although golf started in Edinburgh, St. Andrews in Fife became the home, the arbiter, the shrine of golf with its Royal and Ancient Club and the revered Old Course. The Club takes itself seriously. Officials went into a tizzy in the 1950s when the late Babe Didrikson Zaharis, America's first lady of sports, had the gall to request entry in the British Open. The Club finally decided that, though there was no written prohibition of women, her inclusion would be against the spirit of the thing. They still think so.

It is certainly possible to play golf in Scotland without getting as far as St. Andrews. In fact, it's practically impossible not to play golf. Every town has handfuls of courses; the Ayrshire coast is nearly a continuous line of fairways. We exported this insanity to the rest of the world, but we remain the original dedicated lunatics.

St. Andrews does have another claim to fame—it is the home of Scotland's oldest university, and the scene of

Ducal elegance permeates one of Blair Castle's drawing rooms (opposite), presided over by portraits of the fourth Duke of Atholl and his second wife. The castle and its grounds, open to the public since 1937, today receive more than 100,000 visitors a year.

Swords, shields, and other armaments (top) form a decorative panel in the entrance hall. A bedroom in the oldest part of the castle (center) contains tapestries made for Charles I of England. In the dining room (bottom), a stucco relief depicts the evolution of arms through the ages—a fitting theme for what was once an embattled fortress.

a lot of violent history in the days of the Protestant Reformation. Zealots both Protestant and Catholic were capable of dispatching their enemies by means of incineration, stabbing, or perpetual imprisonment in a bottle-shaped dungeon; you can still see the latter in castle ruins beside the sea. Local legend says that when Patrick Hamilton, a Protestant martyr, was burned in front of the university, his features etched themselves on the stone tower he was facing. There is certainly an image on the stone.

The town shows many other signs of its ancient history: A ruined medieval cathedral where bishops wielded ruthless power; the 16th-century buildings at St. Mary's College that overlook a thorn tree planted by Mary Queen of Scots. But quite aside from golf or history, St. Andrews, with its dramatic coastline, is a lively and popular resort.

Dundee lies on the north shore of the Firth of Tay, 12 miles north of St. Andrews. The stranger is not likely to lust after the city of Dundee, but then the town doesn't really claim to be a holiday attraction. A modern industrial center and busy seaport, it has torn most of its own heart out in the name of renewal; only a few older buildings remain. Dundee was once renowned for "jute, jam, and journalism," and Keiller's tangy marmalade had its origin here.

It was also the home of William McGonagall, the much-loved worst poet in the English language. A weaver by trade, McGonagall reached his fifties and all of a sudden "A flame, as Lord Byron has said, seemed to kindle up my entire frame, along with a strong desire to write poetry." Despite public ridicule he never lost his dignity or his dedication. When the old Tay railway bridge blew down in a gale, McGonagall penned the words:

Alas! I am very sorry to say
That ninety lives have been taken away
On the last Sabbath day of 1879,
Which will be remember'd for a very long time.

The poem ends with the ringing couplet:

For the stronger we our houses do build,
The less chance we have of being killed.

Aberdeen, at the mouth of the River Dee, is Scotland's

largest fishing port. The weather here is noticeably colder than down west. A heritage of fishing those chill waters and dragging a living from the soil has produced a hardy and even a hard race, together with a legend of stinginess that the natives encourage. They say that if you see 20 people getting out of a car, it's an Aberdeen taxi. But Aberdonians are also proud. I was astonished to be approached by a panhandler here until he asked for "the price of a pint, Jimmy" in the unmistakable tones of my native Glasgow.

The Aberdonians have stood fast against the modern trend toward skyscrapers, and my congratulations to them. Much of the city is built of the local stone, earning it the nickname, the Granite City. Buildings glint in the sunlight, and broad beaches of silver sand stretch for two miles to the north. The older section of town crowds around the university and the Cathedral of St. Machar, itself built largely of granite in the 15th and 16th centuries. The city is famous for its gardens too. Beech Grove Garden, laid out by the local BBC station, is a national institution. The American invasion—Aberdeen is at the center of the North Sea oil boom—goes almost undetected, although it's big enough to support an American school.

About 50 miles inland from Aberdeen, along Royal Deeside, stands the royal family's summer home, Balmoral Castle. Prince Albert bought the estate in 1852 and built a grand Victorian country home of white granite, designed in Scottish baronial style. Queen Victoria called it her "dear Paradise." The gardens, a popular lure, and an exhibit hall are open when the royal family is not there.

The Queen attends the annual Royal Highland Gathering in September at nearby Braemar, nestling under the Cairngorm Mountains. It's a good starting point for hikes and climbs through spectacular scenery—Highland scenery, although Braemar is technically in the Lowlands—and is just a 50-mile drive to Aviemore, a ski center.

I did say the place varied a lot. The truth is that it has a bit of everything. If I live out my fantasy of retiring to sunny California, I plan to spend long vacations in the Scottish Lowlands every year to get my sense of wonder back.

Gold from the sea, racks of whiting, haddock, and cod undergo smoke-curing in an Aberdeen processing plant. The fish, bathed in a solution of brine and vegetable dye, are smoked for 12 hours over a smoldering fire of wood chips and then shipped to market.

Though the product is golden, the future of Scotland's fishing industry is not. Rising costs, depleted fisheries, and increasing competition from foreign factory ships threaten to retire the traditional small fisherman.

With both fishing and heavy industry on the wane, many Lowland Scots pin their hopes on a rapidly rising new star—modern technology. Some 200 electronics-related firms have already located across Scotland's central belt, and planners hope that the region from Glasgow to Edinburgh and Aberdeen will achieve success as Europe's "Silicon Glen."

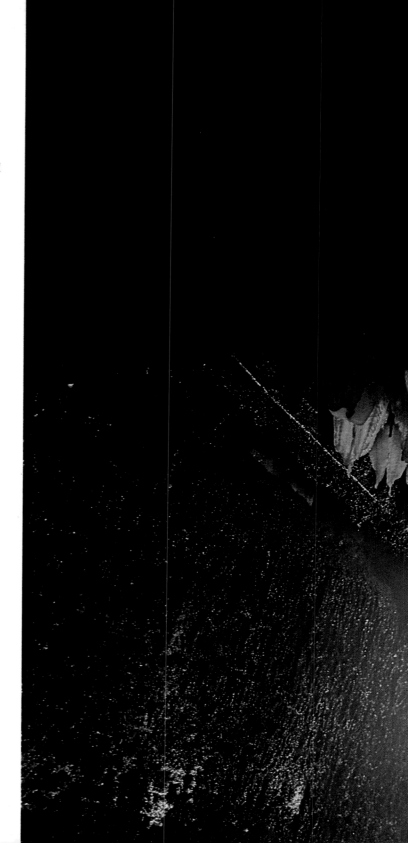

By Derek Cooper
Photographs by Jim Brandenburg

Highlands & Islands

T here are roads and roads that lead to Rome,
But they don't lead down to the sea;
And they take me not to my island-home,
So they're not the roads for me.

ALASDAIR ALPIN MacGREGOR, 1925

Fair Isle, southernmost of the Shetland Islands

Scotland is a baffling country to describe. You think that you have summed her up, that you have assessed her values and reached a decision about her when without warning she suddenly flings a surprise at you.

H. V. MORTON, *In Search of Scotland,* 1929

H*ark, when the night is falling,*
Hear! Hear the pipes are calling,
Loudly and proudly calling, down thro' the glen.
There where the hills are sleeping,
Now feel the blood a-leaping,
High as the spirits of the old Highland men.

CLIFFORD HANLEY, lyrics for the song "Scotland the Brave," 1952

Quite the most spectacular way to escape on a summer jaunt to the Highlands is to take the night sleeper from London to Inverness. When you wake at six or so in the morning and raise the blind, a new and magic scene is revealed. *The Royal Highlander* thunders through a forest of spruce and larch and over a granite viaduct high above one of those whisky-brown burns that rush icily down from the Cairngorms.

The air is crisp with heather and pine, dew drips from trees, a lean-nosed sheep dog barks at the passing train, cattle steam beside a low thatched byre. To the west, the dun bulk of the Monadhliath Mountains rises against a lightening sky; Glen Garry lies behind, Glen Truim ahead. We roll into Newtonmore, and the line curves down the valley of the River Spey through wakening villages, past Culloden Moor, and then in time for breakfast the train pulls into Inverness.

On the platform alongside, the morning train waits to depart on its leisurely and rambling run through Dingwall, Garve, Achnasheen, and the Achnashellach Forest to Loch Carron—a mere 80 miles from here on the Moray Firth to where the sea gulls circle the railhead that overlooks the Island of Skye at Kyle of Lochalsh.

Inverness is a town ringed by hills and anchored on the sea at the eastern end of Glen Mór, the Great Glen. North of this "Capital of the Highlands" there is nothing as urban. Here are the government offices, the neat stone villas of the shopkeepers and bankers—a cozy burgh straddling the broad River Ness and poised on the edge of a great mystery: Is there a monster in the long, deep, dark Loch Ness? If she doesn't happen to surface for you, there is plenty even more wondrous to see. A land of great beauty and wildness surrounds Inverness. Europe's last lung, it's been called. Overstatement? Not really. This is a world apart.

Distances measured in time seem short up here. You could drive from Inverness to Cape Wrath in a few hours, and that's the end of the road. And yet the Highlands and

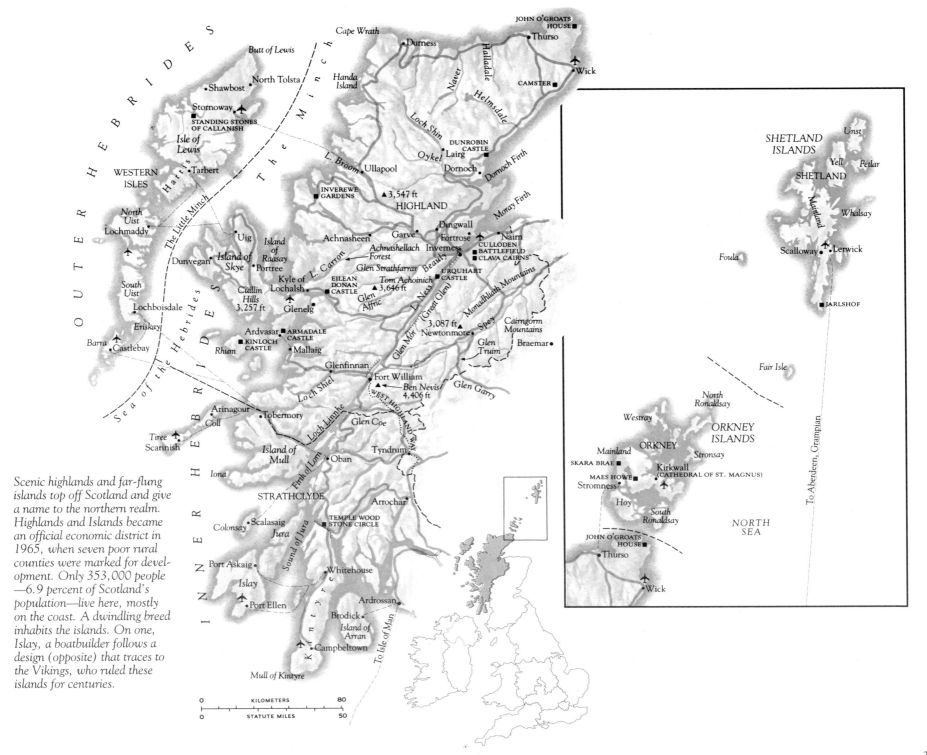

OUTER HEBRIDES

Butt of Lewis

North Tolsta

Shawbost

Stornoway
STANDING STONES
OF CALLANISH

Isle of
Lewis

WESTERN
ISLES

Harris • Tarbert

North
Uist
Lochmaddy

Uig

Island of
Raasay

Island of
Skye

Dunvegan

Portree

South
Uist

Lochboisdale

Cuillin
Hills
3,257 ft

Kyle of
Lochalsh

EILEAN
DONAN
CASTLE

Eriskay

Glenelg

Barra • Castlebay

Rhum

Ardvasar • ARMADALE
CASTLE

KINLOCH
CASTLE

Mallaig

Glenfinnan

INNER HEBRIDES

Sea of the Hebrides

The Little Minch

The Minch

Cape Wrath

Durness

Handa
Island

Loch Shin

L. Broom

Ullapool

INVEREWE
GARDENS

▲ 3,547 ft

HIGHLAND

Achnasheen

Garve

L. Carron

Achnashellach
Forest

Glen Strathfarrar

Tom Achoinich
▲ 3,646 ft

Glen
Affric

Glen
Mor

L. Ness (Great Glen)

Beauly

Oykel • Lairg

DUNROBIN
CASTLE

Dornoch

Dornoch Firth

Dingwall

Fortrose

Inverness

Nairn

CULLODEN
BATTLEFIELD
CLAVA CAIRNS

URQUHART
CASTLE

Moray Firth

Monadhliath Mountains

Spey

Cairngorm
Mountains

3,087 ft
Newtonmore

Glen
Truim

Braemar

Glen Garry

Ben Nevis
4,406 ft

Fort William

Loch Shiel

WEST HIGHLAND WAY

Arinagour

Coll

Tobermory

Tiree

Scarinish

Island of
Mull

Iona

Loch Linnhe

Glen Coe

Tyndrum

Oban

STRATHCLYDE

Colonsay • Scalasaig

Jura

Port Askaig

Islay

Port Ellen

Kintyre

Arrochar

TEMPLE WOOD
STONE CIRCLE

Whitehouse

Ardrossan

Brodick

Island of
Arran

Campbeltown

Mull of Kintyre

To Isle of Man

John O'Groats
House

Thurso

Wick

CAMSTER

Naver

Halladale

Helmsdale

SHETLAND
ISLANDS

SHETLAND

Unst

Yell

Fetlar

Whalsay

Mainland

Foula

Scalloway • Lerwick

JARLSHOF

Fair Isle

ORKNEY
ISLANDS

North
Ronaldsay

Westray

Mainland

ORKNEY

Stronsay

SKARA BRAE

MAES HOWE

Stromness

Hoy

Kirkwall
(CATHEDRAL OF ST. MAGNUS)

South
Ronaldsay

JOHN O'GROATS
HOUSE

Thurso

Wick

NORTH
SEA

To Aberdeen, Grampian

Scenic highlands and far-flung islands top off Scotland and give a name to the northern realm. Highlands and Islands became an official economic district in 1965, when seven poor rural counties were marked for development. Only 353,000 people —6.9 percent of Scotland's population—live here, mostly on the coast. A dwindling breed inhabits the islands. On one, Islay, a boatbuilder follows a design (opposite) that traces to the Vikings, who ruled these islands for centuries.

KILOMETERS
0   80
0   50
STATUTE MILES

their hundred or so inhabited islands stretch, as the migrant birds fly, more than 400 miles from Unst, most northerly of the Shetland Islands, down to the Mull of Kintyre. The Highlands and Islands add up to one-sixth of Britain's total landmass.

In terms of that vast space, the population is minute; the average density is only 24 people to the square mile, compared with 915 to the square mile in England. There are fewer people in the whole of the Highlands and Islands than in Tulsa, Oklahoma.

On the more fertile land, grass grows well in the long northern summer days, but the winters here are dark and dour. Gales scour the coasts, and while city folk lie snug abed, the full force of the Atlantic is breaking on the towering sea cliffs of Cape Wrath and sweeping, often with devastating force, over the mountains.

In this geologically ancient land, you'll not see many crops growing—potatoes yes, and barley, but not wheat. Some islands swept by salt winds are almost treeless, and when you do come across a sheltered plantation tucked in a hollow, it's like stumbling on an oasis. But amid the bogs and bare rocky moonscapes there are magnificent surprises —like the gardens of Inverewe built in the 1860s on a cape almost devoid of soil. It took 20 years to grow the shelter belt of trees here, behind which a laird called Osgood Mackenzie created his famous garden. Warmed by the Gulf Stream, hydrangea bushes and azaleas flourish amid exotic ferns, bamboo, giant magnolias, palms, and agapanthus. Inverewe is a blazing floral affirmation of what ingenuity and determination can achieve on a hostile shore.

The Highlands and Islands have always been peripheral to the mainstream of life. I have found, with the exception of the breathtaking 12th-century Cathedral of St. Magnus in Kirkwall, no remarkable examples of architecture, no relics of high culture. The Romans, who bestowed so much on England, never quite made it here; the Normans stopped short. Not until the beginning of the 19th century was Thomas Telford, brilliant son of a shepherd, commissioned to build 920 miles of roads and numerous bridges in what was then often vaguely called North Britain.

Wild, rugged, inaccessible was how the southerners saw it. Hadrian, in the second century A.D., built a stone wall about 15 feet high, from the Solway Firth on the west to the River Tyne on the east coast of England, to keep the Caledonians from harassing his army.

Keeping them out and keeping them down was the name of the game for centuries. The last big line of defense was built after the rebellion of 1715, when James Stuart, claiming he was the lawful king, tried to regain the crown from the usurping Hanoverians. (The Treaty of Union in 1707 had formally united the Parliaments of England and Scotland under the British monarchy.) James and the army of Jacobites—as Stuart supporters were called—marched as far south as Preston in England, where they were routed. Revenge was swift, and major forts were built across the Highlands to house the redcoated troops of King George I.

The Jacobites tried again in 1745, when the Old Pretender's son, Bonnie Prince Charlie, landed from a French

Look carefully. Is that a rock thrusting from the murky depths of Loch Ness—or is it . . . ? Beginning with St. Columba, who reportedly spotted an "aquatilis bestia" in the sixth century, people have stood on the shores of this long loch and strained eyes and imaginations as they asked that unfinished question. Fans of the unfathomable Loch Ness Monster claim 4,000 documented sightings —and touristry officials happily count 50,000 seekers a year. But "Nessie," as the apparition has been dubbed, still eludes sonar, underwater cameras— even a midget submarine. The loch, 900 feet deep in places, shrouds its mystery in water murky with peat silt and mud.

ship on the island of Eriskay. Supported by Jacobite chiefs, he raised his royal standard at Glenfinnan. In fierce hand-to-hand fighting on the moor of Culloden, the Jacobites were routed again, and the Stuart cause was lost forever. The prince fled to Skye with the aid of brave Flora Mac-Donald, and the troops of "Butcher" Cumberland began wiping out the rebellious Highland clans. The wearing of the tartan was proscribed, as was the bearing of arms.

A sentimental longing for the old days, seen by many Scots today as proud and glorious, still survives, manifested in tartan dolls and a romanticized view of the past, when men were braw and clans were clans. All of this is ritualized in the Highland Games, held not only in Scotland but also in North America, Australia, and New Zealand. The most famous are the games at Braemar, always attended by the royal family. More poignant are the Glenfinnan games, played on the very spot where the old clan spirit breathed its last. The kilt is still worn with a flourish and great feats of strength are performed. Pipers play, betartaned lassies dance, and the splendors of the past are transformed to harmless summer entertainment for the tourists, many of whom are descendants of clansmen exiled overseas.

Some clan histories go back to Viking times. Leod, a Viking prince, is thought to be the father of the Clan Mac-Leod; Somerled, founder of the great Clan Donald, was the son-in-law of Olaf, King of Man. For over four centuries the Vikings dominated the islands, from the Shetlands all the way south to the Isle of Man in the Irish Sea. They came from Scandinavia in the eighth century to burn and loot. They stayed around, never venturing far inland, until Haakon and his armies were finally seen off by the Scottish King Alexander III at the Battle of Largs in 1263.

After the Vikings, marauding was in the blood, and in distant parts beyond the reach of law you made your own rules. The Norse past lingers in geographical names, but the Celtic inheritance dominates the west. The culture arrived with the Scotti from Ireland, who came to Christianize the Picts. Highlanders have never lost their taste for the religion. Eriskay, like South Uist and Barra, is almost

Tranquillity of sea and sailor masks the hard life on Scotland's islands. Home from the sea, a fishing boat (above) passes the sheltering hills of Uig Bay in the Island of Skye, where a veteran islander (right) has weathered 40 years of fishing.

In the harbor of Stornoway on the Isle of Lewis (opposite), a fisherman of sand eels—used for livestock feed—checks for tears in his nets. The boat bears the name of a Lewis town. In the islands, farmers usually fish to make ends meet, and fishermen farm. Shetland fishermen used to row 50 miles to reach the fishing grounds. Sir Walter Scott once wrote, "It's no fish ye're buying—it's men's lives."

entirely Roman Catholic. To the north, the Isle of Lewis and its attendant islands are mainly Protestant, but the Gaelic language forms a much older common link.

On Eriskay, I spent a day with Father John Archie Macmillan, a young priest. I asked him whether living in so remote a place made people more aware of eternity. "It's my own belief," he said, putting another peat on the fire, "that it does affect people's religion, and, funnily enough, the farther north you go in the islands, the stricter the attitudes become. Even the Catholics in the islands are dour in their religion, compared with continental Catholics."

Christianity flourished in the Hebrides after St. Columba arrived from Ireland and landed on the tiny island of Iona in 563. It is said that 48 kings of Scotland lie there, along with 4 kings of Ireland and 8 of Norway. Pilgrims sail across every day from Mull to visit the sensitively restored Benedictine abbey and the little bay where St. Columba may have landed. There is a stillness and calm about Iona that can seize the imagination. A holy island.

At the beginning of the 19th century an intense evangelical movement blew chill fervor through the islands. Fiddles and bagpipes were publicly burnt, pleasure was proscribed. The hour of reckoning has been at hand ever since, and man's all too short travail on earth is seen not as a time for rejoicing and making merry but as a probationary apprenticeship for uncertainties beyond the grave.

Even to walk anywhere other than to and from church on the Sabbath is regarded by many old people as sinful. It is mainly due to the uncompromising ministry of the Free Church that planes do not fly nor buses run on Sunday in the Outer Hebrides. In strict households, the time will be passed in discussing the morning sermon and abstaining from any activities not directly connected with the observance of the Lord's Day. Animals can be fed and the sick attended to. Beyond that, nothing. In the devoutest of families, the bedridden do not even listen to a broadcast church service, for to bring it to them, godless men are working on the Sabbath. In the northern isles, Methodism is more forbearing, Sunday a more relaxed occasion, and

on the mainland on Sunday petrol pumps are staffed, people laugh and enjoy themselves.

But the landscape in many places remains a severe one. There has been so little building, so few attempts to improve on nature that the relics of the past confront you dramatically, almost belligerently. The Standing Stones of Callanish had been in place on the Isle of Lewis for 600 years when Solomon began building his temple in Jerusalem. The 500 and more forts called brochs on the northern coast and islands have been crumbling stone by stone since the Iron Age. Maes Howe, the most elegant chambered tomb in western Europe, lies on Orkney's main island; its great slabs were carved together a thousand years before the Greeks raised the Temple of Hera at Olympia.

In glen after glen you also find the aftermath of the Jacobite risings. You can feel it—an absence of people, miles of empty moorland, island after island left to the seabirds. Wherever you go, you will hear talk of the Clearances, that mass eviction that uprooted thousands from their homes in the late 18th and early 19th centuries. Cottages were burnt, old people pulled from their beds, whole townships were dispersed, all to make way for sheep. Many people emigrated to Canada, Australia, and New Zealand.

The most notorious removals were in the north of the Highlands in a kingdom ruled with czar-like autocracy by what was possibly the richest family in Europe, the Sutherlands. They had inherited huge estates in Yorkshire and visited their northern realm of over one million acres in the summer. They possessed such a fortune that upon visiting the Countess of Sutherland in her London mansion, young Queen Victoria is reported to have said, "I come from my house to your palace."

The northern coast makes you think it's been struck by a plague. I have driven mile after mile over windswept moors, alongside silent lochs, through empty treeless glens. Everywhere the ancient skeleton of rock is breaking through thin surface soil. What isn't rock is bog.

Not a place where you could scratch much of a living. Yet in the 19th century it supported far more families than

A hairy-cap moss and its flanking kin (above) enliven a moor as spring comes to the Highlands. Glen Affric's vast domain west of Inverness encompasses island-dotted lochs, mountains such as sun-grazed Tom Achoinich (opposite), snow-streaked glens, and a virgin forest of pines and birches. Mosses flourish in the wet, rocky moors, where flowering plants are relatively rare. Conifers, including the native Scots pine, cover about 7 percent of the land. Most forests are commercial plantations, many of them growing imported larch and Norway spruce, a 17th-century immigrant.

it does now. After a bad summer—and there were many—famine came among the people like a visitation. It was against this background of distress that the Countess of Sutherland reorganized the economy of her estates.

"The industrious will be encouraged and protected," her agent said, "but the slothful must remove or starve, as man was not born to be idle, but to gain his bread by the sweat of his brow." Thousands were encouraged to remove themselves to the slums of Glasgow or to the new settlements across the Atlantic. From 1807 to 1820, between 5,000 and 10,000 tenants were turned out of their homes. The evictions were so brutal and so devoid of humanity that the people eventually rose in anger. Their refusal to pay rents led in the 1880s to the passage of a law that gave, for the first time, security of tenure to the crofting communities.

By this time the Highlands had become a fashionable playground for the prosperous industrialists of the south. Because huge areas had already been cleared of their indigenous populations, they were ideal for the wealthy. Deer took over from the sheep, and grouse moors, silent most of the year, reverberated in August to the sound of gunfire as dukes and lords, whisky barons, and ennobled brewers descended for the annual round of slaughter.

Many of the old shooting lodges and castles have been turned into luxury hotels; others still serve wealthy sportsmen who jet in from Brazil or Switzerland. And a few remain private—slowly moldering monuments to personal might in the unfettered age of laissez-faire.

I once visited an island in the Shetlands where a Yorkshire wool mogul had built a grand house, complete with battlements, towers, and turrets. The present-day owner asked me, jokingly, "Do you want to buy it?" No, thank you. I prefer another Shetland island, Foula, which is for me one of the world's magic places. By boat the journey to Foula, 27 miles west of Scalloway on the main Shetland island, takes about two and a half hours, though sometimes for weeks on end the islanders can't launch that boat.

Foula lies exposed to the full fury of the winds and lacks a natural harbor. Each time the boat arrives it has to be

winched out of the water away from the restless pluck of the tides, and the 40 or so people who live there rightly regard themselves as the most isolated community in Britain.

For the last few years they've had the luxury of an emergency air service. Loganair, which flies small planes round most of the Scottish islands, has its Shetlands base at Tingwall, only 13 minutes' flying time away. There's a rough landing strip where a little nine-seat twin-engine plane can just set down. Every three weeks during the school year, the Shetland Islands Council charters one of these planes to allow the five teenage Foula children who are at secondary school in Lerwick to go home for the weekend.

Is Foula headed for the fate of the other islands that have been abandoned because life became too harsh, too difficult? Will any of Foula's five teenagers, or indeed the nine small fry in the village school, be living on the island ten years from now? As my old friend Calum Macleod on the depopulated Island of Raasay in the Inner Hebrides said to me once, "When the children have to be taken off the island to go to school, then that very often is the end of the story. Once they go to the mainland they seldom want to come back. It's too dull for them, too slow."

For a youngster with ambition, it isn't much of a challenge to stay on an island that may offer nothing more than a chance to go fishing or do battle with rain and wind to raise a few potatoes. Eighty years ago there were about 200 people on Foula. In 80 years' time will there be any at all?

The cost of keeping these small communities serviced—with a teacher, a nurse, a ferry, a post office, emergency medical help, telephones—is high. Most people see these islands only in summer, when the seas may be calm, the sun high in the sky. Come winter and the real price has to be paid for the magic of living on the edge of the world.

The price was merely money in the days when rich men bought a romantic idea surrounded by water. One of the island buyers was John Bullough, an Accrington machinist and inventor, who in 1888 bought Rhum, which lies in the Inner Hebrides south of the Island of Skye. An 1884 survey said of the place: "Its shores are rough and dangerous, its

Sheep, lamb, and shepherd share an immense landscape unchanged for centuries. On this desolate stretch of moor and loch near Lairg, crofters—farmers of small holdings—can graze sheep, but the rocky soil is too poor for extensive crops. Bureaucratic attempts to govern crofters, nearly all of whom are tenants, inspired a definition of a croft as "a piece of land surrounded by regulations." In the Highlands and Islands, crofts occupy 22 percent of the land.

surface is a trackless upland wilderness and its climate is an almost perennial series of storms, fogs and rain." But in those pre-jet days such a remote island had a preemptive appeal that must have made it seem like a cross between Treasure Island and the Garden of Eden.

When Bullough began taking his friends there for the stalking, there was no one, apart from a few servants, to disturb them, for the previous owner had transported over 300 of the original islanders to North America. When Bullough's son, Sir George, inherited Rhum, he perpetuated the family's feudal regime; no one except invited friends or domestic staff was allowed to land on the island. He hired architects to create Kinloch, a crenellated mansion at the head of the Loch Scresort, one of the most magnificent castles ever built in the Hebrides. Central heating, electricity—it was a red sandstone wonder of the world.

The island now belongs to the Nature Conservancy Council. Rhum's rare alpine plants, Manx shearwater colony, eagles, feral goats, and red deer attract researchers from all over the world. There are day trips from Mallaig, but no transport on the island. If you land, you walk.

The outsiders who brought their opulence to the Highlands and Islands also tried to change the way the people spoke. But, despite all the efforts to stamp it out, the Gaelic language survives. In the old days, every community had its bard; Gaelic poetry and song were handed down by word of mouth. The themes were often on the grand scale: heroic deeds in battle, mythical legends of giants with the strength of supermen, strange tales of the supernatural. Men with long memories could keep a village entertained for hours round the peat fire with stories of mythical water beasts and seal women and witches.

I can't speak Gaelic. All my relatives on Lewis speak Gaelic, and I alone am deprived of access to this ancient language. Gaelic for the outsider is desperately difficult. Soft on the ear, it's hard going when you're trying to learn it. French, German, Latin have all given hundreds of recognizable words to English; Gaelic has contributed only a few, such as *whisky*, *cairn*, *clan*, and *slogan* (originally, a

357

war cry). In idiom and vocabulary Gaelic is totally unlike English. On the page it looks impossible to pronounce.

To hear Gaelic spoken naturally and without inhibition, you must go to the Western Isles. In the shops in Stornoway the women slip easily from Gaelic to English and back again. At shearings and in private gatherings Gaelic is used almost exclusively. Today the language is stronger than it has been in some years, thanks to new feelings of nationalism and pride.

The move to start primary school children in Gaelic and the renaissance of Gaelic as a subject in secondary schools is part of an encouraging awareness of the Celtic heritage—an intellectual "counterdrift," the word the Highlands and Islands Development Board coined to describe its policy of encouraging bright young people not to drift away to the Lowlands, England, or overseas. The board was set up in 1965 to help improve life in the region, pump money, enterprise, and initiative into a part of Britain that for far too long had been ailing economically and socially.

The discovery of North Sea oil and gas has created about 12,000 jobs. And it seems that the new industry has not changed the real fabric of life; an oil worker home on holiday, with hundreds of pounds in his pocket, will still take his turn at the peat bank. This ritual of cutting, stacking, drying, and gathering the peats hasn't changed in centuries. The croft house will have electricity now, and gas for cooking, but the peat stack alongside the house remains a measure of a family's independence.

Just as emotive as the acrid scent of the "peat-reek," the plumes of blue smoke curling from chimneys, is the pungent smell of Harris Tweed. Four million yards of tweed were made in the Outer Hebrides in 1983. Walk through a long straggling township—often not so much a town as a collection of houses strung out on the hillside—and you may hear the urgent clatter of a Hattersley loom, and maybe through an open door see a crofter weaving a length of cloth that might wind up as a jacket in Brooks Brothers.

"You're a weaver?" I heard a visitor saying to an old man in Harris as he rolled a cigarette at the door of a corrugated

Veiled in melancholy, Glen Coe, "the Glen of Weeping" (above), enwraps a murderous memory in beauty. Here King William III, acting on a treacherous charge that the MacDonalds had not sworn allegiance to him, ordered his troops to act. The soldiers, most of them Campbells, first accepted the hospitality of the MacDonalds, then slaughtered 38 MacDonald men, women, and children, including their leader. Legend says the order for the massacre was written on a nine of diamonds, ever since called the Curse of Scotland. In that blood-stained glen, a solitary piper (opposite) plays for coins dropped upon his tartan, adding a poignant elegy to days when clans ruled the Highlands.

Beauty and treachery endure in a glenside sundew (left); its sweet-smelling tendrils attract, then ensnare insects, which the carnivorous plant consumes.

iron shed almost filled by one of these primeval looking looms. "Well yes, sort of," he said gently. "Yes, I do a bit of weaving now and again."

Not modesty this, but fact. Weaving is just one part of a crofter's way of life. It is no longer possible, if it ever were, to make a living solely from a croft. Most of them are less than ten acres and many are considerably smaller. Traditionally the men would fish in the summer, returning to the croft to help with peat cutting in spring and haymaking and harvesting in summer. Young women would often leave the croft too, to take up domestic work or to spend weeks gutting and salting herring in the east coast ports.

Today many crofts are occupied by old people too infirm to work the land. The sons and daughters may well have left the area. But a crofter has always seen his land and his croft house as the anchor of life; other jobs, often seasonal, are to supplement income. One man may drive a lorry, another deliver mail. The loom, too, is seen as part of the crofting way of life—another source of income. But when the sheep need dipping or shearing, when the potatoes need planting or lifting, the loom will be silent.

The specification for a real Harris Tweed—one talks about "a tweed"—is rigidly laid down. It must be made from "pure Scottish Virgin wool, spun, dyed and finished in the Outer Hebrides and handwoven by the islanders at their own homes." Then and only then will every three yards be handstamped with the Harris Tweed Association's famous orb symbol. If the crofter doesn't slip away to lift his lobster pots, help a neighbor mend a fence, go out on the common grazing to gather the sheep, or go to market to buy a cow, then he could make three tweeds in a week.

On Lewis, the woolen mills at Stornoway and Shawbost send each crofter his supply of yarn and the pattern of tweed they want him to weave. The weaver relies on the mill, and in turn the mill can fulfill its orders from the fashion houses only with the cooperation of the weaver. It is an unhurried relationship; more tweeds tend to get woven in bad weather than good, and when the salmon are running, the looms are deserted. (Continued on page 366)

Embedded in the rocks and thin soil of the Western Isles, stone cottages like this one in Harris (opposite) shelter weavers who clack away, "wurrkin' the wool." One, Marion Campbell, weaves Harris Tweed at her old wooden loom. Unlike most other modern weavers, she takes her colors from ragwort, buttercups, bracken, and moss, which she transforms into natural dyes. Genuine Harris Tweed must be made in weavers' homes on the Outer Hebrides. Trucks from Stornoway collect the tweeds for export.

Wild Shores: Mecca for Birds and Bird-watchers

Jim Brandenburg (both)

From a window of my house in the Hebrides, I watch a grey heron standing as motionless as a cardboard cutout on the shore, waiting for breakfast to swim into view. Nearby, some oystercatchers are pecking at mussels. And around the headland, just beyond the cave where the cormorants breed, a pair of golden eagles has an aerie.

I think the seabirds are the most spectacular to watch. The rugged, inaccessible cliffs of northern Scotland provide ideal nesting sites—caves, crevices, and ledges—for colonies of puffins and guillemots, petrels and shearwaters, gannets and fulmars.

For sheer drama, the lonely islands of St. Kilda are incomparable. It's also the most difficult place to get to in Britain—about 40 miles northwest of North Uist (map, page 9). Hirta, largest of the four islands, once supported a small population of fishermen and sheep farmers. Seabirds provided meat and eggs for islanders' tables, oil for their lamps, and down for their beds. In 1930, at the islanders' own request, their numbers having diminished to the point where they could barely raise enough men to launch a boat, they were evacuated to the mainland. St. Kilda today is a nature reserve (and a missile-tracking station).

The number of birds circling these islands would have daunted even Alfred Hitchcock. At least 59,000 nesting pairs of gannets, 40,000 pairs of fulmars, 20,000 pairs of guillemots, 11,000 pairs of kittiwakes, and 100,000 pairs of puffins whiten the stacks and ledges with their lime.

I don't think there is any sight in Scottish waters to equal St. Kilda, but perhaps the sea cliffs of Handa Island, off the western coast, are the

Scotland's coastal cliffs and marshes shelter an astonishing variety of shorebirds like the oystercatcher (left) and numerous species of seabirds.

Jim Brandenburg (also opposite)

Heidi Brandenburg

Black-headed and common gulls (left, upper) number among the species that nest on Scotland's cliffs. Puffins (lower) nest on rocky shores, along with the eider (opposite), the duck treasured for its insulating down.

next best. Handa is a reserve run by the Royal Society for the Protection of Birds. A few summers ago I rowed round the Stack of Handa, a rock towering as high as the dome of St. Paul's. Guano fell in slow motion from on high, like offensive snowflakes. A rank, fishy stench filled the air. But the echoing clamor of the cliff ledges rings in my ears still: herring gulls, fulmars, razorbills, parrot-beaked puffins, kittiwakes, guillemots—each pair noisily guarding its tiny patch of territory.

For ardent bird spotters, the one place to beat them all is Fair Isle, a pinpoint of land between Orkney and Shetland, generally regarded as the most important observatory in Europe. Thousands of birds stop here on their annual migrations, and every one that can be caught is ringed and logged before being released. More than 335 species have been recorded, even North American vagrants such as the song sparrow and

western sandpiper. Scotland's National Trust owns the island. Besides the observatory and research center, there is a hostel for the steady stream of human visitors.

One of my greatest delights is listening to my old friend Dr. Desmond Nethersole-Thompson enthusing about birds. An English schoolmaster, he packed his bags and came to the Highlands 50 years ago. Every spring for decades he and his wife, Maimie, have left their home on Dornoch Firth to study the greenshank—to Desmond "the most wonderful bird that flies." In their pioneering days they had no cash for nonessentials. "We had to go to the nesting ground by taxi or bus, and we always took our stores in an old pram." The research resulted in definitive books on the greenshank and three other species. Now the Nethersole-Thompsons are known throughout the world of bird experts.

Maybe we take all this wildlife too much for granted. The list of diminishing species is long. Sea eagles once nested near my house; they were wiped out at the turn of the century. But nowadays there is a new understanding, a new respect, and new hope for our ornithological wealth.

Derek Cooper

364

Today other Highland products have won appreciation beyond Scotland. When I flew to Islay recently, a lorry waited at the airstrip to load lobsters onto an aircraft for onward flight to the three-star restaurants of Paris, Brussels, and London. At Kirkwall Airport in the Orkneys a week later, I watched a plane being filled with crabs for Scandinavia. In Germany and Belgium the market for Highland venison is insatiable, and the herring that move in shoals from the Hebrides round to Peterhead have been exported to Europe since medieval times.

It's not only the sea that provides a rich Highland harvest. The farmhouse cheeses of the Orkneys, the mutton, lamb, beef, and fresh produce of the Highlands are appearing on more and more menus. Country-house hotels in the Highlands and Islands specialize in fresh local food, simply cooked. All are well worth seeking out.

One woman who keeps the old traditions alive is Rhoda Bulter, a folk poet who lives in Lerwick. Her poetry is not easy to understand—the Norse influence is strong in the Shetland vocabulary. Not for nothing do they claim that their nearest railway station is in Norway. Rhoda provides a glossary for the more way-out words—*hundiklok* for a large black beetle, *sharny bees* for dung flies.

When I called on her on Sunday morning, a warm smell of simmering soup and roasting was coming from the kitchen. "I think the young wives are getting very interested in the old ways," she says. "Like the way we work with our fish and mutton, the same as it's always been, because it's a very good way for working with it. Now that the

The deep past, etched in earth and stone, lives on in Scotland's islands. On Mainland Island in the Shetlands, a maze of ruins at Jarlshof (top) encompasses dwellings from Bronze Age huts to a 16th-century manor. On Orkney's main island, 12th-century Vikings carved runic graffiti (bottom) on the wall of a chambered tomb called Maes Howe, built around 2500 B.C. One inscription says that two Vikings snowbound in the tomb went mad. At Callanish on the Isle of Lewis in the Hebrides, a circle of stones (opposite), erected about 3,500 years ago, may be aligned to the sun, stars, and moon.

366

deep-freezes are in, a great deal of meat is eaten uncured, but the unique taste of the 'reestit' is still very popular."

Reestit mutton will keep for years. You take a leg or shoulder of mutton and put it in pickle. "Just coarse salt and water; it's reached the proper strength when a potato or an egg will float in it. The joints are pickled for about three weeks—you've got to make sure the salt penetrates right to the bone. Then you hang it up to drip, and dry it in a room with a peat fire until it's rock hard."

"O my! Whaat wid I gie eenoo for tattie soup wi reestit mutton," one of Rhoda's poems ends. You boil the mutton, skim off the fat and add potatoes, onion, turnip, and cabbage, maybe some carrots. That soup is delicious.

The Shetlanders threw nothing away. "We always used to eat the insides, or *faa,* of an animal. The tripe was cleaned, then stuffed with sweet or savory meats, then the puddings were boiled and could be eaten hot, or sliced when cold and fried or grilled. Onions and dried fruit would be included in the savory dish, or treacle and spices if a sweet pudding was preferred.

"Every house had milking cattle, and they made their own butter and kirn milk, a sort of cottage cheese but more solid. We sliced it and ate it with rhubarb jam."

> *O foo aften did I lick me lips as a waatched da flesh hang idda reest:*
> *Enjoy me slice a kirn mylk wi rhubarb jam, or a plate a beest.*

The most famous dish in Scotland is compounded of the bits of sheep that less frugal folk might well ignore. Haggis

Male Shetland ponies (opposite) scuffle on the rugged land that produced the gentle, long-lived breed. Small size and shaggy hair suit the hardy horses to the Shetlands' harsh climate. Fair Isle (top, right), a speck of land between Orkney and Shetland, is home to a few people and a stopover for migrating birds that land here by the thousands. Bird-watchers have spotted more than 335 species.

A Fair Isle knitter (bottom) pauses over a sweater whose geometrical pattern resembles Viking designs that have also been found in Norway, Iceland, and in the Soviet Union along the Volga.

OVERLEAF: *"Then light the torch and form the march and sound the rolling drum,"* revelers sing; *"wake the mighty memories of heroes."* It's the Up-Helly-Aa Fire Festival at Lerwick in the Shetlands, when torch bearers set a boat ablaze to end the Yule holidays in a salute to Norse ancestors.

Pages 370-371: Michael St. Maur Sheil

369

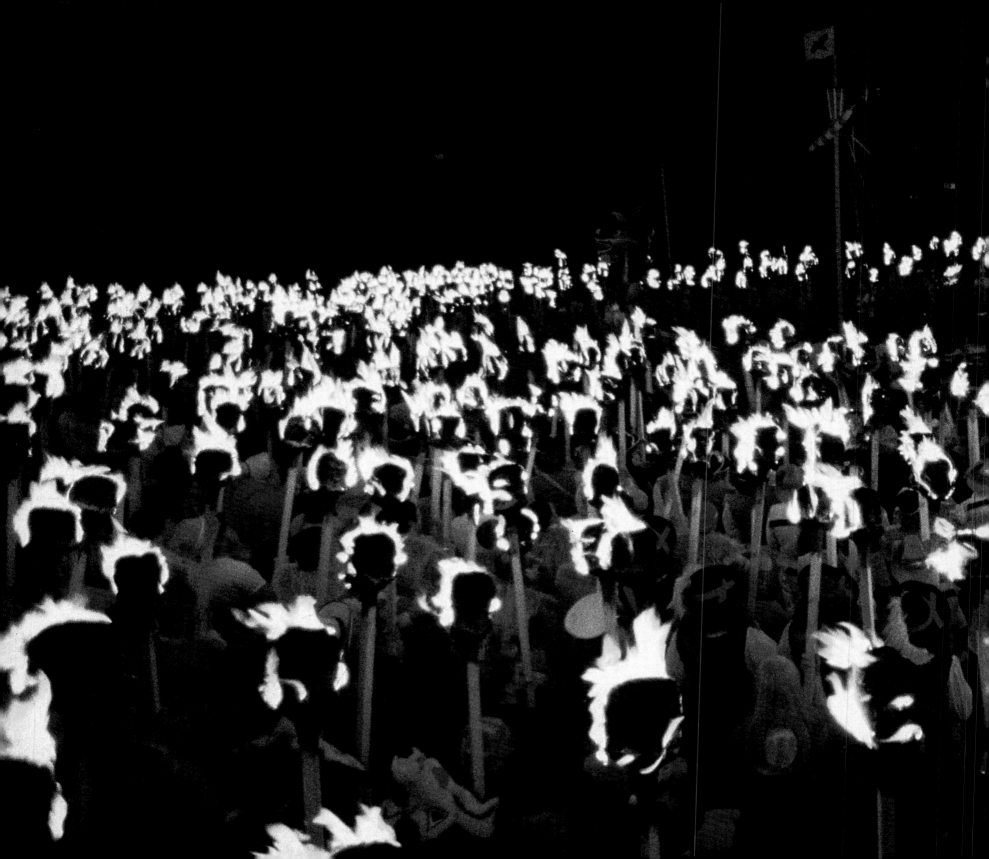

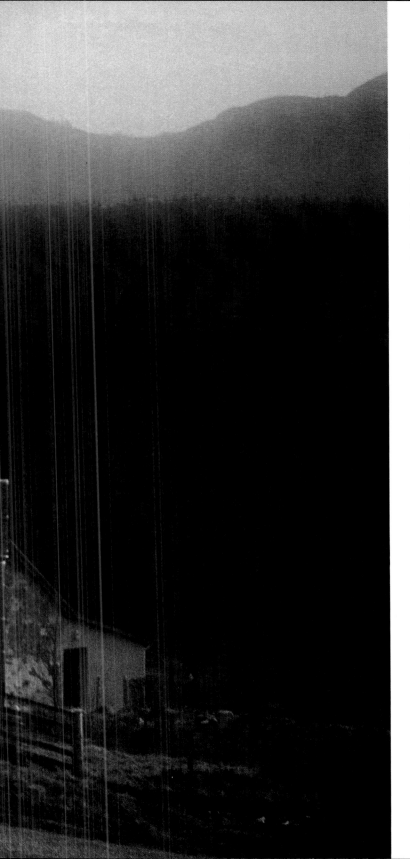

is a round sausage, slightly smaller than a bowling pin, stuffed into the stomach bag of a sheep. (These days, the bag is more likely to be synthetic.) You need oatmeal, chopped mutton suet, the liver of the sheep, along with its heart and lungs, and an onion. When you have toasted the oatmeal until it is crisp, you mix the ingredients together, sew them into the sheep's stomach, and then boil the bag for four or five hours. Haggis is traditionally served on New Year's Eve (Hogmanay) with potatoes and turnips (tatties and neeps) and plentiful libations of good malt whisky.

Today Shetland has a multimillion-pound petrochemical complex and advanced oil-related technology, but it's nice to know that the Rhodas of this world are keeping the old memories alive, even while all about her are tucking into frozen pizzas and Coca-Cola.

Indeed, I see this respect for the past as a very necessary part of the survival kit we all need. Maybe that's why the Highlands and Islands are becoming increasingly attractive to the walking wounded of the consumer society. Even in high summer, when the tourists flock north, there's no sense of overcrowding; the peace and tranquillity is still tangible. Step out of your car, take a turn over the brow of a hill, and you can be alone. Being able to hear silence—that's unusual. Being able to see, from a peak in the Cuillins, the islands of the west, spread out in what Wordsworth called "the silence of the seas among the farthest Hebrides," is well worth the long haul to the top.

Golf, sailing, climbing—it's all there if you want it. And if you want to learn to weave, throw pots—even pan for gold—someone will show you how to do it. In winter the great granite hinterland of the Cairngorms becomes a cross between a tartan-clad St. Moritz and a Highland Sun Valley. Its ski slopes are black with weekend novices and at night the revelries go on into the small hours.

Today the Highlands are peppered with fugitives from the urban jungle. Whether living in so remote a place will make them any happier is up to them. But at least if happiness eludes them, they can be miserable in one of the most magical and awe-inspiring landscapes in the world.

By Thomas B. Allen
Photographs by Colin Jones

The East of Ireland

There is honey in the trees where her misty
vales expand,
And her forest paths, in summer, are by falling
waters fann'd,
There is dew at high noontide there, and springs
i' the yellow sand,
On the fair hills of holy Ireland.

Irish song, 17th century

A patchwork of green hills in County Cavan

A republic eventually came to pass but the
sorrows and the troubles have never left that tragic,
lovely land. For you see, in Ireland there is
no future, only the past happening over and over.

LEON URIS, *Trinity,* 1976

The traveler in Ireland walks paths dappled by the light of the present and the shadow of the past. The welcoming Irish sing songs of yesterday, reciting to the traveler the sweet poetry of past glories and, often with as much ardor, the harsh words of remembered grievances. The past lives in Ireland, unforgotten and unforgiven.

The traveler's map shows boundaries both real and imagined. On this map the imagined realm, Ireland, is a mystical memory, for the reality is two bitterly separated Irelands that call themselves Northern Ireland and the Republic of Ireland. The map also divides the island into the four provinces of Connaught, Munster, Leinster, and Ulster, each the relic of a vanished kingdom, each possessing a proud heraldic shield and, now, little else. The provinces do not exist in the bureaucracy of the island's modern nations; they symbolize an ancient, spiritually united Ireland, untouched by the British, who would one day come as conquerors. The Republic, independent since 1922, encompasses three of the provinces and part of the fourth, Ulster. All of Northern Ireland, still under British rule, lies within sundered Ulster.

My travels in Ireland took me through the two eastern provinces: Leinster, with Dublin at its heart, and Ulster, whose coasts are wildly beautiful and whose shield bears the emblem of a bloody severed hand.

I began in the south of Leinster, in County Wexford. The town of Wexford, deep within a bay, was named and settled in the ninth century by the Vikings. Tall, blue-eyed descendants of those invaders of Celtic Ireland still walk the narrow streets of Wexford. So do the dark-eyed descendants of the Normans, the Vikings' triumphant successors.

One of Wexford's Norman bequests is Nicky Furlong, a writer and historian. He bears the name of a mercenary hired by a deposed Irish king in 1169 to help him fight his enemies. "When the king who hired the mercenaries died, they stayed here, and Henry II was afraid out of his wits that a rival kingdom would be set up," Nicky told me in his

living-history style. "He came to Ireland in 1171 and made all sorts of arrangements with the Irish kings. That was the beginning of the Anglo-Irish problem."

I spent my Wexford nights guarded by the ruined tower of a small 13th-century Norman castle called Killiane. The ruins blended into the walls of a three-story farmhouse that provided an aura of history, along with bed and breakfast. My journeys into the past, usually with Nicky as escort, began there each day. From Norman times we soon moved on to the murderous reign of Oliver Cromwell.

Cromwell, leading his army of English Puritans to fight in Ireland, ravaged Wexford as mercilessly as he did other towns rebelling against English rule. Tradition says that between massacres in 1649 he rested in conquered Wexford at a waterside castle with a notorious "murder hole." Victims were plunged through the hole to a convenient eddy in the harbor. A Woolworth store now occupies the lethal castle. Flashlight in hand, the store's amiable manager took me into his cellar, where we could see the arches and the bricked-up passages of Cromwell's terrible days.

The next visit to the past took me to a crossroad on the outskirts of Wexford and to 1798, when, in a bloody, short-lived insurrection, men armed with barely more than sharpened pikes marched against British muskets. "There were so many killed at this particular point," Nicky said, "that they were simply tossed to the sides of the road. The only side where they weren't tossed was the corner that had a tavern"—he pointed to a spot where a cottage now stands. "They were buried in unmarked graves, and the

Two governments share this island of four provinces—Ulster and Leinster on the east, Munster and Connaught on the west. The Republic of Ireland encompasses all of three provinces and three of Ulster's counties: Cavan, Monaghan, and Donegal. Heavily Protestant Northern Ireland voted to stay with Britain when the rest of the island, mostly Catholic, won independence. In Dublin, capital of the Republic, a girl playing a tin whistle (opposite) marches in support of Irish culture. In the religious battleground of Northern Ireland, violent groups fight over past grievances and future power.

379

National Museum of Ireland: Lee Boltin

land has never been interfered with or plowed or built upon. I think that it's rather sad there is no monument."

Travel in Ireland is time travel. And everywhere there is someone like Nicky, a medium who will summon up the past, who will try to explain the Irish. "There's a great difference between the English mentality and the Irish," Nicky said one day, "primarily because the Irish way of life is Celtic, hooked to a much earlier civilization and way of looking at things. An Englishman may rigidly obey a sign to 'Keep Off the Grass.' An Irishman might ignore the sign if the grass offered a shortcut."

Before I left County Wexford I made an American pilgrimage to Slieve Coilte, the hill graced by the John F. Kennedy Park. By bestowing a commanding height to the President's memory, the Irish gave him their own traditional remembrance for fallen heroes. Row upon row of dark evergreens stood like honor guards on the slope. Families walked about the top of the hill, and fathers stooped to tell their children who was honored here. From the broad summit I looked out to the endless, shimmering greens of distant fields. Somewhere below was Dunganstown, birthplace of John Kennedy's great-grandfather.

From nearly any hill in Ireland you can look down upon villages that gave their sons and daughters to America—more than one and a half million from 1845 to 1859 alone. Talk to any clerk who keeps town records, and he will tell you of the Americans coming in search of their roots.

Like many Americans of Irish ancestry, I know little about my Irish ancestors. "Not unusual," said one of those

High Cross and high art proclaim Ireland's early Christian era, when the new faith inspired works rooted in Celtic tradition. A cross at St. Canice's Cathedral in Kilkenny (right) preserves the design of early High Crosses. Over 150 survive in Ireland and a few in Britain. The circle that typifies most

High Crosses may be a remnant of sun worship, or it simply may be a support. Celtic symbols adorn the robe of crucified Christ (left) in a bronze plaque from around A.D. 700. Eighth-century gold and silver Ardagh Chalice (top), found in a potato field, lists all Apostles but Judas under its gold band.

James P. Blair, National Geographic Photographer

Robert W. Madden, National Geographic Staff

Seeking knowledge of "the goodly race" (as an old Irish poem describes horses), young apprentices watch a farrier at work. He shoes horses and teaches his ancient craft at the School of Farriery in the Irish National Stud near Kildare. National Stud officials decide by ballot which mares are to mate with prize stallions. One Stud stallion sired 57 major winners. Some potential champions bred at the Stud are leased to the President of Ireland and race in his colors. Private studs, such as Ballylinch and Noreland in County Kilkenny (right), also produce new members of Ireland's goodly race.

Cotton Coulson

keepers of the books, a Registrar of Births, Deaths, and Marriages. "People then didn't want to give information about themselves. We were under the British. And the clerks, well, who knows? They worked for the British. Reason enough for keeping quiet."

I wandered northward, following a fitful spring through bursts of sun and sudden squalls, into deep glens, past streams swollen by the rains and the burden of winter's melt. Along the narrow, stone-walled lanes, the first yellow blooms were peeking from clumps of spiky gorse. The sheep had begun to drop their lambs, and white dots punctuated distant greening pastures.

Then, down a road of many turnings, I came upon a medieval town. In the sixth century, long before the British, the Normans, or the Vikings, an Irish saint is said to have founded a monastic settlement that became known as *Cill Chainnigh,* the church of St. Canice. By the 13th century a great cathedral crowned the church hill, and the town was called Kilkenny, frequent site of English-controlled parliaments during centuries of warring between the Anglo-Normans and the subjugated Irish.

Kilkenny, one of the best preserved medieval towns in Ireland, lies along both banks of the River Nore, which, flowing southward, empties into the sea near Waterford. On days as gray as Kilkenny's old stones, I entered abbeys and churchyards, wandered along whimsically named lanes—Velvet, Pudding, Gooseberry—and walked beneath the arches of alleys called slips.

The cathedral, ravaged by Cromwell's troops in 1650 and duly repaired, was being repaired again when I explored its cool, lofty beauty. I was entranced by the mementos of humanity enshrined in its stones: A slab on the floor asks in Norman French that the passerby say a prayer for a man buried in 1280. Other worn slabs bear the carved images of the tools that the dead used in life—a shoemaker's awl, a carpenter's square, a weaver's loom.

During the Reformation, the cathedral changed from Roman Catholic to its present Protestant affiliation. In the time of Cromwell, the Catholic faith went underground in

Little Bits of Ireland that Go up in Smoke

"Buye the dry Turf, buye Turf.... Here's the dry Bog-a-Wood," the turfsellers cried in 18th-century Dublin, selling peat by the donkeyload. Today, huge machines clank across the bogs, harvesting peat by the ton.

Peat, the youngest member of the coal family, is a mixture of dead, partially decayed bog plants and spongelike mosses. New moss grows over the older moss, which dies and sinks under water. Eventually, the layer of peat thickens enough to break through the water, becoming the soggy surface of a bog. At times an undrained bog may look solid, but it is about 95 percent water; there is more solid matter in milk than in raw peat.

Bord na Móna, the Irish Peat Development Authority, scientifically carries on Ireland's long tradition of digging up peat for fuel. The board controls some 200,000 acres of bog and supervises draining and harvesting, as well as reclamation of exhausted bogs for pastureland.

To harvest a bog, the cutting machine scoops up soggy peat from a bank several feet high, chews and shapes the peat into neat bricks called sods, and drops them from its 180-foot arm in long rows (top) to dry. Later, other machines will lift, turn, pile, and eventually collect the sods.

At many such commercial bogs, small trains carry peat directly to power stations. Peat, which has kept Irish home fires burning for centuries, now produces about 20 percent of Irish electricity.

Bogland covers about one-seventh of Ireland. To conserve some of it, places such as Glenveagh National Park in County Donegal are posted as off-limits for peat pickers (bottom, center).

The Irish call self-harvested peat "hand-won turf," which is cut and collected on their own land or in leased bogs (bottom, left). To get a year's supply of turf for an average Irish house—some 12 to 15 tons—a family must work about 160 hours. Peat on the

Cotton Coulson. Below: Colin Jones (also opposite left)

hearth (bottom, right) heats better than wood and about half as well as coal.

Turf cutters carve out sods one by one, using a *sleán,* a special kind of spade. A good cutter slices out a complete sod, or turf, in one clean stroke and "keeps a straight face,"—keeping the side of the bog bank vertical, not ragged. Over the centuries, each region developed its own kind of sleán, and someone might ask a stranger, "What foot do you dig with?" Catholics in some parts of Ireland once called Protestants "leftfooters" because of the way peat cutters in predominantly Protestant northern regions drove sleáns into the turf.

Bogs also yield clues to Ireland's deepest past. Turf seekers have dug up surprises that included well-preserved bodies 500 years old and Bronze Age treasures. "About onethird of the archaeological finds are from the peat bogs," says John Cooke, a Bord na Móna expert on peat. "The acids in the bogs preserve most organic material and precious metals. One of the most common finds in the bogs is butter, usually packed in wooden vessels. The bogs were their refrigerators. Maybe sometimes they just forgot where they put the butter."

THOMAS B. ALLEN

NOTICE

These lands are part of the Glenveagh National Park and are the property of the Commissioners for Public Works, 51 St. Stephens Green, Dublin 2. The cutting of turf and opening of new banks for the purpose of cutting turf is strictly forbidden. Persons found unlawfully cutting turf are liable to be prosecuted.

OIFIG NA nOIBREACHA POIBLÍ

Jim Brandenburg

Ireland; people in Kilkenny will still point out "Mass paths," the secret routes the faithful trod to attend forbidden Mass. Today, in a town where Catholics greatly outnumber Protestants, both faiths work together to repair and maintain Kilkenny's magnificent cathedral.

Alongside the cathedral stands a round tower 100 feet tall, erected by monks sometime in the days of Viking invasions. I climbed the stairs to the windswept roof and looked out upon Kilkenny.

The gray limestone tower of the Catholic cathedral, St. Mary's, rose from another hilltop. Below me I could see brewery trucks passing through the courtyard of an abandoned abbey. At a sharp bend of the Nore stood battlemented Kilkenny Castle, besieged by lawn and garden.

The castle's onetime stables, which I later visited, now house the Kilkenny Design Workshops, set up in 1963 to reawaken interest in Irish arts and crafts by encouraging high standards of design. Displays of exquisite woolens, ceramics, silver jewelry attest to the enduring influence of the designers who inspired an Irish renaissance.

In the village of Avoca, in County Wicklow, I heard how ideas from Kilkenny helped to preserve an Irish craft. I found Avoca on a day when cold winds billowed heavy sheets of rain, a day when people walking in the rain smile, nod to the stranger, and say, with stubborn faith, "It's a grand day." Dripping, I entered one of the long, low, whitewashed farm buildings that house the inheritors of Ireland's oldest handweaving tradition.

Inside the snug headquarters of Avoca Handweavers, I saw, in piles of woven wool, muted colors snatched from Irish fields and skies. Wool has been woven near the mill stream here since the early 18th century, when, so the story goes, the miller began trading his services for the fleece that the farmers brought in with their grain.

"The mill operated until the 1920s," said Jim Barry, who runs the mill shop. "It was run by three sisters. They kept the weaving going when the mill failed. And if anyone was sick, they would come down from the house with a jar of jam and two apples."

He went on to tell how, when the last sister died in 1960, her nephew took over but soon had to sell the mill to a lawyer. "He made all the weavers redundant and said he was going to make the thatched cottages, where they did the weaving, into cottages for Yank tourists." That venture never got started, and the next owner decided to bring back the weavers and try to save the craft. He went to Kilkenny Design, where experts advised him to stick with handlooms and told him what designs would sell in foreign markets. "And we got a production manager from Kilkenny," Jim said, shaking his head at the thought of it all. "It's a frightening operation we have now."

Avoca lies in the glen country of County Wicklow, a tight little realm of coast (Continued on page 394)

Polo players on wheeled steeds tangle at Phoenix Park in the heart of Dublin. Five times larger than Hyde Park, it is one of the biggest urban parks in Europe. In Kildare (opposite), young boxers tangle in a ring set up in the middle of town. On a nearby plain, 19th-century boxers fought bare-knuckle. Ireland and Northern Ireland, though separate politically, unite for boxing and many other sports. Ireland's Olympic Council draws athletes from both sides of the border.

387

Joyce's Dublin, the City that Became a Masterpiece

James Joyce, who gave literary immortality to Dublin's streets and people, once wondered how fair he had been to Dublin. "I have reproduced none of the attractions of the city," he wrote. "I have not been just to its beauty."

But posterity has judged him just, for Joyce wrote of the city's deep and honest beauty, as in *The Dubliners*: "The streets, shuttered for the repose of Sunday, swarmed with a gaily coloured crowd. Like illumined pearls the lamps shone from the summits of their tall poles upon the living texture below which, changing shape and hue unceasingly, sent up into the warm grey evening air an unchanging, unceasing murmur."

Joyce, who lived at more than 15 places in the city of his birth, grew to manhood in a riches-to-rags family. He reflects this life in the autobiographical *A Portrait of the Artist as a Young Man*. Stephen Dedalus, the title character, says his father is "a bankrupt and at present a praiser of his own past." And Stephen says his own soul is "disquieted and cast down by the dull phenomenon of Dublin."

Trinity College in Dublin had produced many distinguished writers, ranging from Thomas Moore and Oliver Goldsmith to Oscar Wilde. But Trinity had a Protestant tinge. Joyce's devoutly Catholic family sent him instead to University College.

In 1904, two years after graduation, Joyce left Dublin, driven into self-exile like so many Irish writers before and since. He summed up the oppression that banished him in a bitter phrase: "Ireland is the old sow that eats her farrow." What he wanted to write—harshly realistic, explicitly

Bettina Cirone. Right: Colin Jones

"A veiled sunlight lit up faintly the grey sheet of water" and "the dim fabric of the city lay prone in haze." The words of James Joyce (death mask, left) enframe a Dublin moment.

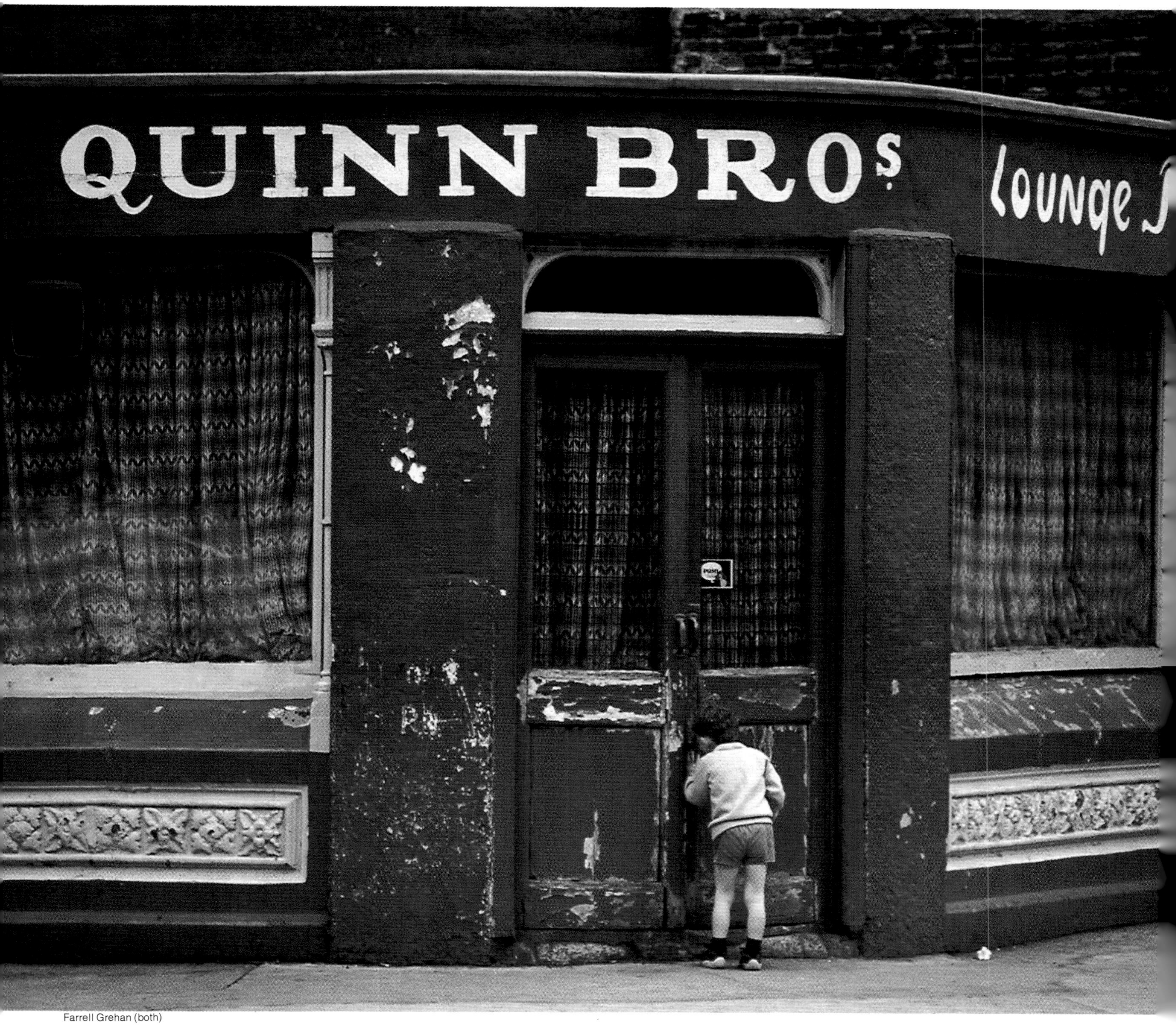

Farrell Grehan (both)

sensual truth about human beings—could not be published in the pietistic Ireland of his time.

Joyce worked in Europe the rest of his life, returning to Ireland only for three short visits. But his writer's eye looked always to Dublin. He wrote to friends and relatives there, asking them detailed questions about the city's streets, buildings, even the species of certain trees. He wanted to create a Dublin so real that if the city suddenly disappeared it could be rebuilt from the pages of his novel. The book, *Ulysses,* was published in Paris in 1922, and if the English language were ever destroyed, it could be rebuilt from this masterpiece.

Just as the first Ulysses, Homer's hero of the *Odyssey,* spends much of his life wandering the isles of Greece, Joyce's hero wanders, but through a maze of city streets and through a single day: Thursday, June 16, 1904.

The 300,000-word tragicomic novel opens at the Martello Tower, where Stephen Dedalus lives (and Joyce himself once briefly stayed). But the focus of the book is on a Dubliner named Leopold Bloom, who begins the day by walking out of No. 7, Eccles Street. As Bloom and Dedalus walk about—and ultimately cross paths—the reader meets numerous Dubliners and experiences moments of their mingled lives.

Working far from Dublin, Joyce used detailed maps, along with a watch to time characters' movements from one Dublin scene to another. He created not only a tightly woven tapestry of a city and its people but also the route for a literary pilgrimage.

Joyceans—devoted fans of the writer—annually celebrate June 16 as Bloomsday, walking where Leopold Bloom and Stephen Dedalus walked, seeking out the places mentioned in the book. The Martello Tower, about eight miles from the center of Dublin, still stands. (The British built the towers against a possible invasion by Napoleon.) The adjacent bathing beach where Stephen and the two other residents of the tower go also still exists. The tower has become a museum, which contains Joyce's

---

Dubliners in Ulysses *pass a myriad of windows and "the sloping mirror of Peter Kennedy, hairdresser." Bloom wondered how to "cross Dublin without passing a pub." Quinn's (opposite) is one of hundreds of pubs in the city.*

waistcoat, his guitar, and his death mask. He died in Switzerland in 1941.

Bloom walked out of a real address to begin his day. The building has been torn down, but the door of No. 7 was salvaged and is displayed at a pub, the Bailey. A haunt of writers and gamblers, it was called the Burton Restaurant in *Ulysses.*

Bloom also walks past "Trinity's surly front" and through the shopping district centered on Grafton Street. The shopping scene has little changed—"Muslin prints, silk, dames and dowagers." But shoppers no longer hear the "jingle of harnesses."

Although much of Joyce's Dublin has disappeared, the city remains a literary landmark for him and for other writers who lived here. The names of many are linked to Merrion Square, a spacious block designed in the 18th century. Georgian mansions line three sides, with a park on the south. Over the years, the handsome Georgian homes with exquisite doors were occupied by the eminent, most of them neighbors only in time: Oscar Wilde lived at No. 1; William Butler Yeats at No. 52 and No. 82; Daniel O'Connell, the great political hero, at No. 58; and the pioneer mystery writer J.

Sheridan Le Fanu at No. 70. Le Fanu's tales of the supernatural are said to have inspired Bram Stoker, the author of *Dracula,* who lived near the square during his Dublin days. Engineers, barristers, and government agencies now occupy the square.

A brass plaque marks the grave of Jonathan Swift in St. Patrick's Cathedral, where he was dean. He lies buried, says his epitaph, "where savage indignation can no longer lacerate his heart."

Dublin's Abbey Theatre gave a stage to Yeats and other dramatists: Lady Gregory, J. M. Synge, George Moore, and Sean O'Casey. Richard Sheridan and George Bernard Shaw were both Dublin-born.

What Yeats said about Ireland's mythical heroes holds true for its literary giants as well, especially in Dublin: They exist because "they lived in the places where we ride and go marketing, and sometimes they have met one another on the hills that cast their shadows upon our doors at evening."

THOMAS B. ALLEN

Busts of the forgotten famous line the soaring Long Room of Trinity College's library, where the Book of Kells is kept.

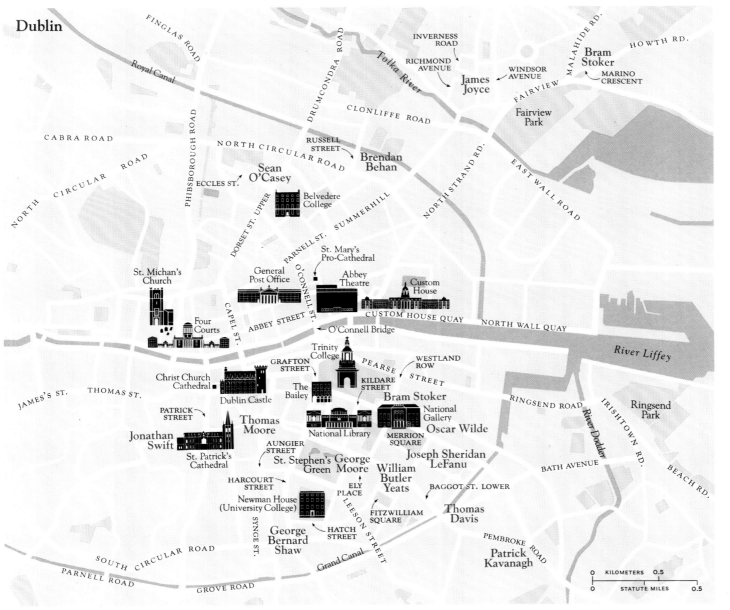

Dublin

FINGLAS ROAD

Royal Canal

Tolka River

INVERNESS ROAD

RICHMOND AVENUE

WINDSOR AVENUE

HOWTH RD.

Bram Stoker

MARINO CRESCENT

James Joyce

FAIRVIEW

CABRA ROAD

DRUMCONDRA ROAD

CLONLIFFE ROAD

Fairview Park

NORTH CIRCULAR ROAD

RUSSELL STREET

NORTH STRAND RD.

EAST WALL ROAD

NORTH CIRCULAR ROAD

PHIBSBOROUGH ROAD

ECCLES ST.

Sean O'Casey

Brendan Behan

DORSET ST. UPPER

Belvedere College

SUMMERHILL

PARNELL ST.

St. Mary's Pro-Cathedral

St. Michan's Church

General Post Office

O'CONNELL ST.

Abbey Theatre

Custom House

Four Courts

CAPEL ST.

ABBEY STREET

CUSTOM HOUSE QUAY

NORTH WALL QUAY

O'Connell Bridge

River Liffey

JAMES'S ST.

THOMAS ST.

GRAFTON STREET

Trinity College

PEARSE

WESTLAND ROW

STREET

RINGSEND ROAD

IRISHTOWN RD.

Ringsend Park

Christ Church Cathedral

The Bailey

KILDARE STREET

Dublin Castle

River Dodder

BEACH RD.

Bram Stoker

PATRICK STREET

National Gallery

Oscar Wilde

National Library

MERRION SQUARE

BATH AVENUE

Jonathan Swift

Thomas Moore

St. Patrick's Cathedral

AUNGIER STREET

George Moore

Joseph Sheridan LeFanu

St. Stephen's Green

William Butler Yeats

Thomas Davis

HARCOURT STREET

ELY PLACE

Newman House (University College)

FITZWILLIAM SQUARE

BAGGOT ST. LOWER

PEMBROKE ROAD

SYNGE ST.

LEESON STREET

HATCH STREET

George Bernard Shaw

Patrick Kavanagh

SOUTH CIRCULAR ROAD

Grand Canal

PARNELL ROAD

GROVE ROAD

KILOMETERS 0.5

STATUTE MILES 0.5

A City of Writers

Brendan Behan, *1923-1964, 14 Russell Street*

Thomas Davis, *1814-1845, 67 Baggot Street Lower*

James Joyce, *1882-1941, 13 Richmond Avenue; 8 Inverness Road; 29 Windsor Avenue*

Patrick Kavanagh, *1904-1967, 62 Pembroke Road*

Joseph Sheridan Le Fanu, *1814-1873, 70 Merrion Square*

George Moore, *1852-1933, 4 Ely Place*

Thomas Moore, *1779-1852, 12 Aungier Street*

Sean O'Casey, *1880-1964, 85 Dorset Street Upper; 422 N. Circular Road*

George Bernard Shaw, *1856-1950, 33 Synge Street; 1 Hatch Street; 61 Harcourt Street*

Bram Stoker, *1847-1912, 15 Marino Crescent; 30 Kildare Street*

Jonathan Swift, *1667-1745, St. Patrick's Cathedral*

Oscar Wilde, *1854-1900, 1 Merrion Square; 21 Westland Row*

William Butler Yeats, *1865-1939, 52 Merrion Square; 82 Merrion Square; 42 Fitzwilliam Square*

From satirist Jonathan Swift, who was dean of St. Patrick's Cathedral, to Brendan Behan, who boasted he was thrown out of every pub in the city, Dublin has sheltered, and sometimes spurned, its writers. All brought their country fame as a place impassioned by words. One poet, Thomas Davis, put this passion into a ballad that still stirs Irish hearts and hopes: "A Nation Once Again."

and mountain, of seashore cliff walks and forest paths, with a 400-foot waterfall and, near Avoca, a tranquil valley celebrated in poetry as "that vale in whose bosom the bright waters meet."

In a wild Wicklow valley called Glendalough, "glen of the two lakes," broken crosses stand over lakeshores where Irish clans buried their kings. And long before that, Bronze Age farmers lived here and kept their animals behind stone walls. Near a circle of those stones a stream flows under a wooden bridge. A path leads from the bridge to the arched gateway of what once was a huge monastic community. Today all that remains are crumbling churches, a graveyard of jumbled headstones, and a round tower.

The shells of churches and the other hallowed ruins trace to St. Kevin, a reclusive sixth-century monk who founded an ecclesiastical city that drew scholars from throughout Christendom. By the ninth century it had become known as the "Rome of the Western World." Plundering Vikings frequently swept down upon it from their stronghold in Dublin, about 30 miles to the north. But the monastery managed to survive until the 13th century.

I clambered up the steep path that led to a spur of rock overlooking one of the two dark lakes. Tradition puts here the stone hut where St. Kevin prayed in solitude and lived on berries and fruit. Farther up, on a cliff face, is a cave known as St. Kevin's Bed. Here, legend says, Kathleen, a beautiful temptress with "eyes of most unholy blue," tried to seduce him. Enraged, he hurled her into the lake.

Down from the hill, making my way through the tilted

A Dublin family pauses near church on first Communion Day, a spiritual milestone for Catholics. In the Liberties—an area near St. Patrick's Cathedral once beyond civil jurisdiction—children scrub a street shrine prior to a procession. Religious holidays fill the calendar of a society that is over 90 percent Catholic. British laws against Catholics strengthened the faith and spurred insurrection. With independence came close church-state ties. They loosened in 1972 when voters abolished constitutional recognition of the Catholic Church's "special position" as "the guardian of the faith."

stones of the graveyard, I stopped and looked beyond to the misty mountains that rose at the end of the long valley. It had been a day of flickering rain. Now, suddenly, the skies began to clear, and across the valley arched a rainbow that vanished as quickly as an apparition.

West of the mountains and the glens of Wicklow the great Central Plain begins. On the eastern edge, near the town of Kildare, is one of Ireland's greatest horse tracks. The Curragh, which means "racecourse" in Irish, gives its name not only to the modern track but also to the 5,000-acre plain around it, where horses have raced for 2,000 years. And here are bred and trained Irish Thoroughbreds.

The Irish National Stud, unlike the other horse farms around the Curragh, is owned by the Irish government. Máire O'Connor, deputy manager and veterinary surgeon, took me with her while she made her rounds one morning. She told me of the Stud's foster-mother service for orphaned foals. Leaning on the fence of a tree-bordered field, we watched a chestnut foal nuzzling a black foster mother. "A foal can be raised by human hands," Máire said, "but a foster mother's better. She'll give a little nudge now and then that says, 'Mind your manners.' "

One night I stood in the doorway of a foaling stall when a mare named American Beauty began pawing at the clean straw. "Better get John," the night man ordered a helper. When John walked into the stall, he pulled on a plastic glove that reached to his shoulder and examined the mare internally as she stood stoically, her eyes unblinking, wisps of steam rising from her body. Soon she dropped to the straw and lay on her side.

John knelt and checked that the foal was emerging properly. "Filly," he said softly. "A nice little girl."

On my way to Dublin from the Curragh, I often saw clusters of battered car trailers along the roadside. Clothing and windblown trash hung on bushes behind the trailers. Children of all sizes ran about piles of junk and burned-out cars. Men and women gathered around wood fires or stared, unsmiling, at the cars passing by. They seemed a breed apart from the other Irish I had met.

When I talked to Maggie Connors, I learned just how apart they were. Disdainfully called tinkers by some, they prefer the name "travelers," and travel is what they do, moving from one place to another, staying where they like for as long as they like.

Maggie, mother of six daughters and four sons, lived in an illegal but tolerated traveler encampment on a highway on the western outskirts of Dublin. Her trailer was one of about 140 parked in a jumble of kids, horses, dogs, and wrecked cars, all engulfed in a surf of litter. The travelers had taken over a mile and a half stretch of the two eastbound lanes, forcing all traffic into the westbound lanes.

Travelers occupy Irish history the way they occupied the Dublin highway: No one knows how they got there; no one knows why they travel; no one knows where to put them. They baffle social workers as well as historians. They are known only as the people of the road, descendants of others like them—the original tinkers, the uprooted of Cromwell's rampages, the hungry of the famines, the men and women fleeing some unspoken fate.

Maggie answered questions with a charming vagueness. How do she and her children manage to get along without water or a bathroom? She has a relative down the road who has "found a spigot," where they can fill large milk cans. "Everybody here has to work out their own arrangement," she said. Arrangements include a nearby river and toilets in the rare shops and pubs that will serve travelers.

"All of the children have received their first Communion, and the young ones go to school," Maggie said proudly. Traveler children usually get little schooling. The boys help the elder males salvage scrap metal from abandoned cars. The girls must help with the babies.

Travelers have far more children than settled families do. A social worker in one camp found three women who had had 20 pregnancies each. A typical family has 10 to 12 children. "The women are the people with the strength," says Maggie, who is raising her children on her own. "The men aren't worth a damn."

I did not feel I had reached Dublin until I saw the gray,

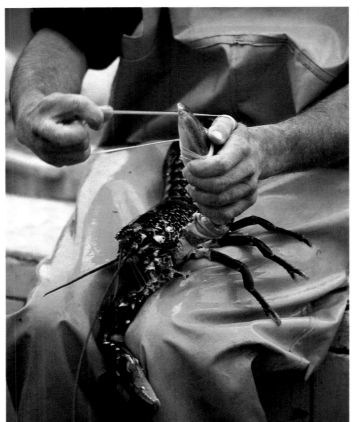

Dunfanaghy, a County Donegal port in the province of Ulster, reflects the tranquillity of a local adage—it's so protected that even the devil cannot enter. Beyond its tight little bay, in the surging Atlantic off the 600-foot cliffs of Horn Head (opposite), lobstermen seek their prey and bind claws of lobsters (left) that closely resemble the American species. Ireland, whose lobster catch ranks behind the United Kingdom and France, exports most of its lobsters live to France. In Donegal, they say someone who lets you down "did the turn of the lobster," slipping from responsibility as stealthily as wily shellfish do when they back out of traps.

397

old River Liffey winding past the quays, until I crossed the O'Connell Bridge on foot. From this hub, the city of Dublin beckons in all directions. But no matter where I walked in Dublin, I was drawn again and again back to the Liffey and this bridge so full of Irish walkers and prams.

The Dublin Tourist Trail begins near a big gray building, where Ireland vowed to become, as the song says, "a nation once again." Here at the General Post Office, on Easter Monday in 1916, the Rising began against British rule. Barricaded in the post office, a band of patriots proclaimed the Republic "In the name of God and the dead generations. . . ." The British quickly put down the rebellion and executed its leaders. But the Rising lived on, through military occupation by notoriously brutal troops called, because of their uniforms, the Black and Tans. After an uneasy truce brought a treaty and independence in 1922, Ireland fought a short civil war over the terms of the treaty.

The Tourist Trail took me on to Trinity College and the National Museum, past Merrion Square (blue plaques marking the homes of Oscar Wilde, William Butler Yeats, and other notables), and around St. Stephen's Green.

I listened to Irish voices in word and song, on the stage of the Abbey Theatre, where the players in Patrick Kavanagh's *Tarry Flynn* spoke in countryside rhythms I could barely fathom; in pubs where men and women sang and where, in one nonstop half hour, an architect quoted me poetry of Ireland, England, and America, analyzed the politics of the three countries, and held forth on the aesthetics of Irish tombs, crystal, and stout.

I walked the inner city, enjoying a pint in rundown pubs renowned for absolutely nothing and recommended by nobody. I strolled the Liberties (so named because the streets once lay beyond the jurisdiction of the Lord Mayor), where sellers cried their wares—"four packets of peanuts for 50 pence"—and some buyers bargained: "Well, now, I'm on a widow's pension. . . ."

I went to a meeting of Concerned Parents Against Drugs in a neighborhood where the young have discovered heroin. The parents' solution was to march on the flats of

accused drug pushers and evict them instantly, without legal formalities. (This inspired the founding of a group called Concerned Criminals. They said that as decent thieves who did not push drugs they were concerned about the breakdown of the criminal justice system.)

Places as well as people wove the threads of my journey. In the faint light of Trinity College Library, I saw the exquisitely illuminated Book of Durrow, which dates to the seventh century, and the ninth-century Book of Kells, which contains the four gospels and some other rare bits of biblical manuscripts. I remembered the mystic beauty of Durrow, in County Offaly, where monks had lovingly created their book. There, in Durrow's monastic ruins, in a deep-shadowed graveyard, against a setting sun, I had seen the High Cross triumphant.

On a warming spring day I visited an even deeper past. About 30 miles northwest of Dublin, in the broad valley of the River Boyne, stand huge circular mounds traditionally called Brugh na Bóinne, the graveyard of the pagan kings. Archaeologists estimate that people lived there as early as 4500 B.C., but these mounds—the great passage tombs—probably date to 3000 B.C.

I joined a group following a guide into the dimly lit Newgrange tomb. At dawn on the day of winter solstice—and only at that dawn—the sun's rays enter through an opening at the tomb's entrance, beam down the 62 feet of the passage, and bathe the corbeled burial chamber in light.

We stood inside a cairn of loose stones skillfully assembled to form a mound 280 feet in diameter and in some

Neighborhoods bear religious labels in Belfast, a city at war with itself. Rows of terrace houses flank Woodstock Road in Protestant East Belfast. In the Catholic neighborhood of Falls Road, sidewalks become the stages for tableaux of latent violence (opposite): a combat-ready British soldier watching for trouble, a camera-shy walker, an inquisitive face in a doorway, another soldier backing up. Down the street, a wire cage protects the patrons of the Blackstaff pub from bricks and bombs. British troops arrived in Northern Ireland in 1969 after several people were killed in sectarian clashes.

Cary Wolinsky

places 44 feet high. Many stones have been incised with spirals and circles. Experts on the tombs believe they are the work of a people whose way of life had gone beyond the survival level. With their time and talent they built something spiritual, the cathedrals of their era.

Ten miles south of the tombs I climbed the great Hill of Tara, where the High Kings of Ireland reigned until, sometime in the sixth century, Christianity took hold in the pagan realm. At the peak of its glory Tara saw splendor unmatched in much of Europe. Annals tell of King Cormac adorned with gold from sandals to shield; of fairs resounding with the music of "trumpets, harps, widemouthed horns;" of a banquet hall 700 feet long, where a thousand people could dine.

Sheep and crows dine here now, but lumpy mounds under the lush grass reveal the long, straight lines of the banquet hall and the ramparts of the Fort of the Kings. Out of one of the summit's mounds thrusts the Stone of Destiny, a five-foot granite shaft. Ancient legend gave the stone a magic voice that roared approval when the rightful aspirant approached it in quest of Ireland's throne. The stone was later moved to mark the burial place of rebels killed in the Rising of 1798. Thus do the Irish forge the links between present and past and deeper past.

Near here history began writing a chapter that remains unfinished today. In 1609 James I began populating Ulster with Protestants, mainly from Scotland, to take the place of Irish nobles who had fled into exile on the Continent (the Flight of the Earls). The Irish peasants were left behind to toil for the strangers.

In July 1690, Protestant William of Orange defeated Catholic James II at the Battle of the Boyne and so won the "War of the Two Kings." Within a decade Protestants, who by then made up 20 percent of the population, owned 86 percent of Ireland's land. Penal laws forbade Catholics to buy land or attend Mass. And the history made at the Boyne has marched on, through risings, through famine, through war, through the unending terrorism and the murders in the North today—the "Troubles."

Victorian Belfast lives again in the Crown Liquor Saloon on Great Victoria Street, a pub of such exquisite surprises (above) it is preserved by the National Trust—and by luck; it survived bombs of the Troubles. You can slip into a snug—a cubicle with a door that shuts out the world—and lift a glass in private. There you can toast the days when newsboys hawked headlines about triumphs in the Athens of the North, as the citizens called Belfast. A politician once denounced them as "a turbulent and disorderly sort of people, whom no king could govern or no God please." They still quote that tribute.

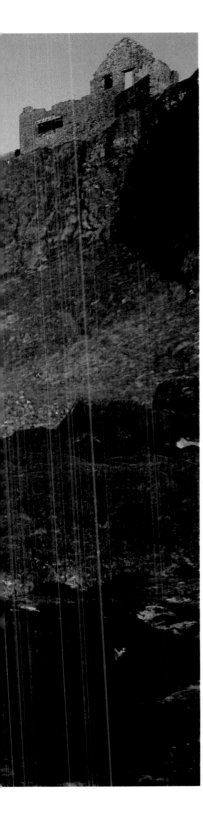

For when Britain granted Ireland independence, the Protestant-controlled parliament of the six northern counties exercised its right by treaty to remain with Britain. Now, every year on July 12, northern Protestants vigorously celebrate the Boyne victory. Many Irish Catholics do not speak of Northern Ireland but of the "Six Counties." Within those borders one faction views eventual unification with the Republic as indispensable, the other, as intolerable. And so they battle on, deep in the long shadow of unforgiven history.

Journeying north, I saw far more splendor than strife. The two Irelands of Ulster—three of its nine counties lie in the Republic—do not confront each other culturally. The tourist boards of the two governments, for instance, have jointly produced one map, which shows the unbounded beauty of the coast they share.

Along Northern Ireland's sea-pounded rim, I wandered the majestic turreted shell of Dunluce Castle, a ghostly fortress clinging to a stark crag. I walked the steep cliff paths and beaches of the Giant's Causeway, where thousands of basalt columns thrust from the sea or rib the cliffs, rank after rank. Glistening, geometrically arrayed stones pave the shore. Basaltic lava, oozing from huge cracks in the earth, cooled so uniformly that the process formed sharply sided, mostly hexagonal columns.

I could easily forget the Troubles at the edge of the sea. From County Donegal of the one Ireland to County Down of the other, the coast has a capricious beauty, shifting from sweeping glen to sweeping beach, from chalk white cliff to grassy slope, from thunderous wave to placid bay. But in the North's cities, patrolled by armed men, I could never forget the Troubles.

In Belfast even the taxis can be sectarian. I took a black taxi from the gritty Catholic neighborhood of Falls Road to the central shopping area. Four fellow passengers—a man, two women, and a young boy—eyed me suspiciously. I learned later I was in a "Catholic" taxi. Identical black taxis carry Protestants to and from their neighborhoods. Belfast's downtown is caged in—block after block of lively

Rampart of rock and castle confronts the sea on Ireland's Causeway Coast, named after a legend about the hexagonal basalt pillars (above): They make a Giant's Causeway, built so he could walk from Ireland to Scotland. The "stepping stones," which formed as lava cooled, also appear on the island of Staffa in the Hebrides. Dunluce Castle (left), three miles west of the causeway, dates from the 14th century. Archers and a drawbridge once guarded the chasm tourists now cross. The castle began falling into ruin in 1639, when a chunk broke off, dropping kitchen and cooks into the sea.

Tattoos on drums and skin mark Belfast's annual celebration of the Battle of the Boyne, on July 12, 1690, when Protestant King William III defeated Catholic James II. William had overthrown James, who tried to regain the throne with an Irish army. A celebrating Orangeman bares his florid back, which hails William, Prince of Orange, "who saved us from rogues and roguery and slaves and slavery, popes and popery. . . ." About 30 percent of Northern Ireland's Protestant men belong to Orange organizations. Bonfires for William light the Belfast night in a Protestant neighborhood (right).

shops and offices, all surrounded by a high barb-tipped fence. Cars are forbidden within, because they might carry bombs. At gateway checkpoints security officers search pedestrians' bags and sometimes bodies for the same reason.

In Derry, as the Catholics call the British-named city of Londonderry, a large billboard at the main bridge across the River Foyle urges people to dial a certain telephone number "IF YOU HAVE ANY INFORMATION ABOUT MURDERS, EXPLOSIONS."

In Belfast one Sunday morning, as I walked into a Catholic church, a police officer handed me a leaflet asking for help in solving the murder of a parishioner who had been shot as she walked home from Mass the previous Sunday. A Catholic terrorist group, the Provisional Irish Republican Army, admitted to killing her and wounding her father because he, as a judge, served the British. The Provisional IRA, like the Protestant terrorist forces, are scrupulous about explaining the murders they commit.

Why does it go on, year after year, decade after decade? I talked to teachers, journalists, government officials, tacit supporters of various terrorists, and the sister of a Derry man killed by a British bullet. "I hated them," she said. "But now I feel Ireland isn't worth a single life. . . ." That was the closest I came to getting an answer.

I talked to a psychologist who investigates "telling"— the ability to tell whether a stranger is Catholic or Protestant. Tests have shown that many children in Northern Ireland learn from an early age to use faces, accents, and first names to identify people by religion.

And while the terrorists have their war, life goes on. I personally never felt in danger, never heard an explosion or a gunshot, or smelled the smoke of urban battle. As one politician said, the statistics on terrorism show Northern Ireland to be safer than London. Tourists cautiously return, drawn by the beauty of the land.

The North's most spectacular scenery flanks the Antrim Coast Road, which dips and rises between shore and sea for 60 miles from Larne to Portrush. Farther south rise the Mourne Mountains, whose varied granites smolder with colors that change in every shift of light from sea and sky. The countryside is not aloof from the Troubles, but it is removed from much of the violence. Beyond the cities and beyond the magnificent coast of the North rolls a landscape of farms and meadows—and estates still called "plantations" in remembrance of the colonizing of Ulster.

The North is a forgotten part of America's heritage. Americans tend to think that immigrants from the Irish island were the Irish Catholics who immigrated in the 19th and early 20th centuries. But about a quarter million Ulster-Scots—also called the Scots-Irish—left Ulster for America in the 18th century.

The Ulster immigrants sired many famous Americans—Davy Crockett, Sam Houston, Edgar Allan Poe, F. Scott Fitzgerald, and ten Presidents, beginning with Andrew Jackson. Theodore Roosevelt said his ancestors were "a grim, stern people, strong and simple, powerful for good and evil. . . ." The same words could be written today in the land of the Troubles.

Most of the people in the North are powerful for good. In Londonderry, at an All-Ireland drama competition, I saw a Catholic priest's players win to Protestant-Catholic applause. "Art easily crosses the border," he said. In a Methodist school in Belfast, a young Catholic woman, hired with state funds, helps students learn to live in a Catholic-Protestant society.

The children. They could be the changers. When I was in the North, schoolchildren throughout Northern Ireland were writing poems for a contest. They created images of the present and visions of the kind of future they may inherit. One saw:

Dappled men charging through the streets
Followed by the avenging stones.

But another poem rang with hope and, in the lilting accent of the North, sang of joy:

Pretty little dancing girl
Swaying to and fro
Show us how to jump and swirl
Birling on your toe.

Peace finds a dominion in Northern Ireland's lakeland as a sailboat glides over island-dotted Lough Erne. The valley of the River Erne was a passageway for glaciers, which left behind rocky debris in the form of rounded hills called drumlins. They appear as domed islands. More than 150 islands, few of them inhabited, are sprinkled through the vast Lough Erne water system. Fishermen come here for salmon, trout, and pike. In boats and on hiking trails, explorers of the past search for Celtic ruins and early Christian monuments.

Cary Wolinsky

by Breandán Ó hEithir
photographs by Farrell Grehan

The West
of Ireland

*Long, long ago, beyond the misty space
    Of twice a thousand years,
In Erin old there dwelt a mighty race,
    Taller than Roman spears; . . .
Great were their deeds, their passions and
        their sports;
    With clay and stone
They piled on strath and shore those mystic forts,
    Not yet o'erthrown;
On cairn-crowned hills they held their
        council-courts; . . .*

THOMAS D'ARCY MCGEE, "The Celts," 1869

The Galty Mountains tower over the Glen of Aherlow in County Tipperary.

W

here glows the Irish hearth with peat
There lives a subtle spell—
The faint blue smoke, the gentle heat
The moorland odours tell

Of white roads winding by the edge
Of bare untamèd land,
Where dry stone wall or ragged hedge
Runs wide on either hand. . . .

T. W. ROLLESTON, 1909

A County Sligo lad loads his donkey's baskets with peat.

At school on the Aran Islands we were told that after the Creator finished sifting the earth between His fingers over Ireland, He dropped the rocks remaining in His hand onto the province of Connaught. On our craggy islands—where in order to grow our potatoes and cereals and grass we had to shape the earth ourselves, by mixing soil from deep crevices in the rocks with sand and seaweed from the shore—it was easy to take the myth seriously.

Two-thirds of what passes for land in western Connaught has never been cultivated at all. In 1653, the first Irish Catholic settlers arrived from their homes east of the River Shannon, banished by Oliver Cromwell with the harsh words, "To Hell or to Connaught!" In exchange for the rich land left behind to the new English settlers, the dispossessed Irish found themselves with marshland and rock, and some of the rock was piled high into barren mountains almost completely devoid of soil. What little soil they did find they cultivated to the last shovelful and treated with a possessiveness astonishing to people whose ancestors were never threatened with starvation.

About Munster, the province south of Connaught, we learned a different myth in school. Here was a tract of land called the Golden Vale, so fertile that if a stick were thrown into a field at night, it would grow up out of sight by morning. Munster contains elements of almost every type of terrain found in Ireland. Around the province's rugged, sea-washed fringes there are mountains that shelter stretches of golden beach. Inland, there are rich pastures, sinuous salmon rivers, and plantations of trees, old and new. The mountains inland are benign—their slopes cultivated to the higher reaches, in contrast to the glistening granite peaks of Connemara. Munster conjures up images of farm produce, well-nourished livestock, Norman castles, and, in the minds of envious urban workers, solid dairy farmers placing hundred-pound bets while drinking glasses of the best brandy at the Killarney races.

Connaught and Munster together account for almost

two-thirds of the country's 234,000 farms of under 100 acres—and half of those are less than 30 acres. These bald statistics come alive for the traveler in the myriad white-washed farmhouses, of all imaginable shapes and sizes, that pop into view in even the remotest parts of this region. They are perched on the slopes of mountains, scattered through isolated valleys, clustered on islands. They huddle near sheltered coves and market towns, and dot the plains like yachts at anchor on a green sea.

For the rural citizens of Connaught and Munster who inhabit these cottages, there are two crucial elements in life—the land they live on and the traditions they live by.

The land was hard won. A class of tenant farmers, led through a struggle in the 1880s by Charles Stewart Parnell, became landowners in a long, gradual process ending in the early 20th century. Since then, these small landowners have acquired considerable political clout.

Many city dwellers regard the farmers as obstacles to change, as dependent on outmoded methods and on a moist, mild, and changeable climate that favors the production of milk—a commodity for which there is a declining market in Europe. As the city dwellers see it, farmers are taking the easy option of dairy farming instead of going into horticulture, like the Dutch.

They will tell you, when no farmer is within earshot, that if Dutch farmers inhabited Munster's fertile Golden Vale, they would be able to feed all of Europe, but if the dairy farmers of Tipperary, Limerick, northern Cork, and northern Kerry lived in Holland, they would drown

Ireland's western provinces, Connaught and Munster, hold the Irish essence—green fields, misted mountains, the Shannon, and Killarney's lakes. Old ways, such as speaking native Irish, live on here in places like the Dingle Peninsula, where yellow gorse lines the lane to a traditional farmhouse (opposite).

415

through neglect of the dikes. My paternal uncle, Tomás, farms a small holding in western Clare. When I repeated this charge to him, he merely pointed to his front gate and said, "In all my life a car has never stopped out there with a city man offering me a fortune so that he could live in comfort and idleness on this farm."

The same tenacity that keeps farming alive has also kept many rural traditions from disappearing in the face of modern attitudes and pressures. Fairs, for example, are still held in Connaught and Munster, but they are now so exceptional as to be special events. Itinerant musicians play, fortune-tellers and three-card-trick men abound, and large sums of money change hands.

The three-card trick, an illegal game of chance, is performed at most large gatherings. A man produces a small folding table and places three cards, one of which is the queen of hearts, face down on the table and says, "Spot the lady for five pounds." He shuffles the cards, shows them face up, and places them face down again. Immediately, a man puts down five pounds and picks up the queen of hearts and wins another five pounds. Some onlookers, not realizing that this winner is an accomplice, start betting, and when the cardsharper feels that it is time to move or when a genuine punter (poor chump) picks up the lady (though, thanks to the sharper's amazing dexterity, that is rare), the sharper dismantles his table and runs, shouting, "Police! Scatter!" and gets lost in the crowd.

Puck Fair is held in August in Killorglin, on the best known scenic road in Ireland, the Ring of Kerry, near Killarney. A wild billy goat, captured in the mountains and enthroned as King Puck on a platform in the town square, presides. Puck Fair officially lasts three days: Gathering, Fair, and Scattering. In my own experience Scattering seems to go on for days and the pubs scarcely ever close.

But Puck Fair is more than a revel. The goat king is a fertility symbol. August is the old pagan festival of the month of Lughnasa, named in Irish after the Celtic god Lugh. Many such traditional celebrations in Ireland possibly derive from ancient pagan rites. (Continued on page 425)

For Jesus, little girls in white finery march through the town square of Westport in County Mayo. The Corpus Christi procession publicly honors a Catholic tenet: Christ is present in the bread consecrated as the Eucharist in Mass. School holidays include Catholic holy days, such as Good Friday and St. Patrick's Day. Though the Irish school system operates with public funds, the Catholic Church runs most primary schools in Ireland; Catholic religious orders run most secondary schools. Education is compulsory between ages 6 and 15.

The Stones
Crumbled, but
Not the Faith

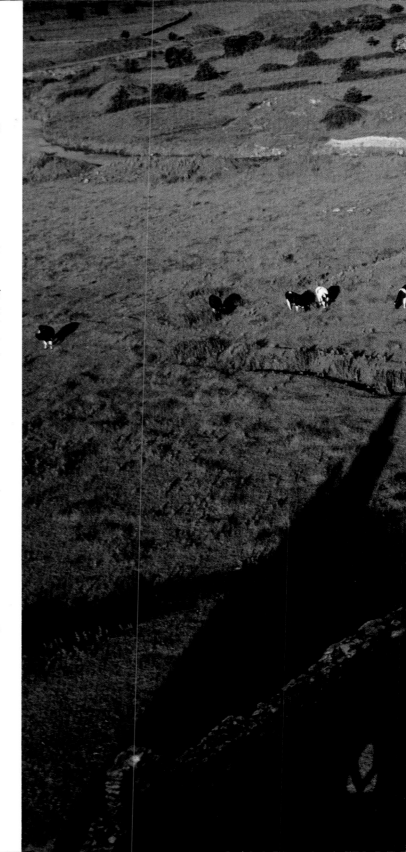

Around the fifth century, St. Patrick and other missionaries from Britain scattered the seeds of Christianity in pagan Ireland. Monasteries began to appear early in the next century, and the religion took root. Today, throughout Ireland, skeletal ruins stand as monuments to those monasteries, which preserved a religion and its worldly treasures.

Irish monks transformed an island of Druids into a realm full of saints and scholars. St. Finnian of Clonard, near the monastery of Kells, sent forth the "Twelve Apostles of Ireland" to establish monasteries from one end of Ireland to the other and on the distant island of Iona in Scotland.

To celebrate the Word of God, monks created brilliantly illuminated books and sacred vessels of gold and silver. As they founded monasteries across Europe, Irish monks spread a reverence for learning through a medieval world besieged by ignorance.

Early monks, inspired by the holy hermits of the East,

lived in individual cells. Some of these beehive huts of stone, though made without mortar, still stand. They would usually cluster around a small wooden, steep-roofed church. The Book of Kells, one of the finest works of the Irish artist-monks, portrays the Temple of Jerusalem as just such a little Irish church.

Monks ate plain food and fasted often. Many mortified themselves, believing in sanctity through torment. They infected themselves with diseases, stood in icy rivers, or knelt hundreds of times a day.

Friaries served as hostels for friars, who, unlike monks, regularly went forth into the world. When an abbot—the term of respect is akin to "father"—governed a religious

Ireland's monastic past lives in the shadows and ruins of Ross Errilly, a 15th-century Franciscan friary; at Rosserk Friary in County Mayo, an angel (left) holds the nails of the Cross.

community, it was called an abbey; an abbess ran an abbey for women. St. Brigid's unique fifth-century community in Kildare had an abbey for men and one for women.

Around the end of the eighth century, the Vikings began plundering Ireland. Monks built tall round towers for refuge and for safeguarding treasures. But more than 200 years of Viking predation destroyed many monasteries, books, and works of art.

During the 12th and 13th centuries, new religious orders—Cistercians, Augustinians, Dominicans, Franciscans —founded large, often prosperous monasteries. Cistercians, who built 38 monasteries in Ireland by 1272, favored order: a rectangle or square with a church on the north, a chapter house (the meeting room) on the east, storerooms on the west, refectory and kitchen on the south.

St. Aidan of Iona built one of England's first monasteries, probably of wood, about A.D. 635 on Lindisfarne, "Holy Island," off the Northumberland coast. St. Ninian, a Scot who went to Rome to study, returned to found Scotland's first church, at Whithorn early in the fifth century; Glasgow grew up around a sixth-century monastery.

The 12th-century monastic

James P. Blair, National Geographic Photographer

Trappists, a branch of the Cistercians, work for their dinner, harvesting eggs and other bounty of their land at Mount Melleray, a monastery founded in County Waterford in the 19th century when France expelled members of the order.

A time-honed cross (above), perhaps a grave marker, stands near the rocky ruins of cells of a monastery on Skellig Michael, a steep-cliffed sea crag off the Kerry coast. The monks, fleeing Viking raids, perched their stone huts on a ledge 550 feet above the Atlantic—but Viking plunderers found the refuge and raided it again and again.

421

Farrell Grehan (also right)

building boom in Ireland crossed the water to England, where most of the Cistercian houses, such as Rievaulx and Fountains, were built.

The end of the monasteries came in 1536, when Henry VIII, as self-proclaimed head of the Church of England and Ireland, began seizing and selling off religious properties. The wealthy made mansions of some monasteries; people quarried others for building stones. Remnants of some, such as the chapter house at Westminster, still exist. Dublin's Monastery of All Hallows became Trinity College.

In the next century, when the Parliamentarians opposed Charles I, many Irish supported him. Cromwell, savagely quelling the Irish rebels, destroyed surviving Catholic churches and monasteries. But the religion survived amid the ruins. Mass was said secretly in farmhouses, in fields—and in the ruins themselves. They stand today as testimony to the keeping of the faith.

THOMAS B. ALLEN

A bridge to nowhere serves the ruins of 12th-century Athassel Priory in County Tipperary. Its grandeur endures, but the town that thrived here has vanished.

Patrick Ward. Left: Farrell Grehan

Selected Monasteries of Britain and Ireland

"Even to the farthest regions, beyond which there lived nobody"—words revered as St. Patrick's describe the boundless vision of missionaries who converted Ireland and Britain and built monasteries throughout the isles. Modern pilgrims visit poignant ruins, such as Jerpoint, one of the finest Cistercian abbeys in Ireland; Dryburgh Abbey in Scotland, which contains the tomb of Sir Walter Scott; and Glastonbury Abbey (left) in England. Annual services are still held at this monastery, which dates from the seventh century.

When St. Patrick embarked in A.D. 432 on his mission to bring Ireland Christianity, he confronted a people immersed in pagan beliefs and rituals. His debates with the Druids—the pagan priests—enliven much of early Irish literature. His most famous debate, recorded in verse, was conducted with Oisín, son of Fionn, leader of a band of warriors called the Fianna. Oisín went to the Land of Eternal Youth, but he pined for Ireland and was allowed to return on horseback for a day, with strict instructions not to touch the earth, or he would immediately revert to his real age. He fell off his horse and became an old man at once.

When Oisín told people who he was, they summoned St. Patrick, who tried to convert him. But Oisín was not impressed. These verses give a taste of the debate.

> Patrick: *Oisín, you sleep too long.*
> *Rise up and hear the psalm*
> *now your strength and health are gone*
> *and your fierce fighting over.*
> Oisín: *My strength and health are gone*
> *because Fionn's troops are dead.*
> *No music but theirs I love.*
> *I have no care for priests.*

St. Patrick finally prevailed. Oisín agreed to be baptized.

Wisely, and diplomatically, St. Patrick helped preserve Ireland's social structure and customs even as he changed fundamental beliefs. When he ascended Croagh Patrick, Ireland's holy mountain in County Mayo, the quartzite peak was sacred to the pagan god Crom. When Patrick descended, after battling for 40 days and nights with a host of evil spirits—including the devil's mother—he declared the summit sacred to the Christian God. The Irish were to continue paying homage here, but in a new form.

So it came about that every year tens of thousands of pilgrims, from all parts of the country and beyond, converge on Croagh Patrick on the last Sunday in July. They climb at dawn, many of them barefoot, to the little oratory on the summit. There they perform penitential exercises, saying a series of prayers while walking around the oratory, kneeling at intervals on the sharp stones.

The view they see is worth scrambling up over 2,510 feet of loose rock and sharp shale (though maybe not in bare feet). The moorland reaches southward in awesome desolation to the mountains of Connemara; westward stretches the Atlantic, in varied shades of blue and green; hundreds of islands dot Clew Bay to the north; and in the east lie the Partry Mountains, Lough Mask, and the plains of Mayo.

Beyond them, if you could see that far, would be the village of Knock—and an example of how the nearness of the supernatural, a mark of the pagan era, remains part of Catholicism in the west of Ireland. For here, on a wet evening in 1879, several townspeople spied the Blessed Virgin silhouetted on the gable of the local church. Now a basilica that seats 15,000 dominates the village, and although no great miracles have been claimed or verified by Catholic authorities, hundreds of thousands of pilgrims, many of them invalids, journey to Knock annually.

The faith of the Catholics in Connaught and Munster (where, in a total population of 1.4 million, there are but 26,500 Protestants) is strong, but practical too. Realizing that all marriages cannot possibly be made in heaven, some of the pilgrims visit the marriage bureau at Knock Shrine.

As I stood near the basilica one day in May, I saw a procession of nurses carrying banners and reciting the rosary. The season of organized pilgrimages had begun. This was the League of Irish Catholic Nurses, arriving in Knock for devotions in thanks for the passage of an antiabortion amendment to the Constitution. The referendum was carried by a large majority in 1983, but the voter turnout was very low. To some commentators this indicated a change in attitude about traditional Catholic morality.

Pilgrims of a different sort take to the River Shannon. For about a hundred miles from Carrick on Shannon south to Killaloe, the unpolluted, surprisingly untraveled river flows from one lovely lake into another. The lakes are speckled with wooded islands, and you may pull in and explore, or moor at one of the little village ports along the river and eat and drink in a local tavern. Just hire a cabin cruiser, stock up, tell nobody, and sail away.

Sticks swinging, a grimacing player from County Offaly and his helmeted opponent from County Galway risk collision during a hurling match before a cheering crowd. They play a hockeylike game that has churned up Irish sod for at least 3,000 years. Counties in both the Republic and Northern Ireland field amateur hurling teams, which compete for All-Ireland honors.

Legal bookmaker Ginger Murphy of Galway may bet on anything, even hurling, but Irish bettors prefer putting their money—"having an interest," they discreetly say—on horses and greyhounds.

OVERLEAF: Fingers of the Burren, Irish for "great rock," reach into Galway Bay. Haystacks dot a stretch of farmland in a region better known for alpine plants and beds of sparsely turfed limestone.

427

Limerick, south of Killaloe, is the only major city on the Shannon. Originally a Norse settlement, Limerick was called the City of Refuge during sieges, for it came under attack during every war fought in this region. King John's Castle, named after the English king who ordered its construction around 1210, is in a good state of preservation.

Downriver from Limerick a new urban center has grown up next to Shannon Airport in County Clare. The airport opened to commercial traffic for refueling in 1945 and became a duty-free zone in 1947. When the advent of long-range jet aircraft threatened the airport's survival, a government-sponsored development company expanded it, set up a major industrial park, and created the town of Shannon, where workers and managers could live within walking distance of their jobs. It was the Republic of Ireland's first new town in over two centuries, and its population of 10,000 is still growing.

To attract tourists, the Shannon Development Company refurbished three old castles—Dunguaire, on the shores of Galway Bay, and Bunratty and Knappogue near the airport—and organized medieval banquets with traditional music and song. At Bunratty Castle there is a folk park, thatched farmhouses, and a 19th-century village street complete with shops and tavern.

To my mind, such "traditional" entertainment can satisfy only the high-speed tourist who seeks to cram as many different experiences as possible into one day. To find the real thing you need not go much farther, for County Clare is one of Ireland's richest repositories of traditional music,

Little bits of Ireland tell much about her people. Tom Ryan's variety shop in Dungarvan, County Waterford, bears his name because Irish shop signs often identify the proud proprietor, not whether he is butcher, baker, or shoemaker. Musicians at a pub (left) in Galway city play for fun, not for pay or tourists, and they sing traditional airs, not "When Irish Eyes Are Smiling." The twin spires of Clifden, hub of Connemara (opposite), belong to two churches, one Catholic, one Protestant. A "landlord town," it was founded in the 19th century by a landowner as a market center for farmers.

song, dance, and folklore. At local pubs musicians and dancers spontaneously perform for their own enjoyment, their audiences merely those who stop in for a drink. These pubs are informal places where customers sit on stools and benches. The musicians will break from their music to have a drink and chat about the next selection of tunes. But they like to gain the respectful silence of the audience for their music, and they can be very sensitive about this.

The little village of Doolin, tucked into the shadow of the imposing Cliffs of Moher, is Clare's musical capital. Growing interest in ethnic music, in Ireland and abroad, brings throngs of musicians and folk music collectors to Doolin each summer. An international village of tents sprouts near the harbor, and the atmosphere hums and throbs with the sounds of fiddles, pipes, concertinas, flutes, and tin whistles.

A short distance north of the cliffs, the terrain changes suddenly. Here stands the Burren, a unique formation of rock and plant life at the northernmost tip of Clare. Ludlow, one of Cromwell's generals, passed through it in 1649 with death on his mind and later wrote of the landscape, "There is not wood enough to hang a man, nor water enough to drown him, nor earth enough to bury him in."

The rounded limestone hills of the Burren, heaved up by great movements of the earth's crust about 270 million years ago, combine with a moist, Atlantic climate to nourish a mixture of arctic, alpine, and mediterranean plants. The hills look gray at a distance, but an explorer on foot finds color in the crevices of the rocks and in the sheltered valleys. Water and soil lie beneath the limestone crust, so that in spring the blue gentians burst into bloom around terraces of gray rock.

The tiny Burren village of Carran was the birthplace of Michael Cusack, 19th-century champion of all things Irish, who became immortalized as the "Citizen" in James Joyce's *Ulysses*. Cusack's most successful achievement was the Gaelic Athletic Association, founded in 1884 to foster and propagate Ireland's traditional games, then in decline.

Because of the GAA, Gaelic football—a combination

432

of soccer and rugby with spectacular long kicking and players leaping high in the air to catch the ball—is Ireland's most popular sport. Hurling also survives, although senior-level teams play in fewer than half the counties in Ireland.

I prefer hurling to football; it is a more ancient game and requires more skill. The sport has been described as a form of hockey for giants, and it is the fastest field game played anywhere in the world. Two teams of 15 each drive a hard leather ball toward their respective goals using ash sticks, about three and a half feet long, with broad, curved blades; they propel the ball along the ground or bat it through the air or carry it on the blade of the stick.

The players battle with great intensity, and I frequently hear foreigners marvel that they are strictly amateur. This is why I regard attendance at a hurling match as mandatory for visitors who wish to fully understand the Irish temperament: They will see a game played with controlled passion, for enjoyment, and for the honor of parish and county. You are more likely to see games in the country than in Galway city. Hurling, banned by city authorities in medieval times, is a rural game, except in Cork city.

I cannot write dispassionately about Galway. After Aran, it is my second home, and I regard it as an essential Irish experience. Its air smells of freshly baked bread, of salty sea breezes, and of Guinness. And, miraculously, it has preserved its central maze of narrow streets, many of which formed part of the old inner city.

Galway's proudest boast is that it has slowed time to a virtual standstill. As they say around here, "When God made time, He made plenty of it." Time is there to be savored—as much of it as possible in the pursuit of convivial company, by day and by night. You can see conversations being conducted across the narrow streets and from the pavement to the upstairs windows.

Many strands of history weave together here. Galway numbers Presidents John F. Kennedy and Ronald Reagan among its Freemen. Christopher Columbus, on a visit to the city, is said to have attended Mass at the Church of St. Nicholas, still Galway's grandest building.

Inisheer, one of the three Aran Islands, wears upon its barren rock the veneer of human toil—whitewashed houses, a maze of stone walls, and soil handmade of seaweed and sand. Beneath the thin green mantle lies a limestone ridge that leaves the land in County Clare and emerges here as the islands, about 30 miles from Galway city. Many stone walls were built without gates; iron or timber was too expensive to haul from the mainland. When livestock need passage, farmers *remove stones to make a temporary opening. The beetlelike Aran boat, a currach (left), is made of tarred canvas stretched over a wooden frame. Currachs sometimes ferry passengers and goods from ships lying off Inishmaan, which has no deepwater harbor. Pigs and sheep travel in the currachs; cows, horses, and donkeys are towed. The islanders make a living from livestock, fishing, and tourism.*

433

Galway is the only city in Ireland where two languages, English and Irish, can be heard in the streets and where strolling musicians play in the afternoons. It all adds up to a strangely foreign but wholly Irish atmosphere, and although it seems like a place where everyone knows everyone else's business, you will find the simplest happening reported in a variety of ways.

Galway lies amid the Gaeltacht—scattered patches along the western and southern coasts where native Irish is the everyday language. Irish belongs to the Celtic language family, closely related to Scottish Gaelic and more remotely to Welsh and Breton. For three centuries before independence, the language was in decline, eroded by the English-dominated school system, emigration, and other economic and social pressures. Because advancement in commerce or the professions was impossible without a good knowledge of English, people regarded Irish as a symbol of poverty and backwardness. With independence, the new government declared Irish the first official language of the state, but efforts to make it the everyday speech of the country have failed.

Only 58,000 native speakers remain, in areas of varying size on the western fringes of Counties Donegal, Mayo, and Galway, and in smaller pockets of Counties Kerry, Cork, and Waterford. Some of these patches of the Gaeltacht are so small that there is little hope for their survival. But the language may not completely die. Irish is still a required subject in the schools, and almost a third of the Irish population claim to have a good knowledge of it.

Like the game of hurling and the native tongue, Ireland's traditional crafts and skills need nurturing. The growth of tourism has led to some revival of crafts, such as weaving, knitting, carving, and pottery. But the slate-roofed bungalow is replacing the thatched cottage, and the traditional modes of dress are disappearing rapidly. Only on Inishmaan, the middle island of the Aran Islands, will a visitor find traditional homespun flannel and multicolored woven belts and shawls. Rawhide shoes—molded to fit the foot by constant wear and ideal for walking over the

"Every article on these islands has an almost personal character," wrote John Millington Synge, who found inspiration for his works in the Aran Islands. On Inishmaan, women walk to church wearing the kind of shawls the playwright saw in the 1900s. Tradition still guides skilled hands in readying rye, yanked out with its roots, for repairing a thatched roof. But nylon cord has replaced straw ropes to hold down the thatch. In "this little corner on the face of the world" Synge found "a peace and dignity from which we are shut out for ever."

fissured rocks—are still popular with the older generation.

A new cooperative on Inishmaan is at work putting old skills to modern use. It makes specially designed traditional garments for export. The young islanders I saw at work in the computerized factory wore American-style T-shirts and jeans but were listening to the Gaeltacht radio station.

Slender wooden boats called currachs are still used in Aran and along the west coast for fishing, particularly lobster fishing, and for transport of goods between islands and between the ferryboat and shore. To curl up in the sharp prow of a currach in a choppy sea—plunging down the side of a wave, landing with a smack in the trough, rising sharply up the crest of the next wave—is to feel the surge and flow of the open sea as a floating sea gull feels it.

My family home on Aran is gone now, and whenever I return to visit friends and relations, I am struck by how material change has left attitudes there unchanged. The Aran of my youth was very isolated. We depended completely on an old steamboat for supplies and transport. In winter the bay was often a boiling cauldron of foam under a pall of mist and spray. Old women peered into it and asked those with keener eyes, "Can you see her?" and groaned when the answer was negative. Now they cock their ears and ask, "Can you hear her?" and, when the drone of the aircraft sounds overhead, they thank God for the comfort that the daily air service has brought.

A relic from the Arans' deepest past overlooks the Atlantic from Inishmore, the biggest island. Dun Aengus (the Fort of Aengus), which stands on the brink of a sheer

Scenes in today's Ireland reflect a 19th-century description— "Beautiful visions crowd on the mind": Evening's light bathes one of the Lakes of Killarney (left). Morning paints a still life at Portmagee, a fishing village in County Kerry (upper). Children by a roadside in County Clare play in a barrel-shaped wagon abandoned by wanderers called the traveling people. Behind the visions lie economic realities: Tourism, a major industry, threatens Killarney's tranquillity; many fishermen are part-timers because they need to earn additional income in other ways; only half of Ireland's population is over 25.

cliff 200 feet above the Atlantic, is the most elaborate prehistoric fort in Ireland and one of the finest in Europe. For years it has defied archaeologists who have tried to date it and identify its resourceful builders. From here you can survey the entire sweep of coast, from the tip of Connemara in Connaught south to the mountains of Kerry in Munster.

Believe everything you read about the limpid Lakes of Killarney; the rugged ravines that wind down toward Glengarriff with its subtropical vegetation; the view of Skellig Rocks from the Ring of Kerry's dizzying mountain roads; the stillness of the forest above the lake at Gougane Barra, so quiet you can hear the chirping of tiny insects; the majesty of the mountains around Bantry Bay at sunset. But realize that there is no substitute for actually seeing the ever changing light, for hearing a summer shower hiss in from the sea, or for getting to know the people.

Far from overawed by their magnificent scenery, the people of Kerry are infectiously lively. Gaelic football is a second religion here, and pictures of star players hang on walls beside the Pope, John F. Kennedy, and Jesus. Kerry folk have a reputation for convoluted language and a quick wit. One man replied to my inquiry about town hotels by saying, "The way it is here is that no matter which one you stay in you'll be sorry you didn't stay in one of the others," and went on, cheered by his own wordplay.

The Kerry wit is applied with enthusiasm to neighboring County Cork. Kerrymen say that a Corkman will not only make a nest in one of your ears, he'll rent the other one out as an apartment. Corkmen counter by telling with relish of the Kerry court where a judge acquitted a man of murder with the words, "You have been found 'not guilty' by a Kerry jury, and you are free to leave with no additional stain on your character."

Cork city rises where the River Lee enters the well-sheltered harbor. Low-lying in the west, the town climbs a series of steep terraces to the summit of a range of hills in the east. Cork city was once the biggest center of industry outside Dublin and Belfast, but in recent years some of the oldest industries, like the Ford and Dunlop plants, have

A master glassblower "blocks" a blob of molten glass (top), starting its evolution into Waterford crystal. Glass farther along in the process whirls into a glistening cake dish (bottom); tongues of flames lick it to keep temperatures even as base fuses to plate. The conical upper portion will be cut off afterward.

A hand-cut plate's starry design sparkles in the hands of a master cutter (opposite). Today's Waterford glass traces back to a factory that opened in 1783 and shut down in 1851 because of British tax policies. The modern factory started up exactly a century later.

The durable, brilliant glass gets its qualities from red lead oxide, mixed with white silica sand, potash, and "cullet" (bits of glass from previous firings). Heavy drinkers especially admired one 18th-century Waterford piece: a decanter with three thick rings in its neck so a shaky hand could hold and pour.

My grief on the ocean
it is surely wide
stretched between me
and my dearest love.
I am left behind
to make lament
—not expected for ever
beyond the sea. . . .
My grief I am not
with my dearest love
on board of a ship
for America bound.

shut down because of a recession—a heavy blow to a city not accustomed to unemployment. But the people are resilient. Their attitude toward life is in tune with their lilting accents, which end every sentence on a rising cadence.

East of Cork the land is flat and fertile all along the coast to Waterford, best known as the home of Waterford crystal, a product that most Irish people cannot afford to buy, but of which they are intensely proud.

Waterford is the starting point for the journey to my favorite view in Ireland. I drive on little-used roads along the foot of the Comeragh Mountains and down past the Cistercian monastery of Mount Melleray, where I pause to admire the carpet of lush grass that marks a partial victory by the monks over the inhospitable mountain. Turning north, I travel through a barren moor, then take a winding road through a gap in the Knockmealdown Mountains.

Suddenly, as if coming out of a dark room into the sunlight, I see before me a vast patchwork quilt of rich pastures stretching west to the Galty Mountains, their slopes as green as emeralds, and north to the Rock of Cashel, which rises from the level plains of Tipperary and can be seen from great distances. A cluster of historic buildings still crowns the rock, which was the principal seat of the kings of Munster from the fourth to the twelfth century. After St. Patrick visited here in the fifth century, the rock became the ecclesiastical capital of the province as well. Here St. Patrick preached the doctrine of the Holy Trinity, using the shamrock as a visual aid to show the concept of three persons in one God. The saint later got so carried away that he rammed his crosier into the ground, through the king's foot. The king never flinched, being much impressed that the new religion demanded even greater fortitude than the one he was about to abandon.

I drive on to my goal, leave the car, and sit down by a most unusual grave—the cairn in which a farmer called Samuel Grubb chose to be buried upright, overlooking the valley. And I who grew up on the bare rocks of Aran, with the thunder of the Atlantic's waves in my ears, share with Samuel Grubb the placid beauty of the Golden Vale.

A Glossary of British English

The American Colonies had barely gained their independence when the British began complaining about America's "barbarous phraseology," which included such outlandish new words as "lengthy" and "belittle."

Unabashed, Americans continued to change their language; crusading lexicographer Noah Webster succeeded in banishing the *u* from words like "colour" and "honour." But usage kept changing in Britain and Ireland as well. Only recently, for instance, did the British begin saying "ill" instead of "sick."

Tourism and television are bringing the languages closer. But problems do arise when an American orders "biscuits" in London, or a Britisher shops for a "vest" in New York. And British drivers in the States are still amused at road signs telling them to "yield" instead of "give way"; Americans smile at signs in Heathrow Airport that say "way out" instead of "exit."

B & B bed-and-breakfast; usually a private home offering accommodations for tourists
badge slogan button
bank holiday public holiday, generally on a Monday
bank note paper currency, as in *pound note*
barrister lawyer who argues in court, as opposed to a *solicitor*, who chiefly works out of court
bath-chair wheelchair; named for the spa town of Bath
bathroom contains bath or shower, not always a toilet; see **lavatory**
bespoke custom-tailored (garment)
biro ball-point pen
bobby policeman
bomb a hit: *The show was a bomb.*
bonnet hood of a car
boot trunk of a car
braces trouser suspenders
braw (Scottish) good, fine, brave
brolly; gamp umbrella

caravan camping trailer
chemist's drugstore
cloakroom rest room
coach a sight-seeing bus, sometimes called a *charabanc*; the tourists are the *coach party*
cotton thread; a *reel of cotton* is a spool of thread

daft mildly insane, or at least ill-advised; also *barmy, bonkers, crackers*
dear expensive
diversion traffic detour
drawing pin thumbtack
dual carriageway divided highway
dustbin trash can

early closing the weekday when every shop in a town or district closes for the day at lunchtime
Elastoplast Band-Aid
engaged (telephone number) busy
estate agent real estate agent
estate car station wagon

fag cigarette
first floor second floor; numbering starts above *ground floor*
flannel washcloth (facecloth); not always supplied by B & B's or hotels
flat apartment; a *block of flats* is an apartment house
flyover highway overpass
football soccer; American football is called *American football*
full stop (punctuation) period

garden yard, with or without flowers (but usually with)
gramophone phonograph

headway overhead clearance
hire purchase installment plan; also known as *the never-never*
hoover generic name for vacuum cleaners; also used as a verb: *to hoover the flat*

ill avoid *sick*, which means nauseated
interval theater intermission
ironmonger's hardware store

joint (at butcher's) roast
jumper pullover sweater

knock up wake up, at hotels or B & B's: *Shall I knock you up at 7 a.m.?*

lavatory; toilet bathroom; *loo, w.c. (water closet)* equivalent to john
to let for rent
licensed alcohol is served
lift elevator
lorry truck
left luggage baggage room

mackintosh; mac raincoat
mad means insane, not angry
motorway freeway
mudguard; wing car fender

nappy diaper
newsagent newsstand
nought (temperature and math) zero; use *oh* in phone numbers
numbers Use *double* and *treble* in phone numbers: *Ring me at treble oh, four, double five* (000-455).
number plate car license plate

OAP Old Age Pensioner
off-license liquor store

panda black-and-white police car
pants men's underpants, not trousers or slacks
pavement; footpath sidewalk
petrol gasoline
pillar box; post-box mailbox
pinafore dress jumper
plimsolls; gym shoes sneakers
plus fours men's baggy trousers gathered below the knee
polo neck turtleneck
post mail (noun and verb)
pram (perambulator) baby carriage
priorities traffic rights-of-way; *changed priorities*: new traffic pattern
public school private school
purse change purse
pushchair baby stroller

queue line of people
quid (slang) pound: *It cost ten quid.*

redundant out of work; laid off
to ring up; to phone up to telephone; *to call* means to pay a visit
roundabout a traffic circle; also *circus*
rubber eraser

saloon (car) sedan
Sellotape Scotch tape
service flat rental apartment with cleaning service

shopping trolley shopping cart
to be sick to vomit
silencer car muffler
single or return? one-way ticket or round-trip?
solicitor see **barrister**
spanner monkey wrench
spend a penny; wash one's hands euphemisms for going to the toilet
sponge bag a small plastic bag in which to carry one's toilet articles
stalls orchestra seating: *I'd like a seat in the stalls.*
state school public school
sticking plaster Band-Aid or adhesive tape for bandages
store department store; other stores are called shops
subway underground walkway
surgery doctor's or dentist's office; also, their office hours
suspenders garters
sweet dessert; *sweets* are candy

ta thanks

CHANGED PRIORITIES AHEAD

Jodi Cobb,
N.G.S. Photographer

telephone box; kiosk phone booth
telly TV
tights panty hose
tin can of food
tip dump; hence *no tipping*
torch flashlight
trunk call long-distance call
tube subway; also called *underground*
twee archly cute

U, non-U usage accepted in upper-class circles, or not; terms popularized by writer Nancy Mitford

underground see **tube**

VAT value-added tax, similar to sales tax, but more insidious; sometimes refunded to foreigners
verge grassy strip beside the road
vest undershirt

waistcoat vest
wash up the dishes, not yourself
Wellingtons; Wellies knee-high rubber boots
windcheater Windbreaker
windscreen windshield

zebra crossing (pronounced ZEB-ra) striped pedestrian crosswalk
zed the letter *z*

At the Restaurant

aubergine eggplant
bill check
biscuit cookie; American biscuits are called *scones*
broad beans similar to lima beans
champ Irish mashed-potato dish with scallions
chips French fried potatoes
coffee, white with cream
courgettes zucchini
crisps potato chips
cuppa; cupper cup of tea
demerara sugar crystallized brown sugar, mostly used in coffee
iced lolly Popsicle
jelly Jell-O
kipper salted, smoked herring
marrow large zucchini-like squash
mince hamburger meat
pasty (PASS-tee) pastry turnover, especially Cornish, filled with potatoes, turnips, and often meat
porridge hot oatmeal
pudding dessert, any kind
scone type of biscuit
serviette table napkin
spotted Dick; plum duff suet pudding with raisins or currants
squash fruit-flavored drink
squashed flies flat raisin cookies
sultana raisin
swede rutabaga, yellow turnip
Swiss roll jelly roll
take-away a carryout food shop
tea generally sandwiches and cakes as well as a beverage; thus *He didn't eat his tea! High tea* is a combination

of tea and supper usually served about 5 p.m.
toad-in-the-hole sausages baked in a batter pudding
treacle molasses
trifle dessert of sponge cake (often soaked in wine or spirit), jam or jelly, custard, and whipped cream
wholemeal whole wheat

At the Pub

ale; beer stronger, heavier, more hop-flavored than American
barley wine extremely strong ale that comes in small bottles
bitter; best bitter dry ales made with pale malt and enough hops to produce a good "bitter" bite
cider sweet or dry, draft or bottled, but always alcoholic; nonalcoholic cider is called *apple juice*
lager lighter than *bitter;* closest equivalent to American beer
mild sweetish, dark ale
neat straight
Pimm's Cup in posh pubs only: a gin drink served on ice with mint and slices of cucumber and lemon
porter a weak *stout*
pub (public house) tavern. A *free house* pub belongs to the landlord; a *tied house* is brewery-owned.
public bar stand-up section of a pub, with some seating, often darts, pool, video games; slightly cheaper than saloon
real ale draft beer traditionally brewed, stored in wooden casks, and hand pumped from the barrel—rather than beers from large breweries, artificially carbonated and stored in alloy kegs
saloon more seats and slightly higher prices than the public bar; in some quarters still considered the only appropriate side for ladies; usually called the *lounge*
shandy lemonade mixed with *bitter*
soda soda water only
stout dark, heavy-bodied brew made like ale, but with roasted barley or malt added
whisky in Britain, usually Scotch; malt whiskies are more favored than the malt-and-grain blended Scotch common in America; *Irish whiskey* has a less smoky quality.

About the Authors & Photographers

Englishman PETER CROOKSTON brings to his **Introduction** experience in covering the British Isles for the *Observer Magazine* in London, as former editor of Britain's *Nova* magazine, and subsequently as editor of books including *Village England* and *Island Britain.*

NORMAN SHRAPNEL, award-winning parliamentary correspondent and columnist for the Manchester *Guardian,* moved from Manchester to **London** in 1958, and has kept a wry eye on the city's changing face ever since. JODI COBB, a National Geographic staffer since 1977, excels at people photography; her work on this book won her the honor of being named White House Photographer of the Year.

English author and travel writer GEOFFREY MOORHOUSE, whose books include *The Other England,* took his appreciation for things fine and traditional back to the **English Heartland,** and found it still measured up—mostly. American DAN DRY, named U. S. National Newspaper Photographer of the Year in 1981, free-lances from Louisville, Kentucky. Artful at camouflage, he adopted native plumage by renting a top hat and cutaway to cover Ascot.

SHIRLEY L. SCOTT, daughter of English parents, and National Geographic staff writer, offers an American visitor's view of the **West Country.** London photographer PATRICK WARD is hooked on Cornwall—so much so that he spends many of his holidays there—shooting pictures, of course.

Best-selling novelist LESLIE THOMAS lives in London and augments his popular novels, short stories, TV plays, and documentaries with travel writing about his favorite spots,

like England's **Southeast.** MICHAEL ST. MAUR SHEIL lives near Oxford, where he attended the University. His work ranges from commercial assignments on North Sea oil rigs to editorial topics such as the Southeast and the **Channel Islands.**

English poet, musicologist, and writer, EDWARD STOREY was born in the Cambridgeshire fens and has been in love with **East Anglia and the Fens** ever since—enough to write five books about the area. MICHAEL S. YAMASHITA, a world-ranging photographer from New Jersey, worried at first about tackling Britain's only flat region. His pictures reveal the surprise he found: an English Holland, full of flowers, dikes, and windmills.

BRYN FRANK, editor of the British Tourist Authority's travel magazine *In Britain,* harbors a fondness for the **Midlands,** which he feels to be an unappreciated part of England. ANNIE GRIFFITHS, a Minneapolis photographer, began her career on the *Minnesota Daily.* Her journalistic approach: strong pictures that tell stories. Since 1978 she has worked on more than a dozen NATIONAL GEOGRAPHIC projects.

FRANK ENTWISLE, author of *Abroad in England,* is a Lancastrian who considers himself an adopted Tynesider. He has worked as newspaperman, documentary writer, and television producer throughout the world. Photographer IAN BERRY enjoyed recording the rich contrasts of the **North Country,** where he was born. "It contains all the extremes of the rest of England," he says. He also covered the **Isle of Man,** where his parents now live.

Welshman NORMAN LEWIS, prize-winning author of 15 novels and 5 travel books, grew up in **Wales** and has since journeyed the globe. His reports of the genocide of Amazon Indians made world headlines. LINDA BARTLETT, based in Washington, D. C., has photographed NATIONAL GEOGRAPHIC stories in

England and on the Dingle Peninsula in Ireland.

Scotsman CLIFFORD HANLEY, who is something of an institution in Glasgow, has celebrated the gutsy spirit of the **Scottish Lowlands** and of the Scots generally in novels, short stories, children's fiction, plays, screenplays, memoirs, poetry —and even the lyric for the anthem "Scotland the Brave." Lowlands variety called for the flexibility of NATHAN BENN, who likes photographing both architecture and a wide range of human situations.

Anglo-Scottish author, broadcaster, and award-winning food and drink critic, DEREK COOPER divides his time between homes in the Island of Skye and in London, where he devotes one wall of his study to books on food, wine, and whisky; the other to books on the **Highlands and Islands**—several volumes his own. JIM BRANDENBERG, twice named U. S. Magazine Photographer of the Year, applied the theme of his life-work—the relationship of man and nature—to Britain's wildest region.

THOMAS B. ALLEN, American author of Irish extraction (and former editor with the National Geographic Book Service), brought an overseas perspective to the historical complexities of **The East of Ireland,** which also attracted London photographer COLIN JONES, long interested in social documentary. His photographs appear also in British and European magazines.

BREANDÁN Ó hEITHIR, Irish down to the Gaelic spelling of his name, was born in the Aran Islands and studied at Galway. Once a fisherman, then an itinerant bookseller, he is now a journalist, broadcaster, and novelist, writing in both English and his mother tongue, Irish. FARRELL GREHAN, a painter and sculptor before turning to photography in 1953, lives in New York. His Irish ancestry teamed with his artist's eye to capture the wistful landscapes of **The West of Ireland.**

Acknowledgments

Our invasion of Britain and Ireland was amiably aided by barmaids and bobbies, shepherds and scholars, and scores of other people throughout these lands. We are especially grateful to the regional and local tourist boards, and in particular to Peter Harbison of Bord Fáilte Éireann; Michael Roberts and E. Anne Moore, Northern Ireland Tourist Board; Adrian Clark, English Tourist Board; Mike Banfield, Guernsey; Stuart Abraham, Jersey; Brian Johns, Sark; Jim Crichton, York; and the staff of British Information Services in New York City, U.S.A.

In addition, the following deserve our special thanks: The Right Honourable the Lord Emslie, the Lord Justice General of Scotland and the Lord President of the Court of Session; the Duke of Atholl; the Duke of Marlborough; Sir David Piper; Canon Paul Britton of Winchester Cathedral; Rear Admiral D. E. Macey and Rian Le Mar of Canterbury Cathedral; Major and Mrs. Peter Wood of Herm; Philip and Elizabeth Perrée and George Guille of Sark; Dr. Anne Ross; Ian Dewhirst of the Keighley Public Library; David P. Hall of the Cambridge University Library; Ronald Sands, of the Lake District National Park; Gerald Craske of Fellwanderers; Niall O'Muilleoir, Bord na Gaeilge; Tim Pat Coogan of *The Irish Press;* Peter Day of Chatsworth; Ann R. Harrison and Guy Norris, Manx Museum Library; the British Waterways Board; Derek Gregg, Thames Water Authority; Patricia Behr, M.B.E., Department of the Environment; R.A.L. Burnet of the Royal and Ancient Golf Club of St. Andrews; Jenny Carter, Edinburgh; the Highlands and Islands Development Board; the Press Office of the Church of Scotland; and the staff of Kodak Limited of England.

Type composition by National Geographic's
Photographic Services. Color separations by
Beck Engraving Co., Langhorne, Pa.;
Chanticleer Co., Inc., New York, N.Y.; Graphic
Color Plate, Inc., Stamford, Conn.; The
Lanman Companies, Washington, D. C. Printed
and bound by R. R. Donnelley & Sons Co.,
Chicago, Ill., and Holladay-Tyler Printing
Corp., Rockville, Md. Paper by Mead Paper
Co., New York, N.Y.

Library of Congress CIP Data

Discovering Britain & Ireland

 Includes index.
 1. Great Britain—Description and travel—
1971-   —Addresses, essays, lectures. 2.
Ireland—Description and travel—1981- —
Addresses, essays, lectures.
I. National Geographic Book Service. II. Title:
Discovering Britain and Ireland. III. Title:
Britain & Ireland. IV. Title: Britain and Ireland.
DA632.D57 1985   914.1'0485   85-707
ISBN 0-87044-598-7
ISBN 0-87044-599-5 (deluxe)

You are invited to join the National Geographic
Society or to send gift memberships to others.
(Membership includes a subscription to the
NATIONAL GEOGRAPHIC magazine.) For
information call 800-638-4077 toll free, or write
to the National Geographic Society, Department
1675, Washington, D. C. 20036.